We Captured a U-Boat

This specially prepared edition, issued in 1958, is for members of The Popular Book Club, 9 Long Acre, London, W.C.99, from which address particulars of membership will gladly be sent. This volume is published by arrangement with Sidgwick & Jackson Ltd., the original publishers

NOTE

REAR-ADMIRAL
DANIEL V. GALLERY, U.S.N.

We Captured a
U-Boat

INTRODUCTION BY
COMMANDER EDWARD YOUNG
D.S.O., D.S.C., R.N.V.(S)R.

THE POPULAR BOOK CLUB
LONDON

To

My Wife Vee

who kept the home fires burning
during the Battle of the Atlantic

S.1058.SC.G.E.
MADE AND PRINTED IN GREAT BRITAIN FOR
THE POPULAR BOOK CLUB (ODHAMS PRESS LTD.)
BY ODHAMS (WATFORD) LIMITED
WATFORD, HERTS

CONTENTS

ILLUSTRATIONS

INTRODUCTION

ALL naval commanders itch to learn afterwards the enemy's side of actions they have taken part in. Few have the fortune to do so. None that I know of has been able to piece together, as Admiral Gallery has, not only the complete history of his opponent's ship from its birth to its capture on the high seas, but also the tactics, the thoughts and the fears of the enemy commander during the days, hours and minutes leading up to the crisis of the engagement. This double viewpoint, switching us back and forth from one side of the action to the other, from the bridge deck of his own aircraft-carrier to the control room of the German submarine, dovetailing the two stories in rapidly shortening flashes, enables him to build up a tremendous suspense and makes his book unique amongst naval documents of either world war, and indeed of any naval war in history.

Nor have I ever before come across any case of a warship captain committing suicide in the very moment of a crisis, as Lange's predecessor in command did so ignobly in the conning tower of the U-505. This was not yet the death-knell of that ill-fated submarine, though it would have been but for the prompt and decisive action of the First Lieutenant, Meyer. It is difficult to conceive by what terrible steps Cszhech stumbled down the slope towards his dissolution, but Admiral Gallery puts his finger on the succession of events which ate their way into the core of his physical and spiritual courage, and leaves the rest to our horrified imagination. This must be one of the most macabre chapters in the long, grim story of the Battle of the Atlantic.

So far as I have been able to discover, Admiral Gallery is the only naval man, American or British, who deliberately set out to *capture* a German U-boat. Many, in both navies, had boarding parties organized in case the opportunity of capture should arise, but, confronted with a surfacing U-boat, the natural reaction of any commander protecting a convoy is to

put as many holes as possible into the submarine and sink it
before it can take any desperate last-ditch aggressive action.
Admiral Gallery worked out a different plan, despite the
scepticism of many of his subordinates, and when the U-505,
damaged so badly that she could no longer remain submerged
and survive, surfaced to allow her crew to escape, he put his
plan into effect with astounding success.

British naval officers may dispute his claim to have made
the only U-boat capture on the high seas, and will point to
the incident of the U-570 which in 1941 surrendered to a
Sunderland flying-boat. The Admiral does not shirk this issue,
but maintains, I think with justice, that the two cases were
different, in that the U-505 did *not* surrender but was taken
by force, code books, secret charts and all. The crew of the
U-570, on the other hand, had ample opportunity to scuttle,
and preferred safety and surrendered their ship. Moreover,
Admiral Gallery did more than merely seize an opportunity
that was offered to him; he created his own opportunity, and
that was the significant thing.

Lest, however, readers should go away with the idea that
he was the only man who thought of organizing a boarding-
party, I must in all fairness put on record the fact that the
boarding party was, from quite early on in the war, part of the
normal stock-in-trade of all Royal Navy anti-submarine ships
—whether they were destroyers, frigates, corvettes or A/S
trawlers. I remember an amusing incident in this connection
when my own submarine was engaged in training exercises
with surface forces. One of the frigates in company made me a
signal that he was sending over a boarding party to capture us.
The rules of the exercise forbade us to submerge, but even as
we saw the frigate's whaler being lowered we prepared our plan
of action. When the boarding party drew alongside us, they
were puzzled to find not a soul in evidence on the upper deck.
Gingerly the first man descended the ominously silent conning
tower. As he dropped down the ladder into the control room all
the lights suddenly went out and a terrifying cacophony of
klaxon hooters, alarm bells and human yells paralysed him with
terror. Within a few seconds invisible hands had bound him

into a strait-jacket and deposited him on the steel plates of the engine-room deck. After a nervous interval the next man came down to see what had happened to his fellow, and suffered a similar fate. When this had happened a few times, the lads up top got rather cross and dropped an asphyxiating smoke-bomb amongst us, at which point I decided the game had gone on long enough and "surrendered". I received an irritable ticking-off from the captain of the frigate for not playing fair.

I have told this story to underline my admiration for the great act of courage performed by Admiral Gallery's men, none of whom had ever been inside a submarine, when they leapt aboard the U-505. They had no idea what terrors might be waiting for them down below, the submarine was settling in the water, so much so that they had to *shut the hatch behind them* to stop the sea from spilling over into the conning tower, and for all they knew their captive was about to up-end itself and take them all to the bottom with it. The thought of it makes your hair stand on end. If ever men deserved medals, they certainly did.

I found this well-authenticated account more enthralling than any fictional "thriller" that has ever kept me from going to sleep at night. Perhaps this has something to do with my having been a wartime submariner myself and being able to put myself under water with the Germans. But I defy anyone, landlubber or not, to read without a pounding heart the passage where Lange sticks up his periscope for the last time and finds himself surrounded by Admiral Gallery's carrier task force. The author has done a remarkable job, for a surface sailor, of explaining how a submarine works and what it feels like to serve in one, and I am sure his amazing story will be equally vivid to all its readers.

EDWARD YOUNG

CHAPTER I

PROLOGUE

EVERY week at the Museum of Science and Industry in Chicago thousands of visitors explore a strange and improbable exhibit. It is the ex-German submarine U-505, once one of Hitler's dreaded fleet of U-boats. Boarded and captured by the United States Navy in 1944 off the West Coast of Africa, it has rested since 1954 high and dry among the trees in Jackson Park alongside the Museum near the shore of Lake Michigan, a memorial to the 55,000 Americans who lost their lives defending their country at sea.

The story of how this came about is one of the strangest of World War II. It takes us back a century and a half in naval history to the days when full-rigged sailing ships with smoothbore guns fought it out yardarm to yardarm, and when the cry "Away all boarding parties" sent gangs of swashbuckling characters scrambling over the rail with cutlass and marlinespike to board and capture the enemy vessel. For over a hundred years such things have happened only in story books. Now naval battles are fought at long range, and when modern weapons hammer an enemy ship into submission she blows up and sinks.

But on June 4, 1944, an aircraft-carrier task group of the U.S. Atlantic Fleet took a page from the story books by boarding and capturing the U-505, 150 miles off Cape Blanco, French West Africa. It was my great fortune and high honour to command the task group that did this job. I could, I suppose, make out quite a case showing how shrewdly I anticipated every move U-505 made during the last week before we captured her, and took proper action to counter it. I would only have to lay her track alongside mine on a chart without comment and let the reader draw his own conclusions from the way they converge to a point at 11.20 a.m. on June 4, 1944.

But I don't intend to do this. The German skipper and I both had what we thought were sound reasons for every move we made that last week. Looking back now, our reasons were wrong in almost every case. It was a combination of errors on both sides in which his mistakes counteracted mine and produced a fantastically improbable result.

This book tells the story of the U-505 from her keel-laying in Germany to her final "docking" in Chicago. The story is put together from interviews with her crew, and from study of her official papers, complete war diary and logs. In telling this story I sometimes quote conversations between crew members of the U-505. Obviously I have no way of knowing whether or not these exact words were spoken. But all the main facts of the story are historically correct and are documented by official records, war diaries and ships' logs. The minor incidents are based on interrogation of prisoners, and on letters I have had from the U-505's crew, who are now back in Germany, but I have occasionally supplied details which cannot be documented but which anyone who fought in the Battle of the Atlantic will agree are probable.

The tale of this U-boat, told against the background of the Battle of the Atlantic in which it played an important part, should help to drive home the moral of sea power which so many people forget, and perhaps some other lessons too. It may show that there was not so much difference between the individual men who met far out on the sea to fight this battle. They were similar human beings with similar motives and emotions, directed by fallible superiors who could make equally bad mistakes. I like to think that our men were fighting for a better cause than the others.

CHAPTER II

THE U-505 COMMISSIONS

THE U-505's story begins in the Deutsche Werft Shipyards at Hamburg, where her keel was laid on June 2, 1940. As they drove the first rivets in this new sea wolf's keel Hitler's panzer divisions were roaring across France sweeping all before them, apparently invincible. They had overrun Poland, conquered Norway and driven the British into the sea at Dunkirk. Two days after the keel-laying, the conquering German armies entered Paris. Hitler danced his little jig in the Compiègne Forest, and there were many who thought that this U-boat and her sisters ships, then being rushed to completion, would never see action in this war.

But there was one barrier left to halt Hitler's conquest of Europe—the sea. In fact it was just a small arm of the sea, the English Channel, only twenty miles across, that barred his victorious armies from England. The big question mark was, could this historic barrier still hold back the crushing power which the Luftwaffe and panzer divisions had just demonstrated to a stunned world?

On many building ways in Germany submarines similar to the U-505, designed to break this barrier, were taking shape.

The fall of France enabled Doenitz to move his U-boat bases from Germany to the Biscay coast of France. This was a welcome break for Doenitz because things were getting too hot for him close to the shores of England. The RAF had learned a lot since the war began, and it was necessary for him to shift his zone of operations farther out into the Atlantic beyond the range of shore-based aircraft. This increased the distance to the hunting ground by about 1,000 miles per round trip, but the shift to Biscay bases evened it up again.

So far, the war at sea had been indecisive, a mere preview of what was to come. The Allies had lost 374 ships totalling

1.5 million tons, but this was hardly enough even to cause food rationing in England. The German seaborne traffic, except with Sweden and Norway, had been completely cut off. But Hitler had conquered so much new territory and acquired so many new resources that he didn't feel the pinch of the Royal Navy's blockade too badly . . . yet. The war had reached a temporary stalemate.

During the first ten months of war the size of the U-boat fleet had remained static. Twenty-three new boats joined the fleet, but twenty-three had been sunk. However, the number of U-boats available for operations decreased because half of the fleet had to be assigned to training new crews for the great building programme then getting into high gear. When the U-505's keel was laid, Allied shipyards were still in low gear but U-boat production was building up to thirty per month. For the next year, the U-boat fleet was growing rapidly and our total merchant fleet decreased by nearly 3 million tons.

When Doenitz moved his zone of operations out into the broad Atlantic, new tactics became necessary. While close to England, where the shipping lanes converged, his U-boats had operated as lone wolves, simply waiting near the bottlenecks for the shipping to come to them. But out in the open sea where the convoy routes could be shifted around, lone wolf operations didn't pay off because too much depended on the luck of the hunt. One boat might intercept a convoy and make a killing while a sister boat patrolling only fifty miles away might see nothing and bring all her torpedoes back to port.

Doenitz had an ace up his sleeve, the *rudeltaktik* or wolf pack, which he had worked out in prewar exercises. This was a revolutionary concept which recognized that to get the most out of submarines they had to be operated as surface vessels most of the time, and which took a well-calculated risk in discarding radio silence.

Doenitz's headquarters took over operational control of the boats at sea and spread them out in a long line on the surface across the convoy lanes. When one of the boats sighted a convoy he no longer drove in submerged and expended all his

14

torpedoes. He stayed on the surface and shadowed the convoy, keeping the masts in sight just over the horizon, reporting by radio to Doenitz. Doenitz rebroadcast the convoy's position, course and speed to other boats on the line and they converged on their prey at high speed on the surface. Often they were guided in by homing signals from the shadower, who, being out of range of shore-based aircraft, could get away with this. When five or six boats had assembled on each flank of the convoy, Doenitz would turn them loose to charge into the convoy at night, overwhelming the escorts by sheer weight of numbers.

This seems very simple and logical as I describe it now. But when Doenitz did it, it was a complete break with previous submarine practice in all navies. Submarines were traditionally lone wolves, and radio silence was sacred. This daring shift in tactics caught the Allies unprepared and Doenitz's new idea met with immediate spectacular success. For the next two years the wolf packs took a terrible toll of our convoys in the North Atlantic.

German histories of the war refer to the nights of October 18 and 19, 1940, as the "Night of the Long Knives". On these two nights a pack of twelve U-boats, led by the three great aces, Prien, Schepke and Kretschmer, ripped into two convoys like a pack of hungry wolves turned loose in a flock of sheep. A nautical version of Dante's *Inferno* was enacted out in the cold Atlantic several hundred miles from the English coast.

After lurking on the surface all day just beyond the horizon, the packs struck with unprecedented fury after dark. Surfaced U-boats charged back and forth through the convoy like the Horsemen of the Apocalypse, firing torpedoes right and left. Star shells lit up the sky, guns of all calibres blasted away, and the muffled thunder of torpedo explosions and depth charges reverberated all night. For hours there were scenes of wildest confusion. Tankers blew up with flash mushroom explosions that were previews of the atom bomb, and subsided into flaming beacons on the surface of the sea that burned for hours, giving a garish light for the continuing nightmare. Ships, manœuvring wildly to avoid torpedoes, rammed and sank each other. Gun crews firing at U-boats racing between columns of the convoy shot into ships in the adjacent column. Escort vessels pursuing the U-boats were mistaken for submarines and shot up by ships in the convoy they were trying to protect. The escorts were utterly futile that night and damaged not a single U-boat. The merchant ships which escaped slaughter did so simply because there weren't enough attackers to sink them all.

Seamen whose ships were shot out from under them did not suffer long in the bitter cold sea that night. After five minutes or so in near freezing water, the body becomes numb and death comes fairly comfortably in about fifteen minutes. Tanker crews' bodies froze while their heads, faces and hands were being burned by the flaming oil that covered the surface of the sea. There were few survivors from torpedoed ships and most of those had both arms and legs frostbitten beyond repair.

For the merchant sailors, these were nights of panic with unseen terror striking out of the blackness time and time again from all sides. Survival was a matter of blind luck as torpedoes fired from the centre of the convoy often missed their intended targets but hit ships in the next column. Blazing tankers illuminated friend and foe alike, but the black submarines with decks awash were much harder to see than the great cargo ships, and a conning tower is a tiny target for a gun crew on a rolling ship.

For Schepke, Prien and Kretschmer, these nights were wild orgies of power and victory. When the grey dawn of October 19 ended the slaughter, 32 ships out of 83 in the two convoys had been sunk. A total of 150,000 tons went to the bottom in the most overwhelming success of the Battle of the Atlantic for Doenitz and his three great aces.

Six months later, in March of '41, the British exacted poetic vengeance for this night of terror. Up to that time they had sunk a total of thirty-one U-boats in nineteen months, but for the past three and a half months had not sunk a single one. Between 8 and 17 March, they sank three. These three sinkings were consecutively recorded on the Admiralty's master list as follows:

16

Date	U-boat	Cause of Sinking	Position
8 March	U-47	HMS Wolverine	60°-47′ N 19°-13′ W
17 March	U-99	HMS Walker	61° N 12° W
17 March	U-100	HMS Walker-Vanoc	61° N 12° W

U-47 was Prien, U-99 Kretschmer, and U-100 Schepke. The three great aces were swept off the board in 9 days! This was the heaviest blow of the war so far to Doenitz and to the morale of his whole U-boat fleet. Prien and Schepke went down with their boats. Kretschmer was captured and spent the rest of the war in prison camp. He is now a Kapitän zur See in the new German Navy.

Kretschmer's capture is of interest in this story of the U-505. He was cornered at night while stalking a convoy by two British destroyers, one of which had just killed Schepke half an hour before. Badly damaged by depth charges while submerged at 300 feet, he lost control of his boat and she started toward the bottom in thousands of fathoms of water. He had the choice of sacrificing himself and his crew by simply riding her down to crushing depth or of blowing his tanks, bringing her to the surface, and giving his crew a chance to be rescued. He chose the latter and broke surface very close to the two destroyers. When he came up he was helpless and intended simply to surrender and scuttle. But there was no way the destroyers could know this, especially at night. Ordinarily, a cornered submarine is treated like a cornered tiger. The British opened fire on U-99 and for ten or fifteen minutes Kretschmer and his crew huddled on deck behind the bridge while the destroyers blasted away. When the British finally realized the U-boat was out of action and ceased fire, Kretschmer sent his crew below to put on warm clothing before going overboard. For another fifteen minutes or so the U-boat and the two destroyers wallowed in the darkness, eyeing each other suspiciously. Finally, one destroyer drifted down very close to U-99 and seemed to be lowering a boat. Kretschmer sent his Engineering Officer below to open the vents and scuttle. The Engineer did his duty well and went down with the boat. Kretschmer and the rest of his men were fished out of the water and taken to England.

The question arises, what would have happened if the destroyers had lowered whale boats and sent armed boarding parties over as soon as U-99 surfaced? There is at least a possibility that U-99 might have been boarded and captured. I bring this up because some people in Germany are critical now of the U-505's crew for "allowing" their boat to be captured. But Kretschmer, the greatest ace of all, lay helpless on the surface for half an hour with destroyers within hailing distance before scuttling his boat. The crew of the U-505 behaved in just about the same way as Kretschmer's crew. The difference in the final outcome of these two engagements resulted not from what the German crews did or didn't do, but from what their enemy did.

Incidents such as the "Night of the Long Knives" and the end of the three aces added colour and drama to the war at sea, but the real battle dragged on methodically and relentlessly day after day with the fate of the western nations at stake. These things, and others that happened on the surface, the great convoys plodding back and forth, wolf packs prowling, hideous night battles, narrow escapes, and drifting wreckage and lifeboats, were all just incidents. The final score was kept down at the bottom of the sea. When the U-505 was ready to go in commission on August 20, 1941, the score since the beginning of the war was as follows:

Allied merchant vessels sunk	1,653
Tonnage lost	8,000,000
New construction	3,000,000
Net loss	5,000,000
New U-boats commissioned	153
U-boats sunk	40
Net gain	113 (plus 57 original boats = 170 total in fleet)

The U-boats were getting the upper hand, food was now strictly rationed in England, and another year or so of blockade by a steadily growing U-boat fleet might force her to the wall. But Hitler couldn't wait. A maniacal urge drove him on and when he was stopped in one direction, he had to lash out in another. He couldn't get across the Channel to finish England quickly, blockade is a slow process, so he launched his attack on Russia. The frantic pleas of his military advisers against the Russian campaign had little effect any more. They had advised against every major move he had made so far, and every move had hit the jackpot. Who could blame him for thinking he had a magic touch and was infallible?

On August 26, 1941, more than a year after France surrendered, the U-505 was commissioned at Hamburg, Kapitän Leutnant zur See Axel Loewe, commanding. By this time the war with Russia was in full swing, but the slogan inscribed on the first page of the U-505's guest book, now in a glass case at the Chicago Museum of Science and Industry, reads, "Wir fahren gegen England" ("We are sailing against England"). Actually, they were going 4,000 miles farther than England— but not even in their craziest nightmares could any of the U-505's crew foresee that she would end up among the trees next to a museum in Chicago.

What they did think about is indicated by the following jingle translated from the early pages of the U-505's guest book. It was written the day she was commissioned, each of the various guests at the ceremony and visiting officers from sister ships composing and signing one verse:

10 proud British merchant men cruising in a line,
Along came U-505 and then there were nine.
Amfert—Oberleut. zur See

9 proud British merchant men with lookouts not awake,
The U-505 caught one and then there were eight.
Engemann, Oblt. Ing.

8 proud British steamers at a quarter past eleven,
When we squeeze the firing switch, then there are seven.
Habberg, Lt. zur See

7 British cargo ships loaded to their sticks,
But after our torpedo hits, there were only six.
Schneewind, Ober Lt. zur See
[Note—son of Raeder's Chief of Staff?]

6 proud British freighters running for their lives,
One lagged behind and then there were five.
                              Wuch, Lt. zur See—U-656

5 big British steamers almost at the shore,
The 505 released an eel and then there were four.
                              Rolph Faustborn, Lt. zur See

4 proud British steamers were sighted by our crew,
We dive and fire a double shot, and then there are two.
                              Boerner, Lt. zur See

2 British freighters a big one and a small,
Loewe shot the big one down so then only one.
                              Hans Schult, Lt. zur See

One little freighter arrived at Portsmouth—then,
The BBC and Reuters announced there were ten.

The moral of this story is "Don't believe what you read
in the British newspapers."

By August of '41, the United States was waging an undeclared war against U-boats in the North Atlantic. Lend
Lease was supplying Britain with arms, fifty old American
destroyers had been exchanged for British bases in the western
hemisphere, and U.S. destroyers were escorting British convoys, hunting out and depth charging U-boats. But Hitler didn't
want to fight the United States at this time and refused to let
his Admirals retaliate. They were now waging unrestricted
U-boat warfare against all non-Axis ships in the North Atlantic,
but he forbade attacks on U.S. ships in their home waters. His
master plan when the U-505 was commissioned was to defeat
Russia, then dispose of England, and to deal with the United
States after that.

I was in England as an observer before America got into
the war in October 1941. I remember well the grave faces in
the Admiralty the morning the aerial photographs of submarine building yards were evaluated, showing that U-boat
production would soon reach thirty per month. England had
plenty of battleships and cruisers to ensure control of the
surface of the sea, but these were useless for protecting convoys

against submarines. They were worse than useless because whenever one of them put to sea she had to have a heavy destroyer screen to protect her against submarines, thus reducing the number of escorts available to escort vital convoys.

The steadily growing U-boat fleet now numbered 200, and the Admiralty was badly scared. Everybody at the meeting that morning did some simple mental arithmetic and their faces got longer when they did. By this time it was apparent that the British people could grit their teeth and take whatever punishment the Luftwaffe could deal out to them. But even the bravest people cannot hold out indefinitely against starvation, and the noose of the U-boat blockade was getting tighter each week. From a long range point of view, this expanding U-boat fleet, to which the U-505 was the latest addition, was a much more deadly threat to England than the Luftwaffe or the panzer divisions.

CHAPTER III

INSIDE A SUBMARINE

BEFORE we go to the Baltic with the U-505 to watch her crew shaking down, let's take a look inside this strange submersible ship. Usually we think of a submarine as a craft designed to spend most of its time submerged, but the World War II submarine was more a surface craft which could, when necessary, operate submerged for short periods of time. In an emergency, to escape an attack, it could go down to five or six hundred feet, but it couldn't stay there long and it couldn't move very far while it was down there. It was a lightly armoured surface warship endowed with a special cloak of invisibility. Like any ship, it had to provide space and facilities for the crew to live, eat, and sleep. It also had to be able to propel itself through the water and to sink merchant ships. It takes a lot of complex equipment to do this and a modern submarine crams more men, machinery and equipment into less space than any other vehicle designed by man.

The "pressure hull" of a submarine contains all the living spaces, machinery and essential equipment. It is a tough steel cylinder, about ten times as long as it is in diameter, divided internally into six water-tight compartments by athwartship bulkheads, with a long narrow fore and aft passageway running from bow to stern. Circular doors three feet in diameter permit passage through the bulkheads. Amidships it has a stubby conning tower sticking up which is also a part of the pressure hull.

Inside this hull the air pressure is always just about atmospheric. Outside is the sea pressure corresponding to the depth at which the boat is operating. At five hundred feet it is sixteen tons per square foot of surface. The pressure hull must be a rugged structure to withstand such tremendous compression and if it ever cracks and admits sea water, the submarine will be on the bottom of the ocean permanently in a very few minutes.

A submarine has two powerful diesel engines, a pair of heavy electric motors, a huge storage battery and many pumps. It has torpedo tubes, complex fire control gear, and intricate radio, radar and listening equipment. When you jam all this stuff inside the pressure hull, plus spare parts, labyrinths of pipes, wires, valves, switches, gauges, plus sixty men and their belongings, plus food and fuel for three months, and then add the streamlining structure necessary to let it make some speed through the water and put a few guns and other useful pieces of machinery on this structure, the cylinder is just barely buoyant enough to float. Only the bridge would stick out of water and her decks would be awash.

Attached to the outside of the pressure hull are large tanks which the submariners call ballast tanks. This term is confusing to the layman because they are really "buoyancy" tanks, which, when empty, supply the flotation necessary to keep the heavy pressure hull afloat with her weather decks dry. These tanks have sea valves in the bottom and air valves on the top. When you open both valves and the vents, sea water comes in, forcing the air out through the vents, the tanks lose buoyancy and the submarine sinks. Theoretically, if you let in just exactly the right amount of water, she will sink until only half an inch of the periscope sticks out of water, but in practice you can't do this. It isn't possible to gauge the weight of the boat and the amount of water admitted that closely. If you admit just a gallon or so too much water, and do nothing about it, the submarine will start sinking slowly, but with a gradually increasing rate until the pressure hull collapses, which in the U-505 type submarine would happen around 1,000 feet. The reason is that sea water is not compressible but steel is. As the submarine sinks deeper and the pressure on the hull increases, the steel cylinder compresses slightly. This small compression decreases the buoyancy, which is already negative, and so she sinks faster.

The sinking can be stopped either by admitting compressed air to the ballast tanks and blowing water out, by pumping it out mechanically, or by driving the boat through the water and using the bow and stern planes to produce dynamic lift and hold the boat up as the wings of an aeroplane do, which is how it is almost always done in practice. When a submarine dives, she admits not quite enough water in the ballast tanks to sink her and then pulls herself down by use of her diving planes. Then if something goes wrong and she loses power, she will float back up to the surface.

Sometimes it *is* possible for a submarine to remain at rest completely submerged without using the diving planes and without juggling ballast. The density of sea water usually is nearly constant, but the sea is moody and doesn't always behave according to its own rules. Occasionally you can find a submerged layer of cold extra heavy water, and if you settle on to it gently enough with just a few pounds of negative buoyancy for the warmer water, the heavier cold water will hold you there suspended motionless. The only other way you can remain motionless submerged is to sit on the bottom in water shallower than your crushing depth.

The ballast tanks are not nearly as sturdily built as the pressure hull because they always have sea pressure both inside and outside, so they have no tendency to crush with increased depth. The same is true of the external fuel tanks which are open to the sea at the bottom. Oil being lighter than water it floats on top of the sea water, and as you use up oil the sea water rises higher in the tanks. Pressure inside and outside of these tanks is equal, as it is in the ballast tanks.

The whole structure of the pressure hull and its ballast and fuel tanks is enclosed in a light steel envelope of "gingerbread" which also never has to resist any unequal pressures. Its main purpose is to streamline the boat, furnish support for the outside weather deck and the guns, and stowage space for things carried externally, such as the anchor windlass, extra torpedoes, life rafts, etc.

A pre-schnorkel submarine of the U-505's type runs on its diesel engines when surfaced. But she must stop the diesels before she submerges. A diesel engine uses a lot of air, and the instant the conning tower hatch is closed for submerging, air becomes a precious thing in short supply. If you slam the conning tower hatch with air inductions closed and submerge with the diesels running full speed, you will suck all the air out of the boat in a few seconds.

Towards the end of the war the "Schnorkel" made it possible for submarines to run their diesels when submerged just below the surface. A schnorkel is simply a long steel pipe that sticks up about as high as a periscope and allows the diesels to suck air down from the surface into the boat. But this great improvement came too late for the U-505.

When she submerged she had to switch to her electric motors which drew their power from a huge storage battery. This battery, weighing over one hundred tons, could drive her for about twenty-four hours at slow speed or a much lesser period at high speed. At her most economical speed there was enough juice in the battery to take her about sixty miles submerged. The only way pre-schnorkel submarines could recharge their batteries was by running their diesel engines, which turned over the electric motors acting as generators and put energy back into the battery. When the battery got low, a pre-schnorkel submarine *had* to surface for two to three hours to recharge the battery. As will be explained later, this was one of the major facts of life about that type of submarine.

A submarine torpedo is a miniature version of the boat itself. Similar in all respects to the parent vessel except that, no crew space being necessary, the whole interior is jammed with machinery, explosives, and mechanical brains.

The standard torpedo at the beginning of the war was driven by compressed air, had a range of four to five miles, and could make thirty knots. This torpedo left a telltale white wake of air bubbles behind it and thereby often gave its target warning of its approach. Later, the Germans developed an electric torpedo driven by a storage battery, which left no wake.

The early torpedoes were straight running missiles which had to be carefully aimed, allowing for the course and speed of the target vessel. If the target zigged or zagged after this torpedo was fired, the torpedo would miss. Later the acoustic torpedo, equipped with mechanical ears which picked up the sound from the target vessel's screws, could manœuvre to make the sound equal in both ears, and thus "home" on the source of the noise. It was only necessary to aim it in the general direction of the target and turn it loose. No careful analysis of target course and speed was necessary and a zig-zagging target didn't bother it a bit. This was a deadly thing until we learned how to counter it.

The counter to this first guided missile, the acoustic torpedo, was ridiculously simple, when the Allies finally thought of it! We just towed raucous noise makers on a long cable astern of our ships. The torpedoes homed obediently on the loudest noise they heard and blew their own brains out harmlessly far astern of their intended targets!

Another type of torpedo, for use against convoys where many ships were crowded together in a small space, ran straight till it got to the middle of a convoy and then darted around like a ferret in a chicken yard making erratic figure eights until it met one of the many ships trying frantically to manœuvre out of its way and at the same time to avoid colliding with each other.

Torpedo exploders also went through various stages of development. At the beginning of the war they were percussion affairs and the torpedo had to hit the side of the target to make them work. If the torpedo depth control mechanism was inaccurate and the torpedo ran too deep, it could pass smack under the target ship and go on harmlessly beyond. Early in the war, the Germans had trouble with their depth mechanisms just as we did, and many a U-boat skipper saw fat targets get away from him after a perfect approach and well-aimed shot because the torpedo ran deeper than the setting he had put on it. These skippers returned to port spouting curses at the torpedo designers—just as ours did. No matter what his nationality, if you give a submarine skipper a defective torpedo, he'll damn your eyes to his dying day.

To counteract erratic depth performance, the Germans developed a new type of exploder which didn't have to hit a ship but merely had to come close. Like the magnetic mine, it was fired by passing through the magnetic field that surrounds a ship. If it passed ten or fifteen feet under a ship it would explode the warhead and break the ship in two. This worked for a while but then it and the magnetic mine were countered by demagnetizing all our ships. We wrapped electric cables clear around the ship fore and aft, and kept a heavy current flowing through them, setting up a man-made magnetic field exactly opposite to that induced in the ship by the magnetic field of the earth, thus sterilizing the ships so they would not fire the magnetic exploders. For a while the demagnetized ships caused the U-boat skippers to damn their own designers again, when they should have been cursing the Allied countermeasure boys.

Another little gadget you find in a torpedo is the arming device. You can't afford to cruise around in a submarine with twenty torpedoes fully armed and ready to explode from any slight jar or some magnetic fluke that could be caused by the aurora borealis. So the detonating cap which originates the explosion of the warhead is kept a few inches away from the hammer which will strike and fire it eventually. Even if the cap fired itself in this position it wouldn't detonate the warhead.

On the nose of the torpedo warhead there is a small propeller-like water vane, which turns when the torpedo drives itself through the water. The shaft of this vane has a screw thread connected to the detonating cap and as it turns it moves the detonator into line with the firing device, completing the alignment after the fish has travelled a safe distance from the firing submarine.

This device may have saved the U-505 from a premature end. One day in 1942, while attacking a ship in the Caribbean, one of her own torpedoes ran erratically, and some of her crew think it turned back and hit her square amidships. But the screw thread hadn't quite finished unwinding and all the submarine got of it was a dent in one of her ballast tanks.

Some people think the ocean's depths are sepulchral, noiseless voids where eternal silence reigns. How wrong they are. If you lower a sensitive microphone into the ocean you can hear many sounds. Water is an excellent conductor of sound—the submarines and their hunters both made constant use of this fact. The noises made by the screws of a ship can be heard many miles in an underwater microphone. The noises of the machinery and people inside her, transmitted into the water by the ship's hull, can also be heard at great distances. Breaking waves make noises and so do many kinds of fish. Schools of shrimp make rhythmic throbbing sounds that are very similar to the screws of a ship. The ocean has temperature, density and salinity layers that sometimes trap sound and channel it for phenomenal distances.

The ability to hear is of vital importance to a submarine, and all submarines are equipped with a sensitive array of listening devices. Very often they can hear an approaching ship much farther than they can see her even when fully surfaced. When a submarine goes deep to evade an attack the *only* way she can tell what goes on up on the surface is by sound.

The principal means used by surface vessels for finding submarines submerged is the sonar or "asdic" gear. The guts of this apparatus is housed in a dome which sticks out a few feet below the keel of the surface ship. A gadget inside the dome makes a "ping" which spreads out in all directions through the water. The sonar operator, in a compartment just above the keel, surrounded by banks of delicate instruments, watches his outgoing ping spread out on a videoscope like the ripple from a pebble on a pond. If there is nothing out there but sea water of uniform temperature, density, salinity and emptiness, he gets no echo and pings again. But occasionally, after hours of endless pinging, he gets an answering echo "pong". All this "pong" tells him is that there is *something* out there besides emptiness, but whether it is a ship, a school of fish, or a temperature gradient, is up to him to figure out. The direction from which the echo returns tells him the bearing of the "something," and the time interval from ping to pong, multiplied mechanically on a computer, by the speed of sound in water and divided by two, tells him its range. An expert sonarman can often tell from the quality of his echo whether he has got a school of fish, a thermocline, or a submarine.

By listening, without pinging, you can often find out a lot more of interest. You can hear the sound generated by a propeller driving a ship through the water, and count the revolu-

28

tions per minute it is making. The sound expert in a submarine can tell the skipper, from the screw noises he hears, how many screws the ship has, and whether it is a plodding harmless merchant vessel which he can safely attack, or a prowling high speed destroyer which he had better avoid. When the sonar operator on a destroyer gets a solid "pong" echo, he listens for screw noises. If he hears them he *knows* he has got a submarine —unless it turns out to be a school of "talking" shrimp.

A friend of mine who had a destroyer squadron out around Guadalcanal in the early days of the war, tells a story about the strange sounds you can hear from the ocean's depths. He says that one day it was the good fortune of his group to witness the most colossal bit of romancing (at least so far as physical bulk is concerned) that ever takes place on this earth—the mating of two whales. This creates quite a commotion in the water because the whales go at it enthusiastically. While all the spectators on the bridges of the destroyers were eagerly training spyglasses and binoculars on this rare sight, the sonar operators down below, conducting their routine probe of the ocean's depth, bounced a ping off the two great fish and reported "unidentified echo", on the precise bearing and distance of the amatory leviathans. Then, in accordance with regular procedure, they quit pinging and listened. My friend swears that his experts on underwater sound reported "screw noises".

The behaviour of sound in water is a field of science which absorbed the effort of some of America's best scientific brains. In water of uniform temperature, pressure and density, sound travels at constant speed in straight lines. But the ocean seldom duplicates standard laboratory conditions. Usually the temperature of the water decreases as you go down, and this will cause a sound beam projected just under the surface to curve down and go deep till it either dissipates itself or hits bottom. Sometimes you get inversions, and the temperature increases as you go down. Then your sonar beam curves up, hugs the surface and you may get echoes from unusually long ranges. A surface vessel with its sonar and "ears" at a fixed depth has to do the best it can with water conditions as it finds them. A submarine can sample the water all the way from the surface down to about three or four hundred feet and cruise at the depth where it finds the best listening conditions on a particular day.

Underwater explosions can sometimes be heard for phenomenally long distances—under proper conditions for several thousand miles. A sinking ship makes characteristic noises as her boilers explode and parts of the hull are crushed in by the terrific pressure as she goes down.

You can tell that sound is of great importance to a submariner from reading any book about submarines. It is full of words designed to suggest the noises heard under the sea. *Kachung, kachung, kachung* is the day-long beat of the diesels. *Thum, thum, thum* is the noise made by high speed propellers approaching for an attack. *Ping* is the ominous warning from a destroyer's sonar gear. *Kerblam . . . crump . . . whang* is a salvo of depth charges close aboard. To a great extent, sound takes the place of sight as the main link with the outside world to the men who live inside a pressure hull.

Radio is another link that connects a submarine to the outside world. Submarines can receive certain types of long distance radio transmissions when they are shallowly submerged, and while receiving them they put out no indication of their location. But to transmit an answering message, they must surface, or at least stick a whip antenna above the surface. When they do, their neck is out as soon as they hit the key of their transmitter because they are then linked to friend and foe alike.

If you have direction finders all around the edge of the Atlantic Ocean, constantly on the alert for any message on the known submarine frequencies, it takes only a few seconds for three or four of them to swing their loops and get a good bearing on the source of the message. These far flung stations flash their readings to a central plotting room where experts can soon lay a small polygon down on your chart of the Atlantic which probably contains a submarine. Many a U-boat went to the bottom a few hours after sending a routine message in mid-ocean because of information furnished by Allied direction finder networks.

Laymen may ask, "Why didn't the Germans set up a similar system to tell their submarines where our killer groups were?" They just didn't control enough of the world's geography to do it. We occupied the whole rim of the Atlantic and could get simultaneous bearings from all around a German U-boat. The Germans in France could only get one bearing on our killer group, and it takes two or more intersecting bearings to give you a "fix".

A layman listening in on a radio circuit hears a jumble of dots and dashes as monotonous and humdrum as rain on a roof. But to a radio operator there is a rhythm and beat to every incoming message that is just as peculiar to the man who is sending it as the sender's voice. Radiomen call this characteristic beat the sender's "fist" and it identifies him to his contemporaries as surely as his fingerprints. Our direction finder operators got to know the fists of many U-boat radiomen, so in addition to locating a U-boat that surfaced to transmit a message, they could often tell you which U-boat it was.

Even a U-boat's radio transmitter also has its own individuality. You can seldom detect this by ear, but if you make a tape recording of a transmission and blow it up many times on an oscilloscope, the experts can put their finger on any other transmissions from that particular radio set.

The moral of all this is, that whenever you touch a radio transmitting key in war time, you are announcing not only your location, but also your name, rank and serial number if the enemy is as alert as he should be. This is why all Navies make a fetish of radio silence.

There is another side to the radio silence business. In the jeep carrier task groups we used our radios almost promiscuously. You can't operate an aircraft carrier, and accomplish anything worth while, unless you do. You've got to talk to your planes in the air to give them landing instructions. You've got to let them test their radio sets right after launching and make sure they are working. Otherwise, when one of them finally spots a submarine a hundred miles from the ship after several weeks of hunting, you experience the utterly frustrating experience of having him fly back to the ship and send you a blinker message saying, "There *was* a submarine out that-a-way an hour ago—but she's gone now."

This business of uninhibited radio traffic with our planes is what we military "experts" call a calculated risk. We knew the enemy might hear our transmissions, but we weighed this chance against the known fact that there was little use flying planes if you couldn't talk to them, and decided to use radio. As things turned out, we were right, so this *was* a calculated risk. The U-boats used their radios too much so this was *not* a calculated risk. The definition of a calculated risk is a gamble which military men take when they can't figure out what else to do and *which turns out to be right*. When it turns out wrong, it was a piece of utter stupidity.

The German scientists were slow getting wise to the facts of life about radar. For a long time they wouldn't believe that British destroyers were equipped with it. German technology was way behind the British in this field, and all the radars their scientists knew anything about were too big to put aboard small ships.

Even after sad experiences convinced the unscientific U-boat sailors that the British had seagoing radar because destroyers were charging straight at them out of the arctic mists, the "experts" in Berlin assured Admiral Doenitz that *airborne* radar was impossible. But it didn't take many attacks on his U-boats by aircraft on pitch black nights to convince Doenitz that the experts were wrong again. At his urgent insistence the scientists developed radar detectors which were eventually installed in all U-boats.

To install active radar sets (rather than detectors) would have been suicidal. Planes and surface vessels would home on the magnetic pulses sent out by such sets. Radar works on the same principle as sonar, except in a different element. A radar set emits an electromagnetic "ping" into the atmosphere, and waits for an answering magnetic "pong" from some reflecting surface. Any time you make a radar "ping" you risk giving away your location the same as you do when you put your fist on a radio transmitting key.

But a radar detector is a passive device which puts out no indication that it is operating. It's like the listening gear of a submarine as opposed to the active sonar of a surface ship. An active radar puts out a pulse of energy, gets an echo and measures the number of microseconds between the pulse and echo. A radar detector simply picks up the original pulse and indicates that a transmitting set is somewhere in the vicinity. It can't tell you how far away the transmitter is because it has no way of knowing just how many microseconds ago that pulse was triggered.

To compensate partly for this, the detector picks up a pulse about twice as far away as the triggering set can detect a usable echo. The detector works on the original outgoing pulse, whereas the active set must detect and measure a weak echo with only a fraction of the energy in the outgoing pulse.

These radar detectors sometimes did more harm to the Germans than they did good. Their warnings saved some U-boats from surprise attacks at night. But they also caused many a U-boat to crash dive for an aircraft many miles away, and to stay submerged for hours when there was no real danger at all.

All a radar receiver tells you when it shows a blip is that there's a radar transmitter somewhere within about fifty miles of you. From about the middle of 1943 on, Allied aircraft were so thick over the Atlantic shipping lanes that it was a fairly good bet there would be an aircraft within forty or fifty miles of any U-boat that surfaced near the shipping lanes, and all the U-boat skippers knew this. But when they surfaced and got a blip on their radar receivers, their heart beat increased and they submerged forthwith. It's one thing to know before you blow your tanks and come up that there will *probably* be an enemy aircraft within fifty miles of you. It's a much more urgent thing, when you break surface, to see a little dancing blip on a scope confirming the fact that you were right, but leaving you in doubt as to whether he is half a mile or fifty miles away. You will probably assume he is half a mile and get below again as fast as you can.

Doenitz and his "experts" finally got so panicky about radar that they conjured up hobgoblins that didn't exist. When the Allies shifted the frequency of their radar transmitters beyond the range of the Germans' detectors, the Nazis wrongly suspected their own passive receivers of putting out signals which the Allies could detect. Several of their U-boats were surprised on dark nights by aircraft equipped with new high-frequency radars which had produced no blip on their detectors. The Nazi scientists jumped to the conclusion that their receivers were somehow enabling Allied aircraft to home on their submarines. They scrapped one type of receiver and developed another called Naxos—of which more later. Actually, we never detected any usable signals from the German radar receivers.

The U-505, Hull 295 of the Deutsche Werft Shipyards, Hamburg, was a type IX-C boat, 252 feet long, displaced 1,100 tons when fully loaded, and carried a crew of four officers and fifty-six men. She could make nineteen knots on the surface running on her diesel engines, and could stay at sea for ninety days cruising at economical speed. She was of the pre-schnorkel type which could not run on diesel engines when submerged, but had to use her electric motors driven by a battery. This battery had to be recharged at least every twenty-four hours, and this could be done only by surfacing and running the diesel engines.

She carried twenty-one torpedoes, each capable of sinking any ordinary merchant ship, and had four tubes forward and two aft. When commissioned, she had a 4.1-inch gun just forward of the conning tower, but this was later removed and replaced by anti-aircraft guns.

So much for the mechanical insides of the U-505 when she started her training in the Baltic. The essential facts about the U-505 type were therefore:

(a) She was primarily a surface vessel.
(b) She was compelled to surface for several hours in every twenty-four to recharge her batteries.
(c) She had no schnorkel.

34

(d) She could go down to about 600 feet.
(e) She had excellent listening gear and only primitive radar detectors.
(f) Her primary armament was twenty-one torpedoes, but at first she also carried a four-inch gun.

CHAPTER IV

SHAKEDOWN CRUISE

On the first of September, 1941, the newly commissioned U-505 went through the Kiel Canal to the Baltic to spend the next four and a half months "shaking down". In this shaking down process a new ship works the bugs out of her machinery and digests and assimilates the men who have moved into her vitals. During this process she is somewhat like a young puppy developing its muscles, eyes, and ears, and learning to run, feed and take care of itself.

There are three major ingredients in the complex reaction that occurs on the shakedown cruise of a new ship, changing her from a floating machine shop into a weapon of war. They are the skipper, the crew, and the machinery. Their relative importance is in the order stated.

The machinery of the U-505 was the best that German scientific and technical brains could produce. The diesels, batteries, torpedoes, listening gear, periscopes and other equipment were the equal of any in the world. If skilfully operated, this mass of machinery would be a deadly instrument of destruction able to smash with one blow great merchant ships twenty times her tonnage and value. With a well trained crew, and fighting on her own terms, she could sink the biggest battleships in the world.

But a U-boat, like any other ship, is just so much cold metal until her crew comes aboard. Then each man in the crew lends her a little piece of his soul to keep as long as he serves in her—and often longer if she's a good ship. These little pieces all added together make up the soul of the ship, bring her to life, give her personality, and make her a member of the sea-going community of ships.

The U-505's crew was a typical cross-section of German youth. At this stage of the war they were a carefully skimmed cream of the crop, fired with zeal for the Fatherland and hate for England. Like most of the German Navy, they were not Nazi party members, but were convinced Germany's cause was just simply because it was the cause of their Fatherland, and were eager to get their U-boat to sea to join their sister ships striking back at England.

The average age of the crew when she went into commission was twenty years. They were born soon after World War I, most of them sired by soldiers and sailors who fought for the Kaiser. In 1933, Hitler took over as Chancellor of the Reich when these war babies were eleven years old. During their most impressionable years, Hitler was practically a god in Germany. Their parents regarded him as a messiah.

Many of them spent their teens in the Hitler youth movement but were too young to be fully-fledged Nazi party members. Besides the Navy discouraged party membership. The career officers who ran the Navy were willing to go along with Hitler and rebuild their service under him, but they avoided joining the party when possible. I fished men from three submarine crews out of the Atlantic and all of them said, "I am a German soldier—but not a Nazi."

Some were inclined to be arrogant after they dried out a bit, but that is understandable. In their brief, unhappy lifetime, they had seen Hitler change their Fatherland from a conquered, helpless country, to the most feared nation on earth. When the U-505 was commissioned in 1941, these youths had every reason to believe that Germany was invincible and they were on the winning side.

I'll say this for them—they were worthy opponents and fought bravely for their cause. They risked their lives to torpedo ships and then steamed off and left the survivors to make the best of their way ashore or to the bottom, as the case might be. They did not machine-gun lifeboats as our propaganda claimed they did. When we sank one of their U-boats and paused to fish them out of the water they were grateful—and surprised. Their propaganda had told them to expect machine-gun bullets instead of rescue! *

* When we tried Admirals Raeder and Doenitz at the Nuremberg war criminals trial one of the charges was that they had ordered U-boat

The U-505 was one of the standard type commerce destroyers which bore the brunt of the Battle of the Atlantic. There were perhaps eight hundred such type U-boats built, and in outward appearance you couldn't tell them apart. But identical sister ships can have totally different personalities. One will be happy and successful, another surly, unlucky, and no good. The skipper makes the difference. This is true of any ship. But in a submarine, even more than in a surface craft, the skipper is literally the heart, soul and brain of the ship. When the chips are down he is at the periscope and often he is the only man aboard who really knows what the score is. His snap judgment on when to take her down, when to blow main ballast and surface, when to attack and when to retire, will mean life or death to all on board. If he is timid, his boat will behave timidly in battle, no matter how tough his crew. If he is daring, his boat can perform great exploits with a comparatively weak crew.

The skipper depends on his crew, of course, and one man who fumbles his own small job can ruin a daring attack for the skipper. But with the right kind of skipper, that man is less apt to fumble. A tough, expert crew can sometimes stiffen the backbone of a timid skipper, but usually whatever influence is exerted comes the other way. The skipper's personality profoundly affects every man in the crew, and each man in the crew, individually, exerts a much smaller effect on the skipper. You will see as this story unfolds how the whole character of a U-boat can be changed overnight just by putting a new skipper aboard, because he alone makes the decisions which determine whether the boat will be a lion or a mouse. The U-505's first commander's name, Loewe, means lion in German. He painted a lion rampant on his conning tower, and as long as he was aboard she behaved like one.

All navies, except perhaps the Japanese, recognized the skipper's importance, and rewarded their top submarine

___

skippers to machine-gun the survivors of torpedoed ships. This was disproved. In the whole war there was only one authenticated case of machine-gunning survivors at sea. This was done by a U-boat skipper named Ems. The British shot him after the war.

skippers handsomely. Prien, Schepke, and Kretschmer were the top aces of the U-boat fleet, acknowledged as such even by the Allies. No one submarine skipper in any Navy has ever rolled up a score to equal Kretschmer's 325,000 tons. Prien, Schepke, and Kretschmer had a far reaching effect on the war at sea by convincing Hitler that the U-boat was the answer to England's supremacy at sea and persuading him to go all out on production of U-boats.

The Germans had a fixed scale of awards for successful raiding operations. Ace U-boat commanders who sank over 100,000 tons of Allied ships, got the Knight's Cross of the Iron Cross from Hitler and were great heroes in Germany. Their crews shared in these awards and were also marked men in the Fatherland. The Americans and British had submarine aces in their own navies.

The U-505's first skipper, Axel Loewe, Kapitän Leutnant zur See, Reichskriegsmarine, was a good one. You would expect him to be good because the U-boats were the elite branch of the service in the German Navy and got the pick of the officer personnel. This U-boat was one of the early ones of the programme that finally produced 1,100. The first skippers of these early U-boats were professional career officers and competition for these commands was keen.

Loewe came from a substantial family in eastern Germany and was thirty-one years old when he commissioned the U-505. His father had been an officer in the Kaiser's Navy who fought in the *Seydlitz* at the Battle of Jutland. The son followed in his father's footsteps, entered the Naval Academy at the age of nineteen and served in surface ships until war broke out. Then he volunteered for submarines, spent six months in the submarine school and made one "makey-learn" war cruise under an experienced skipper before taking command of the U-505. So far as submarines were concerned, his inexperience was comparable to that of his crew. But he had twelve years of regular Navy service behind him; he was a professional, and a good one.

He knew that the best way to advance your own personal interests is to thrust them into the background and make the welfare of your men your first concern. As soon as any crew knows they have this kind of skipper, that ship is on its way to becoming an efficient and successful one. As Loewe expressed it to me in a letter written ten years after the war, "I tried to follow the principle of the British Admiral Nelson and make my ship a happy band of brothers."

Judging from other things in this letter, Loewe is quite a man and a worth-while citizen. Although he lost all his worldly goods in the war and his naval career was abruptly ended, he has re-established himself since. He has now rejoined the newly formed German Navy as a Fregatte Kapitän. He says he considers that his life on earth so far has been lucky and happy because, "I have my health, my wonderful wife has stayed with me, and we are raising three fine children." I think that sentence explains why the man who brought the brand new U-505 into the Baltic in late 1941, soon made her into a good ship.

Loewe spent the next four months in the Baltic, beyond reach of the RAF and the Royal Navy, whipping his boat and crew into shape for the grim work ahead.

Only three of the fifty-six enlisted men in the U-505's crew had ever served in a submarine before. Training submariners is much more difficult than training surface sailors. But when a submarine fleet expands in war time from 57 boats to over 600, keeping as many boats on the hunting grounds as possible and losing trained crews regularly due to enemy action, the level of previous experience in the new boats is bound to be spread mighty thin.

With only three old submarine hands on board Loewe had to start with the ABC of the business. The crew were very willing and specially selected, but they had to be taught everything. Under such conditions the shake-down period is very important indeed.

In a submarine, more than in any other type of ship, each of the men who will live together for a year or so has a very high stake in the welfare and efficiency of this boat—his own life. Every man in a submarine knows that whatever future he has in life is bound to the fate of that submarine. If the boat dies, the odds are three to one he dies with her. He there-

40

fore not only does his own job to the very best of his ability, he checks to see that every other man does likewise. There is no such thing as an unimportant job and everybody knows that a single mistake by any one of them can be the end for the whole lot of them. Everybody resents any carelessness or inefficiency because the guilty party gambles with all their lives when he does anything that risks his own. A crew can be reconciled to a daring skipper who takes long chances and wins great glory for them to share, but they can't tolerate a stupid shipmate who doesn't pull his weight in the boat.

After a submarine crew have made a couple of war cruises together, there is a bond between them that lasts for life. It bridges whatever gaps there may be in their background, education, and station in life, and makes them permanent members of an exclusive club who have shared certain experiences together that no other group in the world have shared. They may not all like each other, but for a certain period they pooled their lives together in a dangerous business and brought each other through it safely. They can therefore make allowances (ashore) for the failings of these shipmates which they wouldn't make for anyone else.

When the U-505 joined the U-boat kindergarten class in the Baltic, the first thing they had to learn was how to handle the boat. It's easy enough in a book of this kind to "explain" how a submarine submerges by opening the flooding valves and vents to fill up the ballast tanks, pulls herself under with her diving planes, and then adjust trim and buoyancy by taking just enough water into the internal tanks of her pressure hull. Anyone can understand that if you close the vents and shoot compressed air in at the top of the ballast tanks, forcing the water out through the flood valves at the bottom, the boat will become buoyant again and come up to the surface.

But before a submarine can dive or surface every man in her crew must become thoroughly familiar with his own little part of the ship's intricate anatomy. This little part may contain dozens of valves, switches, and levers, all of which must be operated not only correctly and in proper sequence, but also in correct relation to what dozens of other men are doing at the

41

same time. It's hard to make a "small" mistake when everything is so closely integrated that one flip of the wrist in the wrong direction can dangerously sabotage a thousand correct operations performed precisely right. Carrying out even a routine manœuvre is a complex operation requiring perfect teamwork of all hands.

When the diving alarm sounds, all hands who are on deck tumble down the conning tower hatch and someone who *knows* how many were topside must check them off as they come down. The last man down slams the conning tower hatch closed provided he is sure the diesels are stopped, as they should be by that time. Then a lot of valves and vents must be opened in exactly the right order, the electric motors must be started, and the men on the diving planes must keep the bubbles in their inclinometers exactly where they should be. The diving officer must know exactly how much water he needs in every trimming tank and must close the valves and vents at exactly the right time. Otherwise he could scuttle the boat instead of just giving it neutral buoyancy.

He must keep track not only of the total weight of the boat but also of the fore and aft distribution of this weight. Both of these vary continuously. The total weight changes as the crew eats up the food and discharges the waste products overboard. Water is heavier than oil, so as you burn oil and sea water replaces it in the external tanks, the boat tends to gain weight. Three men moving from the after torpedo room to the forward one make an important change in the trim of the boat in half a minute. Since the external ballast tanks usually are full when submerged, there are internal tanks inside the pressure hull which are used for final adjustments to trim and buoyancy.

A boat can be in good trim on the surface where it has tons of positive buoyancy, but badly out of trim submerged when the buoyancy is near zero. It can happen if the diving officer doesn't know what he is doing. It did happen once to the U-505.

On the lighter side, a standard joke on almost every submarine in any Navy involves the toilet and the latest recruit to report aboard. When a submarine is running submerged, flushing the toilet (which is, of course, inside the pressure hull) involves a rather complicated sequence of opening and closing water and air valves. All submariners will gravely tell you that to take care of your routine bodily functions you need a degree in hydraulics. Some rather Rabelaisian pranks can be played on a newcomer to the submarine service by giving him only slightly inaccurate instructions as to how to operate the valves the first time he has need to do so when the boat is submerged. Of course, to be sure the newcomer doesn't drown himself and swamp the boat you had better be standing by outside the door of the "heads" after you give him these instructions.

There are two kinds of dives for submarines—a "normal" dive and a "crash" dive. On a normal dive, there is no hurry, everything can be checked and double checked, and you take her down gradually, keeping her on an even keel. A crash dive is an emergency manœuvre when you've got to get down fast to save your skin. When a plane screams down out of the clouds, seconds can mean the difference between life and death. Then a crash dive is a slam bang manœuvre, in which the big idea is to get under as soon as possible, adjusting trim and buoyancy later, before you plunge so deep that your pressure hull cracks. Even on a crash dive you must be sure the conning tower hatch is closed and the diesels are stopped. You will get all the crew below before slamming the conning tower hatch. As will appear later, I encountered one U-boat in the Atlantic whose captain couldn't wait for three of his men to get below when we surprised him. One of those three is the only survivor from that U-boat now.

After the crew of the U-505 had mastered the ABC of their business, they held full power trials and tested their guns, torpedoes, and all other equipment. Then, graduating to a higher class and working with friendly ships and planes, they got into the business of learning to fight their ship. Their radio operators learned how to get quick accurate bearings on any transmissions they picked up in order to track down unwary merchant vessels who broke radio silence at sea. Their sound crews learned to follow an unseen ship by the noise of her screws while she was still beyond the horizon, and to determine from sound alone whether she was a merchant ship for them to

torpedo, or a destroyer for them to avoid. Her "trick" department learned to shoot *Pillenwerfers* out of small tubes to create
chemical bubbles in the water astern which sent back false
echoes and baffled the probing sonar beams of destroyers trying
to hound them down. They practised ejecting oil and wreckage
to convince a gullible destroyer skipper or aviator that his first
attack had made a kill. Loewe perfected his technique for
making a submerged approach and attack on a zigzagging
target. They made crash dives to deep water as they would
have to do when attacked by aircraft. They practised lying
doggo on the bottom in shallow water with all hands practically
holding their breath and not making the slightest sound as they
would have to do to evade tormenting destroyers. They drilled
at creeping away quietly, submerged, their screws barely turning over, while destroyers dropped depth charges on the false
Pillenwerfer bubbles astern. When trying to sneak away in
this fashion, a U-boat crew walks around on tip toes, because
the sensitive listening gear on a destroyer can sometimes pick
up the footsteps of a heavy footed clod-hopper clumping along
on the steel floor plates. They ran submerged at full speed,
making erratic manœuvres to be used only *in extremis* when
noise wouldn't matter because the hellish din of depth charges
close aboard was drowning out all other noises, including the
destroyer's sonar gear. They simulated all sorts of casualties,
pretending that many important pieces of machinery had been
smashed by depth charge attacks, and that they were limping
home in badly battered condition.

During this shakedown period, a change was occurring inside
the U-505 like the change that goes on in an egg during incuba-
tion. Sixty strangers were adjusting themselves to each other,
getting to know and have confidence in their skipper and each
other, giving up pieces of their individuality, and changing
from an amorphous mass of strangers into an integrated, pur-
poseful, intelligent whole, much greater than the sum of its
original parts. Each of these sixty became a limb, organ, or
nerve of the complex body that took shape inside the submarine's tough shell. Each felt that he was an important part
of the new organism and that his destiny and its destiny were

44

one and the same. Loewe was its brain, and about half its soul. As we shall see, so long as he was on board it was a lion that had hatched in the shell of this U-boat.

Finally, the U-505 had to pass a rigid operational test and prove to the Admiral in charge of training that they had learned their lessons and were ready to graduate. Late in November they had their final operational readiness inspection. The Admiral's team of seasoned U-boat experts gave the new ship a merciless grilling, running her through every manœuvre a U-boat can ever be called upon to perform. They sprang unexpected casualties to the engines, torpedoes, and attack director on the green crew and skipper. They pulled critical switches at the wrong time, secretly opened valves that should be closed, and tried every way they knew to sabotage operations. Inspecting officers pretended to get angry at members of the crew and ranted at them to see how they would behave under pressure.

Loewe had done his job well. On 24 November, U-505 passed her operational trials and went back to the yard at Hamburg for her post-trial overhaul and loading of live torpedoes. On 19 January 1942 they were pronounced ready for the final test of battle, and the U-505 shoved off from Kiel to join the Second U-boat Flotilla based at Lorient.

This first operational voyage took them through the Kattegat and Skagerak into the North Sea. In World War I, when both sides of the English Channel were in Allied hands, a mine field clear across the Channel near Dover blocked that passage to the Kaiser's U-boats. In World War II, with the Germans holding the French side of the Channel, it was impossible for the British to lay such a mine field. But swarms of RAF aircraft and Royal Navy motor torpedo boats made it too dangerous for U-boats to use the Channel regularly. Toward the end of World War I, the great North Sea mine barrage, extending all the way from Scotland to Norway, had practically bottled up U-boats in the North Sea. But in World War II, the Germans held Norway and no such barrage was possible. The U-505 avoided the English Channel and took the longer passage north around Scotland, between the Faeroes and Iceland, and into the Bay of Biscay to Lorient on the Gironde River in France.

Although this took them directly across the converging convoy lanes to England, the voyage was apparently uneventful. The leather covered book, now on display in the Museum of Science and Industry, simply records the dates of her departure from Kiel and arrival in Lorient. But the war diary shows that Loewe kept his crew busy constantly for these fifteen days with more drills of every kind, crash dives, and simulated casualties. In addition, regular watches were now being stood, for they were now in enemy waters, and all hands were under a tension they never felt in the Baltic. In this part of the ocean there was no such thing as a friendly ship or aircraft. Submarines were treated as rattlesnakes by anyone who sighted them.

U-boat sailors didn't trust the Luftwaffe any more than Allied submariners trusted Allied flyers. There were recognition signals, of course, for use between planes and submarines. But all submariners used to say, "There's only one recognition signal we really trust—if it flaps its wings, it's friendly!"

As the U-505 reported for duty in Lorient early in '42, and prepared for her first foray against Allied shipping, the Battle of the Atlantic was entering its grimmest year. In 1942 the Germans terrorized the shipping lanes and almost knocked England out of the war by sinking 1,570 Allied ships, totalling 7,700,000 tons.

During this "Happy Time", as the U-boat skippers later called the year of 1942, no outstanding aces succeeded in filling the shoes of Prien, Schepke and Kretschmer. But there were a dozen or more who exceeded 100,000 tons, and the greatly increased number of U-boats at sea more than made up for the lack of phenomenal individual performances like those of the three aces. The U-505 was joining the U-boat fleet just in time to take part in the good hunting that would prevail for the next year and a half.

On her trip to Lorient, the U-505 passed about 200 miles south of Iceland where I had just taken over Command of the U.S. Navy Fleet Air Base at Reykjavik. I was to remain there for the next year and a half, operating a squadron of Catalinas

46

on anti-submarine patrol, helping the RAF to escort the hard-pressed convoys through the toughest stretch of the North Atlantic. During this time the U-505 would make three far-ranging cruises and sink nine ships. Two and a half years later she and I had a strange rendezvous to keep off Cape Blanco, French West Africa. But many things were still to happen before this meeting occurred—and in February 1942, she sailed past me two hundred miles away south bound, unmolested by my Catalinas.

CHAPTER V

ICELAND

I HAD arrived in Iceland on December 31, 1941. I was a Commander then. The undeclared war which we had waged for five months around Iceland was over. Still numb from the shock of Pearl Harbour, we now plunged up to our necks into the Battle of the Atlantic to sink or swim with the British. The Battle of the Atlantic was just entering the black year of 1942, in which things went steadily from bad to worse throughout the year.

Iceland is strategically located to dominate the North Atlantic convoy lanes. It was an ideal base for long range patrol planes helping to fill in the mid-Atlantic gap which our planes based in England and Newfoundland couldn't reach in 1941.*

The Icelanders had sat out all the wars of the world for a thousand years as neutrals, and didn't want any part of this one either. But in a global war the big nations don't pay much attention to International "Law" or the protests of small neutrals. We muscled in on the Icelanders as gently as possible in July 1941 during the undeclared war, brought our friends the British in with us, and stayed there the rest of the war.

My main job in command of the U.S. Navy Fleet Air Base at Reykjavik was to co-ordinate the operations of our Catalina (PBY) planes with the efforts of the RAF and the Royal Navy

---

* When I say "our" I mean Allied forces, not simply the U.S. Navy. Lest readers of this book, in which the U.S. Navy plays the leading role, should get an exaggerated idea of the part the USN played in the Battle of the Atlantic, important though it was, let me hasten to state that the final score on submarines sunk was

British and other Allied Forces	600
US Forces	181
Total	781

to escort convoys through the "gaps" where the U-boat wolf packs prowled. For the next year and a half the Battle of the Atlantic raged from 300 to 500 miles south of us, and my planes helped the RAF beat the wolf packs off many a beleaguered convoy.

We lived primitively in Nissen huts on the edge of Reykjavik aerodrome, and a big part of my job was inventing ways and means to keep the boys from going nuts during the long arctic nights in a cold, strange land.

The command set-up under which I had to work was one of the typical hotchpotches of the early war days. Almost every Allied officer in Iceland senior to me had some sort of authority to issue orders to me. For a while, whenever one of them happened to think of it, he did.

I had five official bosses who could tell me what to do— two U.S. Admirals, one British Admiral, one U.S. General and an RAF Air Commodore. No man can serve two masters, but I soon found that serving *five* is easy. All you have to do is to exercise a little judicious stupidity and get your bosses debating among themselves about their respective prerogatives and about who does what to whom. The situation becomes confused and to avoid any high-level ructions about it, they finally let you write your own ticket. You end up by becoming a small-scale Commander-in-Chief, hob-nobbing with all five bosses on an equal basis and running your own show to suit yourself.

As soon as I acquired this status, I found the RAF Air Commodore was the boss I had to work with to pull our weight in the U-boat battle. For all practical purposes, I joined the RAF, and the Air Commodore's planes and mine worked together over the convoy routes as if we were one outfit.

This didn't happen quite as quickly as you can tell it in one short paragraph. The Air Commodore was inclined to be a bit sceptical of me at first. He took one look at my face, which my friends tell me resembles a relief map of Ireland, and decided that anyone whose ancestry was so obviously Gaelic would probably make things as difficult as possible for His Majesty's representatives. This coolness eventually melted and we became fast friends, seeing eye to eye on every operational question that came up during our year and a half of close association.

An amusing incident helped us to break the ice and make friends with the British. One day when a blustery wind was blowing, the first shipment of recreational gear for our camp arrived from the United States. Opening up the boxes of this consignment like a bunch of kids on Christmas morning, we found, among other things, a push ball which we promptly blew up to its full five foot diameter. Exploring the crates for more loot, we left the push ball sitting outside the storeroom unattended.

You should never leave anything as big and light as a push ball unattended in Iceland, because the wind comes along and blows it away. This happened to our push ball. I emerged from the storeroom just in time to see it go skipping down the road, bounce over the bluff into the water, and start sailing across a small inlet on which our camp was located. It soon grounded on the opposite shore where a British anti-aircraft battery had its camp.

I wanted that push ball back, so I picked up my field telephone to call the CO of the AA battery and ask him to hold my push ball till we got over there and reclaimed it.

Our field telephone system consisted of a labyrinth of wires laid out over marshy ground. Short circuits and earths were frequent, and strange things happened on this command circuit. Connections often got crossed—as they did this time.

Just as I picked up my phone, I heard my friend across the way calling Royal Navy Headquarters and reporting. "The biggest bloody mine you've ever seen in your life has just washed ashore at our camp, and will you *please* send a mine disposal squad over to deal with it?" I hung up without saying a word.

After a few minutes I called the Royal Navy Headquarters and reported that I too had seen this huge mine wash ashore, that I had a qualified bomb disposal party at my place, and that if the RN wished me to do so, I would be happy to deal with this situation.

There was nothing in the world that the Royal Navy wanted more at that time than to have someone else take this nasty job off their hands. The Officer of the Watch promptly replied that this would be "quite satisfactory".

I burst into our Officers' Club, rounded up about a dozen helpers, explained the situation to them, and we organized a bomb disposal squad on the spot. We had all read enough about bomb disposal to know what sort of equipment we needed and how to go through the proper motions. We scrambled around the camp grabbing half a dozen rifles and commandeering a stethoscope, a voltmeter, a field telephone set, and a couple of tool boxes. Dumping this equipment into jeeps, we roared over to the British camp, where we found a crowd of our gallant Allies standing back at a respectful distance, casting nervous glances at the "mine".

The arrival of the American "experts" obviously relieved the tension. We immediately stationed our sentries and shoved the crowd back to a safer distance.

Leading out our field telephones we placed one at the mine and another about a hundred yards back, so that our mine disposal boys could phone back every move they made to be recorded in a note book, in case they made the wrong move and blew themselves up.

Then, after a few minutes of hocus pocus with the stethoscope and voltmeter, much telephoning back and forth and scribbling in the note book, we finally gave the signal that the big moment was at hand.

While the crowd watched in awed silence, we unscrewed the valve, let the air out, and then got the hell out of that camp in double quick time.

I was always getting into "situations" with the British. One icy day in January, I accompanied Admiral Dalrymple-Hamilton to a conference with Commander-in-Chief, Home Fleet, on board his flagship anchored near Reykjavik in Hvalfjördur.

When we departed from the great battleship, the guard and band were drawn up on the quarterdeck to send us off with appropriate ceremony in accordance with time-honoured naval custom. In deference to the foul weather, two sailors were also stationed at the foot of the gangway to help the visiting brass into the boat.

As our boat was shoving off one of the sailors slipped on the icy gangway and plunked into the near-freezing water. His buddy promptly hauled him back on the gangway platform and then, though both were drenched in icy brine, they snapped to attention and stood at salute till the boatswain's mate finished piping the barge away.

I complimented Admiral Dalrymple-Hamilton on this "good show . . . traditions of Nelson, and all that sort of thing".

"Nothing at all old boy," the Admiral replied modestly, "I'm sure any of your sailors would have done the same thing."

"I suppose so," I said, but then all my Irish ancestors rose up in their graves and compelled me to add, "Except, of course, that none of my sailors would have fallen overboard in the first place."

Don't think from all this monkey business that life was just fun and games in Iceland. In January '42 The Battle of the Atlantic was mounting to a smashing climax, and we were smack in the middle of it and brand new at the business. This was the heyday of the wolf packs, and the outcome of World War II hung in the balance a few hundred miles to the south of us. Our planes flew fourteen-hour patrols every day, taking the weather as it came—and it came in stinking doses of fog, wind, and freezing rain. Our pilots, flying lumbering PBY's, often spent ten hours going and coming from a convoy, but during their four-hour patrol around the convoy they kept the wolf packs down, forcing them to use up their precious batteries and to lose distance on the convoys.

The logistics of an operation of this kind are worth looking at, since military men are so frequently accused of padding their requirements outrageously. To keep one PBY over a convoy 500 miles away twenty-four hours a day, you have a perfect right to demand a twenty-six plane squadron. This probably sounds a ridiculous overestimate, but I can really justify that one. Your planes spend ten hours on each sortie going and coming to put in four hours on the convoy, so it takes six planes to do the twenty-four hours of flying time over the convoy.

You've always got to have at least one spare plane sitting on the line with its crew briefed and ready all day long, so that makes seven. The six planes that flew fourteen-hour hops yesterday are being overhauled today for tomorrow's operations, so that makes thirteen. In the flying business you hope there will never be an accident, but you know there will, so you add a certain per cent for "attrition". Let's say you are really conservative and only demand one extra plane for this factor. That makes fourteen. After a plane has flown let's say 1,000 hours, it has to be laid up for a major overhaul, which takes a month as opposed to a routine check of one day. This means you will always have about two planes in the workshop, so now we are up to sixteen. Just as Doenitz always had 50 per cent of his U-boats in training, you have to back up your operational force with plane crews in training. Being acutely cost-conscious and frugal with the taxpayers' money instead of demanding an equal number of planes "on the line" and in training as Doenitz always did for his U-boat fleet, I'll settle for only half as many, which brings our total up to twenty-four. Any sensible military man always adds a certain percentage to the best honest guess he can make as to what he needs, and, again being a thrifty soul, I'll add only ten per cent. So we wind up with a requirement of twenty-six planes to keep one over the convoys in the mid-Atlantic gap.

Some critics have accused the military of being profligate wastrels because we didn't win World War II by killing the last Jap with the last bullet we had in our ammunition locker. I would much rather defend myself against such charges than try to explain to my three kids why we lost our liberties because military planners didn't want the war to end with a lot of surplus junk on our hands.

So if you ever have to fight wolf packs, operating from a base in Iceland, don't settle for a squadron of less than twenty-six planes. (I had to get along with sixteen.)

Many of our pilots in Iceland flew hundreds of hours around the convoy before sighting their first submarine. Sometimes it seemed to them that it was utterly futile and useless to stick their necks out flying through foul weather only to bore holes in the air around a convoy with no submarines anywhere in sight. But the U-boats were there, *submerged,* and by keeping them submerged we were doing a lot to help defeat the wolf packs. My boys needed their first kill to boost their morale and enable them to rub elbows with their blooded partners in the RAF without any inferiority complex.

Early in 1942 we sighted three U-boats but fumbled the opportunities for a first kill due to over-eagerness, bad luck, and inattention to seemingly minor details. I called all the pilots together and read the Riot Act to them. At the end of my tirade, I announced that our recently opened Officers' Club was hereby closed and would remain so until we got our first kill. This was cruel and unusual punishment, but I had decided I would rather be a bastard and help win the war, than help lose it and be thought a "swell guy".

Soon afterwards one of our pilots, Lieutenant Hopgood, en route to meet a convoy out of England, caught the U-464 surfaced about 50 miles from the convoy. His attack crippled her so that she couldn't submerge, but could still limp along on the surface.

Hopgood had dropped all his depth-charges on the first attack and his single thirty-calibre machine gun was useless against the thick hull of the U-boat. He radioed to the convoy and a British destroyer broke off at full speed in answer to Hoppy's plea for help. Meanwhile the crippled submarine went alongside an Icelandic fishing vessel, and as Hoppy circled the Germans abandoned and scuttled their U-boat, took over the trawler and headed for Germany. Hoppy duly reported all this by radio and spent the next couple of hours shuttling back and forth between the trawler and the on-rushing destroyer coaching her how to steer.

This was an exciting three hours for all of us back in Iceland. Hoppy's electrifying message that he had a cripple on his hands but couldn't finish it off brought everybody piling into the RAF operations room where we sat with our ears glued to the radio following the dramatic developments at sea.

Hoppy's radio reports right up to the end were terse and official giving a clear and complete picture of what was happen-

54

ing out in the Atlantic mists. His next to last one was "Destroyer is alongside trawler and has taken off 52 prisoners." We were still cheering and slapping each other on the back when he came through with his final one in plain English—"Personal for Commander Gallery. Sank sub, open club."

We opened the club all right. We almost blew the roof off the joint that night, and while this celebration was at its height we conceived the happy idea of getting a suitable trophy of this victory to grace the lounge of the club. Obviously the most suitable trophy would be the U-boat skipper's pants.

Next morning I addressed an official letter to the First Lord of the Admiralty in London, outlining the previous day's action, explaining the American expression "Caught with your pants down" and its obvious application to what had happened, and requesting that when the British destroyer arrived in England with the prisoners, the German skipper's pants be forwarded to the Fleet Air Base for framing. To make this deal legal and prevent leaving the German skipper in an embarrassing position, I sent a pair of my own pants along with this letter and forwarded the correspondence via the British Admiral in Iceland.

At first the Admiral was horrified at the idea of addressing the First Lord with such an irregular proposal. But the Air Commodore persuaded him to "bung it on into London." By return mail I received a very pleasant letter from the First Lord congratulating us on our first kill and saying he had instructed the Admiralty "to deal with" my request.

A month or so later a very stuffy communication arrived from the Director of Naval Intelligence, quoting several sections of the Geneva Convention about humiliating prisoners, etc., etc., and regretting that my request could not be granted.

I took a very dim view of the matter. I didn't mind the stuff about the Geneva Convention so much, but I did resent the outrageous injustice of *not even getting my own pants back!*

In any story of Iceland the ordeal of the Murmansk convoys clamours for a hearing. The merchant sailors who survived that murderous run from Reykjavik to Murmansk and back (back only if you were lucky) were the unsung heroes of the war. In winter the Arctic Ice Cap extended down nearly to Bear Island and forced the convoys to cruise well within bomber range of the Norwegian coast. In summer the midnight sun gave both U-boats and planes twenty-four hours of daylight to find their targets and do their deadly work. Our planes escorted these convoys as far as they could and often the Luftwaffe planes practically relieved us "on station" at the limit of our range. Thus the convoys had air escort all the way to Murmansk and back, but most of the way it was hostile. The Russians made sweeping promises about heavy fighter escort for each successive convoy as soon as it came within their range, but they made no attempt to meet their commitments. Our ships were bombed by the Germans even when they were unloading at the docks in Murmansk.

If the Luftwaffe and the German Navy had been able to co-operate harmoniously, nothing would have got through on that run. On the few occasions when they did work together, such as on convoy PQ17, they decimated our convoys. Luckily for us Goering and Raeder hated each other, and the U-boats seldom got the help they needed from the air.

The ordeal of PQ17 is one of the saddest chapters of the Battle of the Atlantic. Several Murmansk convoys had been roughly handled, and as PQ17 assembled at Reykjavik in June 1942 there was unrest among the merchant sailors, some of whom refused to sail with their ships. To quiet the unrest, word was passed that we were going "all out" on PQ17. It would have a close escort of six destroyers in addition to the usual dozen corvettes. It would also have a covering force of four heavy cruisers escorted by three destroyers to beat off surface raiders. To top all this, a task group of the newest British and American battleships, *Duke of York* and *Washington,* plus four heavy cruisers, plus a dozen destroyers, would follow close behind them to trap and destroy the *Tirpitz* in case she was rash enough to venture from her hide-out in Norway. This is probably the most formidable escort any convoy was ever given, or more accurately, was ever promised.

On 27 June 1942 thirty-four merchant ships sailed from Reykjavik for Archangel, their crews lulled with a sense of security that the combined naval might of Britain and the U.S. would see them through. The ships were loaded to the gunwales with tanks, planes and ammunition—all badly needed in Russia.

What followed is a shameful page in naval history, and I must say that so far as the ships in this operation were concerned, all they could do was obey the peremptory orders of the Admiralty in London.

One of the many things that the merchant sailors didn't find out until after they sailed was that when the Admiralty said the battleship force would be "close" behind the convoy, they meant 150 miles—at least five hours' steaming at full speed. They also meant only until the convoy reached Bear Island, at which time the big ships would turn home.

On July 1st, when the convoy was just passing Jan Mayen Island and was still six hundred miles from Bear Island, the Germans located it by air, and shadowed it from then on. On July 4th, when the convoy was passing between Bear Island and Spitzbergen, the attacks began and four ships got sunk.

I'll never forget that 4th of July in Reykjavik if I live to be a hundred. The Air Commodore and I met in the RAF operations room early that morning and spent most of the day watching the drama unfold hundreds of miles to the northeast. Early in the forenoon we got a flash from London saying, "*Tirpitz* is proceeding to sea." So far as we knew, our two great battleships were still following "close" behind the convoy. The *Tirpitz* was heading into a booby trap.

The Air Commodore turned to me and said, "It looks like this is going to be the best 4th of July since you blokes declared your independence." I agreed. All afternoon we anticipated the coming triumph. As we found out later, by this time our battleships were on their way back to Scapa Flow.

Late that unforgettable day we intercepted the message from London, "All warships retire to the west at high speed. Merchant ships scatter and make best of way to Archangel." Too stunned and ashamed to say a word we just drifted out of Headquarters, went back to our huts and wept or cursed.

When the U.S.S. *Washington* came into Reykjavik some

weeks later her people wouldn't come ashore. They didn't want to face their friends, although God knows all they did was carry out orders from London which left them no discretion.

Fortunately, the merchant sailors in the convoy never saw our battleships, so it was a long time before they found out how the battleships deserted them. But they did see four heavy cruisers turn and run, taking the six destroyers assigned to escort the convoy along with them and leaving the convoy to its fate. The merchant ships scattered in accordance with the Admiralty's orders and did the best they could in lone battles against the Luftwaffe and the U-boat fleet. Only 11 out of the 34 ships which sailed from Iceland ever got to Russia. Some of them limped in months later, having hidden themselves in the ice pack to repair their damages. Out of 200,000 tons of vital cargo in this convoy, only 70,000 got to Russia.

Much as I deplore the conduct of our naval forces in this action, I must, in justice, state the Admiralty's side of the case. Singapore, where the *Prince of Wales* and *Repulse* got sunk, and Pearl Harbour were still fresh in their minds. Many of our finest surface ships had been sunk in the previous seven months and British dockyards were jammed with badly damaged battleships. The whole future of surface navies seemed to be at stake, and the heirs of Nelson in the Admiralty were taking no chances on having two more new battleships caught out on a limb where the Luftwaffe might nail them.

Perhaps this explains why the two battleships were told to stay 150 miles behind the convoy. But I'll never understand why the four cruisers and a dozen destroyers were ordered to run for home as soon as the *Tirpitz* was rumoured to be coming out. (Actually, the *Tirpitz* turned back soon because the Wilhelmstrasse could make just as big blunders as the master minds in London.)

Churchill in his book, *Closing the Ring,* said of PQ17, "The consequences for us were painful." This was a classic understatement by one of the masters of the art. He said that this cruiser force would not have had a chance against the *Tirpitz*. Perhaps in theory he was right. But on 13 December 1939 three small cruisers wrote a glorious page in British naval history when they defeated the German pocket battleship *Admiral Graf Spee* in an all-day running fight and drove the big ship into neutral waters at Montevideo. In theory these three frail British cruisers were foolhardy to venture within gun range of the *Graf Spee*.

Churchill also knew, perhaps better than anyone, that to win great victories you sometimes have to take long chances. Even after the Admiralty pulled the battleships out of PQ17's escort, the four cruisers and nine destroyers still with the convoy *might* have written another page for the history books if the Lords of the Admiralty had had as much guts as their compatriots at sea.

Soon after the PQ17 fiasco, we stopped running the Arctic convoys until the long winter nights set in again. When we started again, Berlin soon proved that the Nazi bureaucrats could hamstring their sea-going forces just as badly as the Admiralty could. While attempting a raid on a Murmansk convoy the great cruiser *Hipper* and the battleship *Lutzow*, obeying orders from Hitler, turned tail and ran for shelter when a few destroyers peeled off from the convoy and made what they expected to be a suicide attack on their huge opponents. The odds against these destroyers were at least as great as those against the escorts which abandoned PQ17. But despite the odds these bantamweights went in and routed the heavyweights.

One incident that occurred in Iceland before we got up there has a place in this story of the U-505. It is the strange business of the U-570. This submarine, although of a later number than the U-505, was at sea on her first cruise when the U-505 was being commissioned in August 1941.

One morning, three hundred miles south of Iceland, she surfaced simply to air out the boat for a few minutes. It was her bad luck to pop up half a mile in front of an RAF plane returning to Iceland after a fruitless anti-submarine patrol with all her depth charges still in the bomb racks. Within seconds the plane plastered the U-570 with a full salvo of depth charges which shook her up severely and, although doing no fatal damage, crippled her so that she couldn't submerge. Then to the amazement of the circling pilot, as the U-boat limped along on the surface, the whole crew came scrambling up on deck holding their hands aloft and waving a sheet in token of surrender!

The plane had no more depth charges left, and there is no way in which the pilot of a land plane can negotiate surrender terms with the skipper of a crippled submarine. The pilot sprayed machine-gun bullets in the water to let the U-boat crew know that he was in charge here and could take disciplinary action if necessary, and then sent them a blinker message to steer for Iceland. The U-570 meekly obeyed! For the next twenty-four hours the RAF kept planes circling the U-570 as she plodded through the stormy weather towards Iceland, and the Royal Navy rushed a tug out from Reykjavik to meet her.

I can see why a skipper who was not yet willing to die for the Fatherland might be reluctant to scuttle his U-boat in the North Atlantic hundreds of miles from land with nothing in sight but an aeroplane. There was a gale blowing, even in August the water is cold, and the circling aeroplane could do little for fifty men in the water. But when the British tug appeared a new situation was presented. The British were well aware of this and had prepared for it.

As the tug neared the submarine the Royal Navy skipper hailed the Germans and expressed grave doubts that he could rescue any of them in the prevailing heavy seas if the U-boat happened to sink. He urged them to keep her afloat at all costs. I'm sure he stayed within the limits of the Geneva Convention, but he must have been a very persuasive man, because the German crew accepted a towline from him and continued their voyage towards Iceland.

Just off the south coast of Iceland the towline broke in the heavy weather and the U-570 with her crew still on board was washed ashore on a sandy beach. By this time her crew had thrown her codes and secret papers overboard and had smashed most of her secret equipment. When the storm abated, the British salvaged the U-570, towed her to England and eventually repaired her and operated her in the Royal Navy as HMS *Graph*.

I have related this story in detail because some British naval officers will dispute the claim that the U-505 is the only German submarine ever boarded and captured at sea. There is no doubt whatever about what happened to the U-505. She didn't surrender, we took her by force. I don't know how to classify what happened to the U-570, but it was a different sort of thing entirely.

This strange tale does have a bearing, even though remotely, on the story of the U-505. The arctic nights are long, the social whirl in Iceland was slow, and we often gathered around the fireplace in the Officers' Club after dinner to swap tall stories about our flying experiences and to discuss global strategy. The strange story of the U-570 was hashed over many a time. One night after Hopgood's exploit with the U-464 and the Icelandic trawler, and while a marvellous aurora borealis display outside made all things seem possible, a fantastic plan was hatched. Somebody tossed the question out on the hearth—"Why can't we board and capture a sub with one of our PBY's?"

If you analyse this idea now it seems crazy—in fact, next morning when we got up in the dim arctic light, it seemed a little bit far-fetched. But when you are gathered around a fireplace in Iceland with a dozen active young imaginations at work on an idea, and especially when the bar stays open late, small difficulties are solved immediately and big ones are soon whittled down to small ones.

We started from the known facts that a depth charge attack which doesn't sink a submarine may cripple her so that she can't submerge, and that submarine crews had a strong desire to stay alive. We all knew that you can land a PBY in a pretty rough sea and get away with it—much rougher water than you can take off from afterwards.

We visualized another situation like Hopgood's with a cripple limping along on the surface. We decided we would circle close aboard for a few minutes peppering the hull with machine-gun bullets to convince the crew they had better stay below. Meantime, we would crack off a previously agreed code word to the base which meant, "We are about to board and capture a submarine—send destroyer out to accept prize from us." *Borealis* was to be the magic word.

Then our PBY would land in the water just short of the

U-boat's stern, taxi rapidly up and hook her wing over the deck just abaft the conning tower. All this time the bow gunner would be beating a tattoo on the conning tower with his machine gun. The plane would, of course, be equipped with boat hooks, tommy guns, and about a fathom of steel chain.

While the pilot kept his outboard engine going to hold the plane alongside, the rest of the plane crew would pile out of the side gun blister on to the deck and, after lashing the PBY securely to the U-boat, rush up to the conning tower. The man with the chain secures one end on deck and heaves the other down the conning tower hatch, making it impossible to close the hatch and submerge in case the Nazis are able to effect repairs. His pals fire a few shots down the hatch from their tommy guns to convince the boys below that it isn't safe to try and come up on deck. Then the only thing left is to pound out another message to base on our portable transmitter asking, "What the hell is the delay in getting that destroyer out here?" About this time the bar closed and we all went to bed.

Call this plan fantastic if you will. I suppose it was. But it is the germ from which an equally fantastic plan sprouted two years later—a plan that put the U-505 on the end of a towline astern of a jeep carrier and eventually alongside the Museum of Science and Industry in Chicago.

CHAPTER VI

LOEWE'S FIRST PATROL

On 11 February 1942 the U-505 and the veteran U-68 sailed from Lorient, the U-505 on her first war mission and the U-68 on her fifth. Escorted by a minesweeper to the hundred-fathom line, they parted there to proceed independently as lone wolves to their assigned hunting ground off Freetown, just above the Equator in the big bulge on the west coast of Africa.

The shipping lanes for traffic going round the Cape of Good Hope pass close to Freetown, and there was a lot of traffic going that way now. The battle for Egypt was raging along the northern rim of the Sahara Desert, with Rommel and the British chasing each other back and forth from Bengasi to El Alamein. The Mediterranean was practically closed to Allied shipping and all supplies for the British Army had to go all the way round Africa. Doenitz, keeping a shrewd eye on shipping and on the deployment of Allied naval and air forces, had found a spot off Freetown with heavy traffic and weak defences. The hunting would be good there.

As Kapitän Leutnant Axel Loewe took the U-505 to sea for her first raiding mission, he had every reason to look forward eagerly to the future. He had a splendid new U-boat, and a crew which he had trained himself. His orders to operate as a lone wolf gave him an independent command and made him the master of his own destiny as much as it is possible to be on this earth. He had reached the highest point to which any young German could aspire at this moment in world history and had a better opportunity to win fame than any of his contemporaries in the Army or even in the Luftwaffe. Within a few months he might be a hero of the Fatherland like Prien, the giant-killer who sank the *Royal Oak*. Prien was now on the bottom of the sea, but Loewe didn't let his mind dwell on things like that. All aviators expect to die in bed and so do U-boat skippers starting off on their first cruise.

Loewe had nineteen torpedoes on board and it took only 50,000 tons of enemy ships sunk to win an Iron Cross. If he was lucky, if most of his torpedoes hit, and if his targets were average-sized ships, he might make it on this cruise alone. Hessler in the U-107 had sunk 90,000 tons on one cruise. The U-68, now also en route to Freetown, was already well on her way to 100,000 tons and a Knight's Cross for her skipper. The luck of the chase would, of course, play a big part in the score that Loewe would make on this cruise. But he had drawn a good hunting ground, so his own guts, skill and intuition would play a big part too. Every U-boat skipper who ventured out of Biscay was crossing the doorstep of destiny and Loewe must have had a few dreams of glory as he stood his night watches on the bridge working his way south.

The crew were just as anxious as the skipper to get into action. Up to now Germany was certainly winning the war and none of them doubted final victory. They were anxious to play a part in it which they could boast about in later years. Members of famous U-boat crews were great heroes in Germany now. During their eight-day stay in Lorient, the unproven crew of the U-505 had been tolerantly patronized by the combat veterans of the U-68, U-124, U-515, and some of the other famous boats. With a little luck they would be able to do some patronizing themselves next time they were in Lorient.

For the first two days out of Lorient, Loewe crept along at low speed submerged all day and ran at high speed on the surface all night. Then, with about four hundred miles between him and the RAF bases in England, he ran surfaced all the time except for about an hour a day of test dives and drills. At this time the proposition that Britannia ruled the waves, and the air over them, was merely a patriotic idea in the minds of some old-fashioned Englishmen. A bold eager beaver like Loewe, who had confidence in his lookouts, could cruise on the surface any time he felt so inclined. As we shall see, when the U-505 headed for Freetown the next time—two years later—it would be quite a different story.

The one thing that the new U-boat, its Captain, and the crew needed to fuse them finally into an effective combat unit was a successful brush with the enemy. No matter how well a new ship does at drills, these are make-believe affairs. Until the chips are down and you play for keeps you can never be sure that there isn't a weak link aboard who will get butter-fingered when his life is at stake.

The U-505's first chance to prove herself came within two weeks, when she was passing west of the Cape Verde Islands.

At 4.30 in the afternoon on February 24, Loewe sighted a smoke cloud twenty miles to the east. When he tried to close it he soon found it came from a fast south-bound convoy making fifteen knots. Such a convoy would have been hard to catch in any event because even when running on the surface the U-505 could make little over eighteen knots. When you are trying to close twenty miles on a convoy, holding a position abeam of it, as you must to make a successful attack, a three-knot margin in speed is just barely enough. But in this case the convoy had air escort and Loewe was driven under several times when the planes made routine sweeps out in his direction. Apparently the planes never saw him, but their approach forced him to submerge. His submerged speed being only three or four knots at best, he lost distance on the convoy rapidly whenever he was driven down. Loewe hung on till one o'clock the next morning, by which time he was still twenty miles from the convoy but had dropped astern of them. Then he lost the convoy in the darkness, and he surmises in his war diary that the convoy made a sudden change of course to the east which he failed to detect. He also records for the information of his superiors, "My fault that we lost contact." This sheds a lot of light on the man's character. All his superiors could ever know about this episode was what Loewe told them, and he could easily have told them a better story to explain his first failure if he had been built that way.

Of course, the crew knew pretty well what was going on during this ten-and-a-half hour chase, and knew it really wasn't the skipper's fault that this convoy had escaped. They knew you can't always attack every target you sight. A lot depends on the speed of the target and your position relative to its course when you first pick it up. If there are planes buzzing around the convoy you'll only get in a shot if your first sighting happens to be from a lucky position. So the crew of the U-505 didn't blame their skipper for the convoy's escape. But they still needed their first kill, and Loewe knew very well that you don't build morale on good alibis for missed opportunities.

But sometimes you *can* build it on strange things. Next morning a lookout sighted a Sunderland bomber near the horizon about five miles away. "Alarm! *Flugzeug!*" he cried, and the four lookouts plopped down the hatch into the conning tower. The officer of the watch pulled the diving alarm and the whole boat sprang into action.

Both diesels coughed to a stop as the *maschinistenmaten* spun their throttle valves and slammed the main air inductions shut. Electricians threw in the switches on the big board in the motor room and the whine of electric motors replaced the throbbing of diesels as the shafts kicked over again.

"Ready to dive," bawled the officer of the watch as he dropped from the bridge into the conning tower, pulling the hatch down over his head. On the level below in the control room men stood tensely at the flooding and vent manifolds, their hands on the valves ready to go into the routine that would take her down.

The diving officer made a signal with his right hand. The men began spinning valve wheels in a carefully predetermined sequence.

The boat had been "riding on the vents", which means that the sea valves in the bottom of all ballast tanks were open but the air vent valves in the top were closed. Sea water had therefore entered all tanks through the open sea valves, compressing the air trapped in the top of the tanks until the air pressure equalled the sea pressure and the water stopped coming in. All ballast tanks were about half full of water and the boat was, in effect, being kept on the surface by the cushions of air trapped in the top of each ballast tank.

To take her down, all they had to do was to pop the vents open. The air would rush out, the water would surge in through the bottom and down they would go. You get under a little quicker if you nose the boat down about ten degrees in the

66

process, so it was standard procedure on U-505 to pop the forward vents open first, letting water in forward to trim the bow down, and then pop the after vents. Meanwhile the men on the diving planes watched the bubbles in their inclinometers and wrestled with the big wheels on the forward and after diving flippers to keep the boat at the desired angle.

A dozen operations must be performed at exactly the right instant to make a good crash dive retaining full control of the boat. When they are, your boat is completely submerged in about thirty-five seconds, she has levelled off at about forty metres, the bubbles are centred, the trim tanks adjusted, and you settle down for a normal submerged run.

This time on the U-505 there was a slight hitch. Willi Bunger, an eighteen-year-old farm boy on the after ballast tank vents, missed a signal and didn't pop his vents open when he should have. Willi knew that he should open his vents at a certain point without further signal after the diving officer gave the order "Take her down." But always in the past the diving officer had motioned with his left hand when he wanted the after vents. He did this time too, but Willi didn't see it and the diving officer failed to check. Willi waited about ten seconds too long before popping the vents on his own initiative. As a result, for fifteen or twenty seconds, water was pouring into the tanks up forward but none was coming in aft. This made the boat very nose heavy.

As Loewe climbed into the conning tower the boat had just reached its normal ten-degree nose-down trim. "Sunderland aircraft, 5 miles bearing 270, Kapitän," reported the officer of the watch.

"Very well," said Loewe. "Hold her at this angle."

The angle increased to fifteen degrees. "Bow planes full up . . . Stern planes full down," ordered the diving officer. The angle increased to twenty degrees, the diving officer checked quickly to see that the after vents were open—and by *this* time they were. "Close forward vents," he yelled.

Normally this would have straightened things out fast. The inrush of water up forward would stop, water would continue to pour in aft and proper balance would soon be restored. But

Willi Bunger had waited so long before popping his vents that by the time he did it the stern was clear out of water and the after flood valves were a foot above the water. Instead of more water coming *into* the after tanks, the water already in them was gurgling out. When he opened the vents, it just made things worse by letting the water pour *out* faster.

Down, down, down went the bow. At thirty degrees Loewe shot a glance at the depth indicator, saw that it still read zero and realized immediately what was happening. The boat was pivoting around the conning tower with the bow going under and the stern coming out of water.

"*Ausblasen,*" he yelled, taking over from the diving officer. "Blow all tanks." As the shafts began to race he added, "Stop motors."

High pressure air to expel water from all tanks began hissing through the boat, but she kept right on tilting till she was forty degrees nosed down. Before she reached that angle the men and all loose gear started sliding along the floor plates and piled up against the forward bulkhead in each compartment, making the boat more bow heavy. Water was still pouring out of the after tanks faster than it was being forced out of the forward ones.

For two minutes, in order to stand erect, Loewe had to brace one foot on the forward *vertical* bulkhead and one on the deck of the conning tower. A few more degrees increase in trim would have forced him to shift both feet to the bulkhead. Any instant he expected to feel the smashing impact of bombs from the Sunderland.

Finally the increasing trim stopped. The boat hovered at a crazy angle for half a minute, and then began settling back again. When she was within ten degrees of being level again, Loewe ordered, "Cut off the air, open all vents, start motors." The U-505 settled back in the ocean, water rushed in equally forward and aft, and the boat disappeared under the sea.

To all hands in the crew it seemed that their heartbeats had stopped and they hadn't breathed for five minutes as they were waiting for the blows from the air which hadn't come. Now, at forty metres on an even keel, everyone let out a sigh, looked at each other silently and relaxed.

In Loewe's war diary the following entry appears: *"Eine schauderhafte Situation. Gottsei-dank hat das Flugzeug nichts gesehen."* A liberal translation is—"A hell of a fix. Thank God the plane didn't see us."

Ten minutes after getting squared away again, Loewe and the diving officer had reconstructed the whole sequence of events and figured out why it had happened.

"Tell Bunger I want to see him," said Loewe.

Willi Bunger was in his bunk, his face buried in the mattress and his whole body quaking, when they shook him and said, "The Captain wants to see you."

Willi pulled himself together, dried the tears on his skivvy shirt and made his way forward to the conning tower.

"Seaman Bunger, sir," he said, snapping to attention.

Loewe looked at the bloodshot eyes and tear-stained face. "Well?"

"It was all my fault, sir," blurted Willi. "I missed a signal and . . ." Willi choked up and began crying again.

After a pause Loewe asked, "Did you do it on purpose?"

"No, Kapitän," said Willi.

"Will you ever do it again?"

"No, Herr Kapitän," said Willi emphatically.

"Good," said Loewe. "We must have looked very funny with our head in the water and our arse up in the air, like an ostrich." Even Willi couldn't stop an embarrassed grin at this absurd picture. "Go below and get some coffee, Wilhelm," said Loewe.

Although only the Captain and Willi had been present in the conning tower during this interview, every word spoken was known to every man in the boat within a very few minutes. Each one of them said to himself, "I must be careful not to fail this Captain."

From that day forward Willi Bunger responded cheerfully to the nickname "Ostrich" and never made another mistake on the vents.

On March 2nd the U-505 arrived in her assigned area off

Freetown, and three days later, at 6.30 in the evening on the 5th, the lookouts sighted a 6,000 ton cargo ship, 120 miles off shore bound for Freetown. This time Loewe was lucky. The ship had no escort, it was just before sunset when he sighted her, and he could remain on the surface and make his attack under cover of darkness. For four hours he stalked her deliberately and just before 11.00 p.m. fired his first torpedoes at a live target, a double shot from the bow tubes at point blank range of 600 yards. They both missed! But a third shot didn't. It hit the unsuspecting steamer smack amidships, and she coasted to a stop sending out a frantic SOS saying, "S.S. *Ben Mohr* torpedoed," and giving her position. The U-505 had finally tasted blood. In the light of a nearly full moon, Loewe waited while the *Ben Mohr* got her boats in the water and then finished her with another torpedo that broke her back and sank her. He then made off on the surface at high speed leaving the lifeboats to make the best of their way ashore. The ship had sent off an SOS and on such a fine moonlight night there might be planes out there any minute, so it was advisable to get away from the scene of the sinking. In fact, three hours after the sinking they had to crash dive to avoid a Sunderland obviously sent out in response to the *Ben Mohr's* SOS. The SOS had given Loewe all the information he needed for his sinking report, and that night he entered in his war diary, "5.3.42— Englische Frachter Ben Mohr 6000 BRT." From the point of view of a U-boat skipper and his crew, the above terse entry contains all the information of any importance in connection with an incident such as this one.

It is not quite as simple as that for the survivors in the lifeboats. But if they are only 120 miles from Freetown in good weather, the outlook isn't too grim. If they are in the middle of the Atlantic, that's something else, and they have an ordeal to go through before they can be sure they are survivors.

As the U-505 steamed off to the southwest from the scene of her first kill, she was a different U-boat and every man in the crew a new man. Up till now they had been on trial but hadn't proved themselves. Now they had come up with a clean kill and wouldn't have to be bashful any more in the presence of the older crews of the Second Flotilla around the bars in Lorient. It was a jubilant group of novices that had tasted their first blood that night.

Their next opportunity came sooner than they had any right to expect. At 9.30 the next morning, only about forty-five miles from the spot where they had sunk *Ben Mohr,* they sighted a heavily laden tanker also inbound for Freetown. She was zig-zagging widely, evidently having been warned about the sinking of the *Ben Mohr* in this same area a few hours before. But it didn't take Loewe and his navigator long to analyse the zigzag and determine that she was headed for Freetown and that they were right on her basic course. Loewe submerged and waited for her devious path to bring her in front of his tubes, and two hours later she lined herself up with his periscope cross hairs. He fired a double shot at her as she disappeared in a rain squall and heard two explosions at the time when his torpedoes should have hit. Ten minutes later, when the squall lifted, there was nothing but a huge cloud of smoke where the tanker had been. Loewe surfaced and approached the cloud, noting that the water was covered with oil and wreckage, and finally spotting two rafts and a lifeboat. He came close enough to the rafts to determine that the survivors were all soaked with oil and that some were burned and needed medical supplies. But as he prepared to go alongside and give them morphine, salve and bandages, the lookouts sighted an aeroplane. He had to submerge and get out of that area.

The entry in the log for that day's work was "6.3.42 Engl. Tanker, Name Unknown, 8000 BRT." The sinking of 14,000 tons in two days started dreams of glory dancing in every head on the U-505. They had 13 torpedoes left and if they kept on at this rate the torpedoes would soon be gone and they would be on their way home to get Iron Crosses at the end of their first cruise! They regarded themselves now as seasoned U-boat veterans.

But Loewe, although pleased at these first two successes, knew that he and his crew hadn't really been tested yet. They were all still apprentices and would be until they got shaken up. There is nothing heroic about sinking a couple of unescorted merchant ships any more than there is in shooting sitting ducks. It requires a certain amount of technical skill in operating the boat, alertness by the lookouts to spot the game, and skill in adjusting and aiming the torpedoes. But it is no real test of the crew's ability to perform under pressure. That would come later when exploding depth charges slammed the hull with stunning blows, when each man had to grit his teeth and find the right valves in the dark with the ocean quaking around him.

It was Loewe's duty to postpone this testing as long as possible. His job was to make his attacks so that the enemy had the least possible chance of doing any harm to him. The more one-sided and certain he made this business of sinking unescorted merchant ships, the better he was doing his job. In submarine operations, as in all fields of military endeavour, the ideally planned and executed operation is an ambush where you kill the enemy from a position of complete safety yourself. A commander who takes any unnecessary risk is a fool.

Submarine warfare is a business in which the advantages are all on either one side or the other and the odds can change quite suddenly from one extreme to the other. The very nature of a submarine requires it to operate by stealth, and so long as it remains undetected until its torpedo blows the bottom out of an unsuspecting victim, the odds are all in the submarine's favour. Even Prien's great and daring feat of sinking the *Royal Oak* depended on stealth and surprise. But the moment a destroyer or an aircraft spots a submarine the odds swing the other way. Its only real defence is to submerge and make itself invisible. That first convoy the U-505 sighted, just after leaving Biscay got away simply because an aircraft circling around it forced the submarine to submerge and hide.

Submarines seldom get into a fight, properly speaking, except when cornered. A fight is a two-way battle in which the opponents stand up to each other and slug. Submarines are supposed to roll with the enemy's punch, dodge and squirm, and to get away rather than counterpunch. Even the wolf packs which charged into convoys on the surface at night did so under cover of darkness, depending on surprise and confusion to enable them to hit and run.

I don't mean to imply that the U-boat crews were not brave men. They were. But they had a different kind of courage from the kind we usually associate with military exploits. Their courage was tested not by the sinking of helpless merchant ships, for which they got their medals, but by the uneventful weeks of prowling in enemy waters between sinkings when nothing was happening. Even if they went for months without encountering enemy opposition, this was no guarantee that in the next ten minutes they might not be fighting for their lives, struggling to bring their boat to the surface and get overboard before her battered hull went to the bottom. Loewe knew that it took a few depth charges close aboard to sort out the men from the boys in his crew and finally make the U-505 a tested veteran.

After sinking the tanker, Loewe patrolled back and forth across the shipping lane from Freetown to Cape of Good Hope eager for the next victim. But for the next ten days he had the whole ocean to himself, and his jubilant crew had to settle down again to the tedious monotony of routine life at sea in a submarine.

Landlubbers who spend their lives ashore where they have plenty of elbow room, and can have all the privacy they want any time they feel grumpy, find it hard to believe that sixty men can live together for three months inside a pressure hull no wider than a tube train.

It's a cramped, confined life, in which all hands get to know each other much too well. But so is life in a monastery or a prison. Men can get used to it, and, counting all navies of the world, perhaps 100,000 men did it in World War II.

When you are on patrol and the hunting is bad, one day is almost exactly the same as the others. You could simplify the calendar by boiling the week down to three days—Yesterday, Today, and Tomorrow.

The sixty men who go to sea together in a submarine have got to make more personality adjustments than most psychiatrists have ever heard of. Before the cruise is over, every man

73

on board will know every joke that every other man on board has ever heard. He will listen to plenty of bragging by his ship-mates about their amatory exploits and probably do some himself. To three or four intimates he may let his hair down and tell them what he really thinks. But although plenty of serious thinking is done on a long cruise, little of it comes out in words. A garrulous deep thinker would be a menace to the morale of a group who know they are never sure of half an hour to live. Raconteurs are what you need on a U-boat—not philosophers. A misfit can make life hell for all on board. A claustrophobe would, of course, be unthinkable—the longest walk you can take is two hundred feet in a narrow passageway from the forward to the after torpedo room.

With sixty men living at such close quarters, little things assume great importance, and an irritating personal quirk that might be overlooked ashore can quickly antagonize all your shipmates. If you sip your soup too loudly, the fellow who sits next to you for ninety days may want to strangle you at the end of the first month. You can make life-long enemies by occupying the "heads" for more than your fair share of time. This, incidentally, is the only place on a U-boat where anyone is ever alone, all by himself—except for the skipper, who can pull a curtain across the door of his cubbyhole cabin and pretend he is getting some privacy.

A thief on a submarine is simply unthinkable. I heard of a man on a U.S. submarine during the war who didn't think it was safe to leave his money behind on the paymaster's books in Pearl Harbour when he went off on a war patrol to Japan. He drew $1,200 in cash the last day in port and kept it in his clothes locker on board.

An unusually funny quip or noteworthy comment of any kind gets through the boat almost as fast as if it had been broadcast on the loudspeaker system. Sometimes the crew can tell the skipper gently but firmly something which he ought to know. A new skipper on an American submarine in the Pacific muffed his first attack because he stuck the periscope up too far out of water, and his prospective victim spotted it and got away. For the next day or so, he overheard snatches of conversation mentioning a nickname which he didn't recognize as belonging to anyone in the boat. Finally, he asked one of the Chiefs, "Who is this guy I hear the boys calling Old Totem Pole?" The Chief had to tell him, and he never stuck his periscope up too far again.

Bathing facilities are primitive on a U-boat. There is no such thing as a bath tub, although you can take a salt water shower in the cooling water for the diesel engines, *after* it has done its cooling and is maybe too damned hot to interest you. A submarine must make her own fresh water by distilling sea water, which uses up her precious fuel supply or battery. Fresh water is carefully rationed and each man in the crew gets half a bucketful per day. After a while, you learn to brush your teeth, shave, scrub your clothes, and take a sort of bath every now and then, all in half a bucket of water. You don't have to be too particular about bathing, because when *everybody* smells a little bit gamey, nobody gets a dirty look unless he is really ripe. Submariners say, "If you think you smell someone standing behind you but find nobody there, then you'd better take a bath."

Space is at such a premium on a U-boat that they can't provide a bunk for each man. As soon as one man gets out of a bunk, another one crawls in. This is known as the "hot bunk" system. At the start of a cruise with all torpedoes on board, some of the upper bunks have torpedoes stowed in them. Some bunks are shared by three men, being occupied around the clock. Officers double up in a small compartment with upper and lower bunks.

In accordance with the long-standing custom of the sea, the Captain lives in solitary grandeur in a private cabin. He has a desk, wash bowl, locker and bunk all jammed into a space six feet square. But at least he has it all to himself, and is therefore the only man on board who can have some privacy when he wants it. Of course, he is always alone with his indivisible responsibility, and probably often wishes he could share that with somebody.

The galley on the U-505 was little bigger than a telephone booth. It had a three-burner stove on which all the cooking was done for sixty men. The food was good—the very best that Germany could produce was given to the U-boats.

What to do with spare time is quite a problem on a submarine. You can't just sit around thinking during off-duty hours, and there is certainly no use in writing letters home. Whenever possible, a skipper will run close enough to the surface to stick up a whip aerial and get the radio news. It helps relieve the hemmed-in feeling of isolation to hear what is happening elsewhere on this planet. Most U-boats carried a record player which they could hook into the loud-speaker circuits. By the end of one cruise the discs would be worn out and the melodies etched into the brains of the crew for the rest of their lives. Books and magazines were read over and over until they became dog-eared. Decks of cards continued in use long after they were worn out, and checkers and chess were popular pastimes.

Any military man from a spit and polish unit would be shocked by a brief glimpse inside a submarine after it settles down on a war patrol. He would certainly assume that this was a ragtime, undisciplined outfit. He would be wrong about the discipline—no U-boat lives long unless its crew is thoroughly trained to instant and precise obedience.

Life is certainly a bit informal in submarines. When on patrol, U-boat sailors looked more like pirates than members of the Third Reich's Kriegsmarine. All who could, grew beards, and you could make a pretty fair guess as to how long a U-boat had been away from base when you fished its survivors out of the water, from the length of the crew's hair.

The "uniform of the day" in the tropics was sneakers and a pair of drawers. When sixty men live as close together as a U-boat crew does, you don't need any insignia of rank to tell the others who you are. And when all you wear is a pair of skivvy pants, it cuts down the laundry problem. So conventional uniforms went into the lockers when they left Lorient and didn't come out again until they came alongside the dock to be received by the Admiral on return.

After ten days of the Yesterday, Today, and Tomorrow

routine, Loewe finally spotted another steamer early one morning. It was unescorted but zigzagging widely. Loewe stalked it for seven hours, manœuvring on the surface just beyond the steamer's horizon to get into a position ahead for a good shot. At mid-afternoon he submerged, closed in for the kill and fired a double shot. Both shots missed because the ship took an unexpected zig directly away from him just as he fired. The water was glassy and the steamer may have spotted his periscope just in time. At any rate, he had to retire beyond the horizon, surface and manœuvre for firing position again. Had this happened at night he could have regained position quickly on the surface. Several hours later, when he had worked around ahead of the steamer again, an aircraft appeared forcing him to submerge prematurely and the steamer got away.

This futile day's work highlights the fact that U-boat operations depended completely on stealth. Whenever a prospective victim saw the U-boat more than a minute or so before a torpedo hit, she simply had to turn away to frustrate the attack. The submarine would then have a long haul getting into position for another attack. (*Note:* The acoustic homing torpedo later changed this.) The escape of the steamer after the aircraft arrived on the scene also underlines the fact that boats like the U-505 were essentially surface vessels. Whenever they had to stay submerged any length of time their victims got away.

For the next twelve days the only events to break the monotony were several crash dives in the daytime to escape planes which the U-boat's alert lookouts sighted before the planes saw them. Theoretically, a plane can see a submarine much farther away than the submarine's lookouts can see the plane, and in peacetime manœuvres they usually do. But it often happens the other way in wartime because a submarine's lookouts have a much greater incentive for alertness than the plane's lookouts. When the plane sees the U-boat first and sinks it, everybody in the plane gets a medal—but everybody in the U-boat usually gets killed.

Loewe's lookouts also sighted a corvette on the horizon, but since she was all alone and proceeding at high speed, Loewe avoided her. His mission was to sink merchant ships and he could not afford to waste fuel getting in position to pick a fight with a small but deadly warship.

March 28 began like any other routine day, but turned out to be an unusual one. Shortly after midnight on that day the British made a daring naval raid on Saint Nazaire aimed at destroying the only dry dock in France that could take the great battleship *Tirpitz*. They broke into the inner harbour with the ex-U.S. destroyer *Campbeltown* and rammed her into the dock gate where she remained with her bow wedged fast until the next afternoon. Then, while many German engineering experts were aboard trying to figure out how to get her out of there, pre-set time fuses solved the problem for them by blowing her to smithereens and scattering pieces of highly trained experts all over the outskirts of Saint Nazaire—and putting the dock out of commission for the rest of the war.

When the *Campbeltown* rammed the dock gate, a jittery staff officer in Doenitz's headquarters jumped to the conclusion that the British were making a major landing and released an urgent radio signal saying "All U-boats east of twenty-nine degrees West proceed towards Lorient at high speed".

On the U-505, 3,000 miles away off Cape Palmas in Africa, they woke Loewe up at 3.00 a.m. and handed him this dispatch. His longitude was twenty degrees West, so this was a peremptory order from Doenitz, telling him to head for Lorient. It was obviously meant only for boats in the Bay of Biscay, but this was Loewe's first command and he didn't feel justified in reading between the lines. He felt it necessary to send a signal to U-boat headquarters referring to the panic message and saying, in effect, "Who, *me*?"

By the time this query got to headquarters, order had been restored and he got a prompt reply telling him to remain on station. Kapitän Leutnant Merten in the nearby U-68, being a veteran skipper, had merely dismissed the panic message with a contemptuous comment on chair-borne strategists ashore and gone on about his business.

When things quietened down in Saint Nazaire, Doenitz, whose communiqués were usually pretty factual, sent out a message to his U-boats, recorded in U-505's war diary, saying, "British attack driven off."

This is comparable to the communiqués of all governments after an air raid had blasted one of their cities off the map, and when the enemy bombers were finally going home, "The enemy aircraft were driven away."

Later on that day Loewe got sucked into a succession of incidents that nearly lost him a few tail feathers. Twice after sunset on the 28th, he had to crash dive to avoid aircraft. Just before midnight he sighted another aircraft and a corvette. Sniffing around the area to find out why there was so much activity he finally spotted a large merchant ship headed for Freetown.

Manœuvring on the surface in the moonlight he was just getting into position to shoot when the steamer suddenly headed right at him as if to ram. He had to crash dive and let her pass over him, thus putting him astern of her where it was useless to fire torpedoes. Apparently this was a chance manœuvre by the steamer and she hadn't actually seen him. He surfaced and trailed her for four hours waiting for the moon to set. But again an aircraft drove him down and must have seen him and called the corvette back from its position ahead of the ship. Soon Loewe's sound man reported, "High speed screws approaching," and a little later, "Sonar pulses, growing louder."

This was *it*. Now he was the quarry instead of the hunter and would soon find out what his crew were made of. His only defence was evasion. He couldn't use his torpedoes without exposing himself to almost certain destruction.

Loewe took her down to six hundred feet, slowed to creeping speed, and an expectant hush came over the boat. All hands in the submarine can hear the increasing noise of the enemy's propellers as he approaches the firing point and the decreasing beat as he passes it. There follows an interval of perhaps half a minute while the depth charges are sinking, when everyone braces himself, and almost everyone, no matter what his background, prays and promises God he will do better from now on IF . . .

Then suddenly, massive sledgehammer blows strike the hull. The steel plates transmit each shock to the very marrow of every man's bones. But unless the explosions are very close indeed, all they do is smash the lights and jar large flakes of paint off the bulkheads. If the skipper is a tough man, he knows within a few seconds whether his boat is really hurt or not.

The skipper of a cornered submarine faces a grim dilemma in deciding how he will try to escape. If he stays near the surface, he is easier for the sonar operators to find and easier to hit with depth charges. But he is under less water pressure than if he goes deep, and if his pressure hull is cracked he may have time to surface and give his crew a chance to escape before she sinks.

If he goes deep he will be much harder to find and more difficult to hit. But he loads his hull with tremendous water pressure. A mere tap from a depth charge too far away to hurt him at a depth of ten fathoms may crack his pressure hull at 100 fathoms. Then, even if he blows all tanks, the water may gush into the pressure hull faster than the air can expel it from the ballast tanks. In that case they all go down, down, down until the sea pressure crushes them flat, and the end is like a beer can full of flies that gets run over by a truck.

When the increasing screw noises and sonar pings told Loewe that the corvette was almost at the firing point, he ordered full speed on both motors and put his rudder hard over, hoping to run out from under the depth charges while they were sinking to their set depth. Half a minute later hell broke loose all round them. The ocean trembled, great blows smashed against the hull, and the men were thrown against the sides of their steel cigar like dice rattling around in a box. For a few seconds discipline and panic scuffled with each other inside every man but soon panic was overpowered and shoved back into the depth of his subconscious. A few seconds after the battering subsided the reports were coming into the control room. "No serious damage forward." "Engine room's OK. . . ."

Loewe kept on at full speed for ten minutes and then reduced to creeping speed again. For about fifteen minutes after depth charges rip the ocean apart, reverberations, eddies and gas

80

bubbles disturb the water so that a corvette's listening gear is useless. Her sonar man straining his ears for tell-tale noises cannot pick up the sound of a U-boat's propellers over the rumbling and re-echoing that goes on in the depths. During his ten-minute speed run Loewe had moved about a mile from the scene of the attack and was still down at six hundred feet. As the ocean began to quiet down the sub's sound man was straining his ears too, and soon he reported, "Propeller noises medium distance." A minute later he said, "Propeller noises decreasing," and all hands took a deep breath and grinned at each other. At last they were indeed members of the inner circle of seasoned U-boat veterans.

That night Loewe wrote in his log, "Baptism of fire. Crew behaved excellently." But he didn't seek any more trouble with that particular steamer and her escorts. He remained submerged for two hours after the screw noises died away, then surfaced and moved off to the south.

Next day Loewe made a nice little gesture to his crew by dipping down across the equator for half an hour. No sailor is considered a real shellback until he has crossed the line and they all like to brag of having done so. In his war diary, Loewe records, "Appropriate ceremonies were observed modified to meet existing conditions." Even in the midst of an all-out war, seafaring tradition required that proper deference be paid to Neptune.

After another uneventful week, Loewe hit the jackpot again two days in a row. On the first day, he entered in his war diary: "4–3 2132 Stmr West Irmo (Amerikaner) 5775 BRT." This ship was escorted by two corvettes and Loewe had to stalk her for twenty-nine hours before he got her. He missed her once with two torpedoes and neither she nor the escorts even knew it. But when he hit her, he had to slink away and elude the escorts so he didn't actually see her sink. He claimed her only as a "probable" because he heard the torpedoes hit and ten minutes later heard the unmistakable noises produced when a sinking ship is being crushed by the pressure in the depths of the sea.

Next day he got a Dutchman, the "SS Alphacca, 5759 BRT."

This one was a sitting duck, unescorted. He sank her with one torpedo early in the evening in a surface attack, and then stuck around for a while to gossip with her crew in the lifeboats. He notes in his war diary, "Boats well equipped and provisioned. Crew spoke German. Upon parting we wish each other 'good sailing.' . . . Irony of war, we fight against men who speak our own language."

Twelve days later the U-505 started back for Lorient and had a comparatively uneventful passage. One day she had a brush with an aircraft that dropped twelve bombs around her in the course of a couple of hours but they did no harm, although the first one must have been close to her just as she was submerging. They later found a fragment of its case on the conning tower.

Four hundred miles out of Lorient they were again attacked by aircraft, but crash dived in time to get nothing but a shaking up from the bombs. Two hours later Loewe received a radio from Doenitz telling him an inbound U-boat had just been attacked in his exact position. Evidently the Germans were reading the coded reports from RAF aircraft over Biscay at this time. Loewe comments on this dispatch, "Fast intelligence work."

On May 7, the U-505 tied up in Lorient. On her maiden cruise she had sunk 26,000 tons of Allied shipping, a pretty fair record even in the banner year of 1942. Actually, it was close to the general average of all U-boats at sea during the ninety-two days she was out. For a new boat on her first cruise, to equal the average was a very creditable performance.

She fired fourteen torpedoes of which eight hit. She sighted seven possible victims and got four. She crash dived to avoid aircraft twenty-four times and was only bombed twice. She had felt depth charges exploding close enough to expose any weak members in her crew and none had let the side down.

One significant statistic of this cruise, showing how well the war at sea was going for Germany at this time, is the summary of miles steamed, "12,937 surfaced, and 316 submerged." This means that the U-505 travelled forty times as far as a surface vessel as she did submerged.

The comment of Admiral Doenitz's staff on the U-505's war diary for this cruise was: "First mission of Captain with new boat, well and thoughtfully carried out. Despite long time in operations area, lack of traffic did not permit greater success."

CHAPTER VII

HAPPY HUNTING-GROUND

THE exultant U-505 returned to Lorient on 7 May 1942, to overhaul her engines, get a new load of torpedoes, oil, and stores, and to let her crew blow off steam. For the next month life was fast and easy—plenty of fresh air and sunshine, no more constant tension, and other faces than the sixty that had grown so monotonously familiar. Many of these faces were pretty, female, and willing.

The repairs needed by the U-505 were minor. She was soon reloaded, and on 7 June she sallied forth again, this time bound for American waters. Reports in Flotilla Headquarters had told an amazing tale of the slaughter the U-boats were making along the U.S. coast, and Loewe was eager to join the fun and run up his score.

The United States' entry into the war brought a major shift in Doenitz's strategy and tactics. There was nothing static or hidebound about the Admiral. He was a shrewd man who knew his business, and when new situations came up he reacted to them quickly. He was constantly probing for weak spots where he could make an easy haul. When he found one, he shifted his area of operations and concentrated on it until the sinkings mounted so alarmingly that the Allies had to rush reinforcements there. Then he would shift to another weak spot.

When Pearl Harbour plunged the U.S. into the shooting war, we Americans were babes in the woods so far as anti-submarine warfare was concerned. True, we had been fighting an undeclared war for five months with Doenitz, but on a very limited scale, and far away from our own shores. In general, we were totally unprepared at home in organization, training and equipment to protect shipping close to our own coasts.

The lights of our coastal cities still blazed at night, silhouetting coastwise ships for pot shots by U-boats. Our ships jabbered promiscuously on radio. There were no convoys in U.S. waters, we didn't have enough planes or destroyers to do a proper escort job, and our people simply wouldn't believe that this war that had raged for two years in far-off Europe could reach to our shores. Actually, the only reason why it hadn't got there long before was that Hitler hoped to keep the United States out of the shooting war until he finished conquering Europe. Despite our undeclared war, he had forbidden Doenitz to go beyond the mid-Atlantic.

Pearl Harbour surprised the Germans almost as much as it did us. But Doenitz reacted rapidly. Within a month he had recalled his wolf packs from the mid-ocean gap, revised his whole strategy, and was redeploying the packs as lone wolves against the U.S. coastal shipping. In January, his battle-seasoned U-boats ripped into the Atlantic seaboard shipping like hungry wolves turned loose among a flock of sheep.

Ships were sunk within sight of our city streets. On some nights the flames of burning tankers were even brighter than the city lights. Our beaches, from Sandy Hook to Key West, turned black from oil scum as the slaughter mounted. After several months of this, we finally dimmed the shore lights, organized coastal convoys and went to war. Then Doenitz simply shifted further south and had happy hunting there for many more months than I care to tell about.

Just before the U-505 sailed on her second cruise, Doenitz, keeping a sharp eye on the "exchange rate" between tonnage sunk and U-boats lost, had detected a levelling off in the exchange rate along the U.S. coast as we began to learn our business, and had just shifted to a virgin territory where the opposition would be feeble—the previously untouched Caribbean. This was Loewe's assigned area.

The U-505 made another easy transit out of Biscay, and as soon as he got out into the mid-ocean gap Loewe put on speed and ran surfaced as much as possible. He didn't want the happy hunting in the Caribbean to be over before he got there.

This run across the Atlantic was a picnic. The jeep carriers had not yet appeared in the Battle of the Atlantic. You never saw an enemy aircraft out there except for high flying, harmless

transport planes, heading for the Azores. The U-505 ran surfaced nearly all the way and Loewe let his crew bask in the
balmy sunshine all day long. Everybody could have a salt water
bath on deck every day, and as a gesture of contempt for their
enemy, they even set up a mess table and served lunch on deck.
They could always depend on sighting a surface vessel first,
so with no aircraft to worry about this was indeed a garden
of Eden.

Just three weeks after they sailed from Lorient and while
still several hundred miles from the Caribbean, they found their
next victim. One forenoon the sunbathers were brought to
their feet by the port lookout's cry, "Masts on horizon bearing
twenty degrees on port bow."

"All hands below except the bridge watch," ordered the
officer of the watch.

The crew tumbled down the escape hatches to the forward
and after torpedo rooms and the deck was cleared by the time
Loewe scrambled up on the bridge and trained his glasses on
what the lookout had seen. It was a spar no bigger than a
broomstick, poking up over the horizon at the limit of visibility.

"Good work, Muller," said Loewe to the port lookout. Then,
to the officer of the watch, "I'm going to close a few miles on
him first before submerging."

Loewe headed directly for the spar and noted that it grew in
height with gratifying rapidity. With his powerful glasses he
saw a crow's nest emerge over the horizon, but there was no
lookout in it, so he remained surfaced. Doenitz was right in
thinking that the enemy would be careless in this new territory.
After half an hour the top of the pilot house showed over the
horizon. Soon Loewe would be able to see the bridge and, by
the same token, those on the bridge would be able to see him.

"Take her down," he ordered and dropped down the hatch
into the conning tower, followed within six seconds by all four
lookouts. The last one slammed and locked the hatch, and in
another forty seconds they were submerged with nothing but
the periscope sticking out.

The eyepiece of the periscope was now ten feet lower than
Loewe's eyes had been on the bridge. The steamer had dropped

below the horizon and only the masts were visible again. But Loewe had her course worked out to half a degree by this time. She wasn't even zigzagging, and all he had to do was wait for her to climb over the horizon and steam smack in front of his loaded torpedo tubes. This would be shooting fish in a barrel.

That's exactly what it turned out to be.

Date	Type	Name	Tonnage
28.6.42	Am. Frachter	Robin Hood Class	6900 BRT

This time Loewe fired a double shot and both hit. He remained submerged after his first fish hit, giving the crew about an hour to lower boats and get clear. Then he finished her off with a third shot, surfaced after she sank, and continued on his way to his assigned area.

So, on the first day near his new area, Loewe hit the jack pot again. The U-505's lucky star was still rising. On the second day the jack pot repeated.

Date	Type	Name	Tonnage
29.6.42	Am. Frachter	Thomas McKean	7400 BRT

This time he surfaced, after crippling the ship with his first double shot, let the crew lower boats and then finished the job with his four-inch gun. After setting her on fire he photographed the sinking ship and one of the lifeboats, and gave the boat medical supplies and directions to the nearest land 360 miles away.

As the U-505 wishes the survivors luck, and disappears over the horizon in search of new victims, let us now look at the other side of the picture in this war against shipping.

Statements obtained from all survivors of ships sunk during this period are on file in Washington with the Maritime Administration of the Department of Commerce. I reproduce below extracts from two of these statements from the *McKean*. They tell the story as only seamen can tell it.

Thomas McCarthy, Chief Engineer, made the following statement:

On Saturday morning, June 20th, the vessel dropped down and went to anchor off of the Statue of Liberty, and the next morning,

June 21st, we left New York in convoy bound for the Delaware Breakwater. We arrived at the Delaware Breakwater about half-past eight or nine o'clock in the evening of June 21st, where we anchored for the night. At 4.20 the next morning, June 22nd, we left in convoy bound for Lynnhaven Roads, where we arrived that evening about 11.12 p.m. and where we remained until the following morning.

The following morning at 4 o'clock, June 23rd, we left Lynn-haven Roads and proceeded to sea on our destination, which was Trinidad, where we were to take on bunkers. We proceeded alone and not in convoy. Everything went well until the morning of June 29 when, at 7.20, a violent explosion occurred between No. 5 hatch and the steering engine room, starboard side. At that time, I had just gotten into the bathroom and was preparing to take a shave. My room is forward, on the port side on the boat deck. The first assistant, Mr. William McClintock, was on watch in the engine room. Oiler Shepard and Water Tender Hendeley were also on watch, both being in the engine room.

On this ship there was no bulkhead between the engine room and the fireroom. It is all one compartment. There was no fireman on watch as such, but the water tender is a combination water tender and fireman. In other words, just those three men were in the engine room. The engine room is amidships and the explosion did not affect the engine room—that is, it did not occur in the engine room.

When that torpedo hit I knew darned well what it was because I had just got torpedoed about six weeks previous, and I had my face all lathered up, and I was just getting the old razor out and "Wham!" I put on my sneakers and I immediately went down in the engine room, and when I got there the first assistant, the oiler and the water tender had evacuated. After she hit they took and got out of there.

In other words, when I was going down they were coming out, so I took and turned around myself, and to take and make sure that I knew they were all out I made a round of the quarters to check up to see all the men were out of there, because the fire alarm, or the emergency alarm was ringing continuously. Somebody had thrown that in from the wheelhouse and everybody was going to their boat stations, or the various stations at which they belonged, so I went back up and the engine was still running at this time. I did not stop her because I went up to the skipper and he said, "How hard are we hit?" and I said, "It looks to me like the whole stern is gone,"

88

and he said, "Take and climb over and see what you can see." And we had these cargo nettings alongside of each lifeboat so you could crawl down instead of going down the ladder, and fifteen or twenty men could crawl down into the boats at once, so I crawled down abeam of starboard boat No. 1 and I saw the ship was completely shot.

The skipper at that time was on the boat deck and hollered out, "What does it look like?" and I said, "It looks like she is finished." And he said, "Where are your men?" And I said, "Nobody is in quarters and they are evidently by the boats." So I said, "All right, I will shut off the engine," because the engine was still going like the devil, but she was not making any progress. So I went down and shut the engine off and came back up. The water tender, Short, who was on the 8 to 12 watch, shut down the service pump, that is the pump that supplies the fuel from the tanks to the burners in the boilers.

From the place where the torpedo hit, the torpedo evidently was very low. I would say offhand the torpedo hit her about 15 feet below the surface from the way she acted. She hit very low and she just took and broke the stern right off. She opened her right up in a perfect V, because I could see it very plainly when I was in the netting talking to the skipper, because I was standing in there and looking along the shell of the ship, and I could see the whole stern had dropped down. It was perfectly visible from the deck, but what we wanted to look at was how bad it was and saw she was finished.

I went back up and I took and secured the engine there and shut off the throttle valve, and that is accessible from the main deck in a small compartment there. After I shut her off I went down in the engine room to see what damage was down there. Then I went back up to the skipper and he said, "How is it lined up now, Chief?" I said, "Well, we are a dead pigeon." And so he took and said, "I will heave the papers over and you grab a case of cigarettes," and he passed them to me to throw in the lifeboat.

As soon as the torpedo struck Sparks got a message off right away, a wireless message, because I asked the captain about it, he said, "Yes, the message has gone out that we got hit," and Sparks got a verification on it from the various Naval Bases who picked it up and who were listening in. So after we got the cigarettes and threw them in the boat, the Skipper said, "Is everybody accounted for?" I said, "Yes," and he said, "Pull away and we can check up on those other boats." I didn't get a chance to get anything. I went in Boat No. 1, as all of the other boats had pulled away. After we got off the ship about fifty feet or a couple of boatlengths away Sparks came running out on deck, but there was no use to turn around because she was starting to sink back aft all of the time, and he crawled back aft, and by that time the painter on our boat got afoul of the rudder and we told Sparks to jump, and the skipper cut the painter loose and Sparks jumped then, but he didn't want to jump, and we pulled him in the boat and we squared the boat away, and hauled back aft in case anybody was back aft, and if they were they should have been in the water, but there was nobody there.

After we got about six or eight boatlengths off to the starboard quarter we came right around and the stern of the boat was completely off, and we pulled around the starboard quarter and we went by where she was blown off and we took and laid there. Just as we started to slack off the submarine broke surface right abeam of us, but she come up about a mile off. It was the first time I had seen her. She started shelling the ship and the first four shells were short, because she was too far off and the range was too great. She had a four-inch gun and a three-inch gun, and they kept moving in and firing all the time until they got right up on her, and they started to work.

They started and they took and raked No. 1 hatch. That was where we had the dynamite and that 50 calibre anti-aircraft ammunition, and then after they shelled that for a while they moved to No. 3—they didn't touch No. 2, but they moved to No. 3. That is where we had the highly inflammable gasoline and various accessories for planes and tanks, and after they got going good in there and got a fire started in there, they moved back to No. 4 hatch. They stayed in that position but they shifted the guns. Then they blew up the deep tank, the fuel oil tank; they knew where everything was. I think only one shell hit the engine room.

It took about an hour, between an hour and a quarter and an hour for the vessel to sink. I saw her go down completely. We were about a quarter a mile off and No. 3 boat was alongside of the submarine. She had an injured man in her, one of the gunners had an injured hand, and they gave him a package of medicine. After she shelled the ship, after she shelled her for about a half hour, then she went by the stern and cruised around and came back up again, and then she let that 3-inch gun, the aft gun, have a little target practice. The 3-inch gun fired about twelve or fifteen rounds, and the ship was settling all the time, and then the submarine went back and stayed in its original position until the ship sank. After they had shelled her there and had her afire, the ship was laying

90

down by the stern. Then the submarine came from this position amidships where she had been shelling her and moved around the stern right by our lifeboat, and then they let the after gun, the 3-inch gun, have a little fun with her, and fired 12 or 15 rounds at her, and then the submarine went over and stayed in its original position until the vessel sank, and after the vesel sank it went back to where the second mate's No. 3 boat was.

Of course, the boat was plainly marked "Thomas McKean, Baltimore," but the submarine wanted to know where it was from, and I believe they told him. The submarine gave No. 3 boat some kind of sleeping potion for the man that was hurt and some first aid equipment. We saw him for over two hours, because he talked with the second mate in No. 3 boat and then he proceeded southeast and he was still afloat, still on top of the water, when he went over the horizon.

There were three naval men on watch in the pillbox on the starboard quarter and after the explosion we did not see any of these three men. There was another man, one of the crew, whose name was Russell Funk, a wiper, who was sleeping on No. 5 hatch. He was injured very severely, and he died and we buried him at sea. A sailor from No. 3 boat picked him up from off the deck and put him in the lifeboat. I can not tell you the name of that sailor, but he was a Canadian. He is a naturalized American citizen now. I can not say definitely whether this man Funk was dead when he was put in the lifeboat. There was also a gunner stationed in the pill box on the port side aft, and he was blown completely overboard, but he swam back to the ship to help out. He later got into No. 2 boat, the first mate's boat. He was cut around the head very badly and also on his left leg, and he had lacerations and abrasions all over his body. He was taken care of in the boat and he was left in Norfolk at the Naval Base. There were a few others who received small cuts and abrasions, and there was one other gunner who had his left hand severely injured, and it was that man to whom the man on the submarine gave some aid. That man was in No. 4 boat. I understand all of the other men have been accounted for.

After the sub had left and the ship at that time had completely gone out of sight, she was sunk, we took and pulled over near the second mate's boat to check up on how many men he had on, and how many were injured. So he said, "I think I got a dead man here, Captain," and everybody was a little bit upset about it, so the skipper said to me, "Chief, you had better look at him."

So I asked them what tests they had made to find out whether he was dead, and after they had told me what they had done I said, "All right, did you burn his feet with a cigarette butt?" They said, "No." I said, "All right, let's try that." We tried that. I put my finger on his pulse to try to get any reaction, but got none, and I watched his eyes, and then we burned his finger tips, and there was absolutely no sign of anything in his eyes or anywhere else, and you could see that rigor mortis had already started to set in. So we took the hooks out of the lifeboat that he was in and took the hook out of our lifeboat, which was No. 1, and we took the after hook out of No. 3 boat and made a couple of lanyards out of No. 7 thread line that we had in the boat and secured the hooks to his ankles and dropped him overboard.

We took an account of the men again, and the Captain said, "All right, now, we are here on the chart." All of the boats were equipped with charts, each boat had a sextant and necessary equipment with regards to water and food and medical equipment, each of them had everything, and the captain said, "All right," and he told the three mates, "Here we are, we are about 66 east and 20 north." So he said, "All right, we will have to make it southerly as much as we can to land in the Islands," because it was a westerly set there, which was swinging us to the westward, and there was an easterly wind there all the time—I think they call it Trades.

We started, we got under way, we got the sails rigged in each of the boats and we started off.

The above is a typical sailor telling his story exactly the way a sailor tells it. No fiction writer could match his description of the torpedoing. Very few would think of having a Chief Engineer go back down below for a last look around while the ship is sinking and being abandoned, just to see what damage had been done. And very few real engineers would be able to resist the urge to do exactly that. A good novelist could easily make a chapter out of the Chief's terse statement about the radioman who went back—"but he didn't want to jump."

His description of the manner in which the U-boat shelled the ship, and his conclusion that the Germans knew exactly what was in each hold, is typical of what many sailors thought at this time. However, Loewe's encounter with the *McKean* was by pure chance and he certainly knew nothing about how she was loaded.

The first and most successful captain of U-505: Kapitän
Leutnant Axel Loewe

Survivors of S.S. *Thomas McKean* in No. 2 lifeboat

S.S. *Thomas McKean* burning and sinking, photographed from U-505

I don't know why it's important to tell how they rigged the dead man for burial, using "No. 7 thread line", but no seaman would omit this detail from his tale.

Roland L. Foster, Jr., Second Officer, made the following statement:

I was asleep in my room and the explosion woke me up. I jumped up right away and looked at my watch and it showed 7.29. Well, the first thing I did was my licence was laying on the corner of the desk and I grabbed it and my life preserver and rushed out on deck to my lifeboat station, No. 2. That is on the starboard side aft, and I released the strap around it that holds it on to the side of the ship. By that time the A.B. and the boatswain were up to take the falls, and I went on the bridge to get my sextant and chart, and then I came back and they had the boat waterborne when I got back. When I went on the bridge I told them to lower away, and I went to get my sextant and chart and when I came back I got in the lifeboat and we took a wounded man in the boat at that time and we shoved off from the side of the vessel at 7.36.

Everything was orderly and there was no confusion and everybody went to his boat station. Each officer and the captain got away in his respective boat and it was pretty generally true that there was no confusion.

When I first saw the submarine it was 7.45. That was the first time I saw him. Whether he had been on the surface before that or not I could not say. The second engineer said he saw him before we left the deck of the vessel, but I did not see him. When he surfaced we were between him and the ship. We were in his line of gunfire. He waited for us to row our lifeboat out of the way before he started firing, and the first shell hit very close to our lifeboat and fell in the water, and that was the only shell that missed in the entire firing. The fellows in our lifeboat counted thirty-nine other shells, which were fired in three periods.

After the second period of firing he came alongside my lifeboat and he came up and the commander of the submarine hollered through the megaphone, "Please come alongside," in English. That is all the commander said, and then his interpreter, I cannot say what he was, he only had on shorts and had a big red bushy beard and no other identification, no identification as an officer at all. I do not know what he was. All I know is he was the interpreter and he asked us whether we were an American ship and I said, "Yes."

He wanted to know what kind of an American ship and I said, "An American merchantman." And he said, "Gut," in German, and he wanted to know if there was anything he could do for us. He gave us first aid bandages for the wounded man. He wanted to know where we were bound, and before I had a chance to say anything, some member of the lifeboat crew, or a passenger, one or the other, said, "Trinidad," and that is all that was said about that.

Then he said, "You are carrying munitions? Yes?" And then he looked at every one of us in the lifeboat with that wicked eye he had, as much as to say that none of you had better say "No" to that, and I would say approximately thirty of those shells were fired at the hold where the munitions were in, and that looked to me suspicious, but maybe it was not. And I asked him what was the course to the nearest land; and he understood me to say I wanted him to tow me to the nearest land. I said, "No." He said, "No, we can not do that. We haven't got the time." I said, "I didn't say that, I said the nearest course to land." He said, "Steer mit the wind." He turned around to the commander and he said, "He says he is going ashore, he says he is going ashore." He shouted it out the second time. I am sure they were Germans, mostly young. They had a very large submarine. I read in the paper this morning where some other fellow said it was 250 feet and I would say it was about 200. She was very manœuverable, and I would say it would do 22 knots. She had a Swastika and a German ensign, and she also had a lioness painted on the side of the conning tower. This lioness was standing on its hind foot, I believe its left one, and in its front paw it had a big hammer, and in its tail it had a torch. They were all the markings on there. Her paint looked very good. Some of the fellows were very sun tanned and the majority looked like they had been faring pretty good in those islands down there.

It was very nice weather that morning. The rest of the trip, it went on well because we got in all right, but we had very rough weather and we landed at the northernmost tip of Anguilla, British West Indies, on July 5, at 11.10.

Notice in the above statement the things that a sailorman grabs first when he gets jarred out of his bunk by a torpedo explosion—his licence, and *then* a life preserver. This ship may be on the way to the bottom but to get a job on the next one he's got to have that licence.

94

Note also that by this time the U-505 has a lion rampant painted on the conning tower.

Comparatively speaking, the survivors of the *McKean* had an easy time of it. They were only 240 miles from land when they got sunk, two boats were picked up within four and a half days, one got ashore in seven, and the last after nine days. This was a picnic compared to the crazing thirsty hell that many others went through.

Only four lives were lost in this sinking out of a total of fifty-nine. But some inkling of the slaughter among ships then going on can be gained from the fact that this was the second time within six weeks that the Chief Engineer had been sunk. The reader will also note that there is no statement from the Captain of the *McKean*. He was picked up safe and sound, but on his way back to the States on another ship he got sunk again and was drowned.

CHAPTER VIII

U-505'S LUCK TURNS

THE U-505, with two kills in rapid succession, now had six sinkings totalling 40,300 tons. Two more of similar size would put them over the 50,000 mark, win Loewe an Iron Cross First Class and give Iron Crosses Second Class to many of the crew. With six more weeks to patrol in an area where ships didn't even zigzag, this should be easy. If they could economize on torpedoes by using their deck gun as they had on the *McKean*, it was even possible they might stretch their tonnage close to 100,000.

Some will say that it must be a brutal type of man who thinks simply in terms of statistics when the lives of human beings are involved. This is a mistaken way to look at it. The U-boat crews were average human beings, products of our western civilization whose destiny on this earth put them in a spot which demanded that rational human beings become ruthless about certain things. You can't conduct submarine warfare in a kindly humane manner any more than you can blast a sleeping city off the map benevolently. Allied submarines followed the same rules of warfare as the Germans and rolled up some impressive statistics.

So far, the U-505 had killed perhaps several dozen men and left about 300 more to make their way to land, if they could, in open boats and rafts. But that was incidental, merely one of the loose ends in the normal way that nations work out their differences. The duty of a U-boat crew was to sink ships. What happened to the little men who ran up on deck after the explosion, scrambled into boats and rowed away while the ships were sinking, was a problem for the survivors to work out with *their* destiny. When the U-boat crew got home from that cruise, if they did, they would be just as kind to their wives and children as they had been before.

So, after her second kill, the U-505 continued happily on

her journey looking forward to a busy time and a rich haul. But it didn't turn out that way. They spent the next month prowling through the Caribbean seeing nothing but aircraft. They crash dived for planes thirty times but only had bombs released at them once, and then not accurately.

The contempt in which they held American planes at this time is clearly shown in their war diary. They seldom spent more than one hour out of twenty-four submerged even though they were averaging one aircraft sighting per day! Our airmen in the Caribbean, when they happened to see a submarine, would scatter a few depth bombs around, note that the submarine had disappeared and fly back to base grinning from ear to ear to boast of their sinking.

It was for this reason that we set up Assessment Boards in Washington and London to analyse all attacks on U-boats and decide which ones had damaged submarines and which ones had merely shaken up the fishes.

The most hard-hearted and cynical bunch of sceptics that I have ever known sat on these boards. They wouldn't believe their own grandmother under oath unless she was able to produce oil samples and photographs of thirty identifiable Teutonic types in the water.

Their word was final. Their decisions often infuriated us who were fighting the Battle of the Atlantic and left us weeping into our beer at the Officers' Club between cruises and muttering "we wuz robbed." But at the end of the war when we got hold of the German Navy archives we found that they had been uncannily right most of the time.

These board members had good reason for their scepticism —and they weren't necessarily calling you a liar when they reduced your claim of a sure kill to "possibly minor damage". The very nature of anti-submarine warfare is such that the boys working at this trade will always firmly believe that they are doing better than they really are.

When a surface ship drops depth charges on a submerged submarine, the ocean reverberates with echoes of the explosions for a long time and it is impossible to ping again for some minutes. Meantime, a skilful U-boat skipper, who was merely shaken up by your attack, may give you the slip and get away. A depth charge must explode very close to a submarine to crack the tough pressure hull. But any destroyer skipper who had a good solid sonar echo when he dropped his charges, and had all the dials on his attack director screaming "Fire" at him, and who got no further echo, is going to swear that he made a kill—especially if the submarine ejected oil, garbage and maybe an old pair of pants from its stern torpedo tubes right after the attack.

Aviators have been held up to scorn as being flagrantly over-optimistic in their claims. In general they *were*, but in anti-submarine warfare there was much more excuse for it than in the bombing of surface targets when the "wild blue yonder" boys claimed any bomb that landed in the outlying suburbs of a big city was a direct hit on the city hall. Whenever a plane dropped a bomb within half a mile of a surfaced submarine, the submarine naturally pulled the plug and "sank" forthwith to a safe depth. When the flyer returned from that hop and swore that he had "sunk" the submarine, he was merely stating the facts truthfully as he had observed them.

The Assessment Board had to sift the facts, with the above and many other things in mind, and determine whether the intrepid birdman had really killed the submarine or had merely frightened him into submerging. Photographs of fifty Germans clinging to bits of oil-soaked wreckage were the best evidence. Pictures of a salvo of depth charges exploding close to a U-boat on both sides were the next best. A huge oil streak that kept spreading hours after the attack was sometimes good enough. The noise heard by listening gear when a hull was being crushed by water pressure a minute or so after the attack carried a lot of weight. Many U-boats went to the bottom in very deep water with all hands, leaving no evidence whatever behind until a day or so later when oil began seeping to the surface. The Board had to score these attacks, as well as the ones in which the photographs showed the submarine with its stern end sticking straight up out of the water and the crew plunging overboard. In both cases the U-boat was dead, but in the first one the evidence of death was inconclusive. At the end of the war we found that the Board's crystal ball had been a lot more accurate than any of us would believe it was when these chairborne bureaucrats were rejecting claims that we "knew" were true. The Board only allowed me ten sure kills, although I still claim eleven.

During the next month while Loewe ranged from one end of the Caribbean to the other, crossing and recrossing the regular traffic lanes, the Yesterday, Today and Tomorrow routine could have been even further simplified by eliminating Yesterday. There was no use remembering Yesterday, because luck was always bad, or rather they had no luck whatever, good or bad. Tomorrow, of course, always promised to be better.

Little incidents assume great importance at a time like this. One morning there was a muffled explosion behind one of the diesels. The man on watch spun his throttle closed and the chief engineer was soon squirming his way through the crates of canned provisions stored between the diesel and the pressure hull, to find out what was ailing his engine. He finally traced the explosion to a case of canned frankfurter sausages which couldn't stand the tropic heat plus that of the diesel engine.

This casualty placed a command decision squarely in the skipper's lap. Ordinarily a U-boat would run out of food before she ran out of fuel. When preparing for a cruise, every nook and cranny of the boat was stuffed with provisions after she got her torpedoes and other war supplies aboard. Her stay in the operational area was planned on the basis that she had food for ninety days aboard.

Napoleon said that an Army marches on its stomach. So does a U-boat. When a whole case of frankfurters explodes, it upsets a lot of carefully laid logistic plans. Loewe's command decision was a clear-cut but touchy one, profoundly affecting every man in the boat. Should he eat up this case before it went bad—feeding his boys *nothing* but frankfurters as long as they lasted—or should he heave the offending hot dogs overboard and cut short his operations by a week? He decided, as any good military man would, to stuff his men (and himself) with frankfurters for a while.

Being a smart Captain who kept his crew briefed on the

overall strategy of the war, Loewe broadcast this decision to all hands. He said, "Enemy flyers can't drive us home by the explosions of their powerful bombs, I'll be damned if I think we should be driven home early by the explosion of a case of our own canned goods." The crew all nodded reluctant agreement, each man ate a couple of fathoms of hot dogs in the next week, and probably had a family row next time a frankfurter appeared on his table at home.

Perishable items, like eggs, had to be eaten up early in a cruise. The U-boats put to sea with the passageway through the boat cluttered with crates of fresh eggs. By the end of the first couple of weeks, the crew all had a bellyful of eggs, and had eaten their way into a little more elbow room in the passageway. While the eggs lasted, the messenger on watch used to turn over each crate once a day, the crates all being marked with a circle on the side that should be up on even numbered days, and an "X" on the side for odd days. I am told that this procedure postpones the day when the eggs begin tasting like moth balls. Whether it does or not, it adds an extra little chore to keep the boys busy when nothing much is happening during the first ten days or so of a cruise.

Loewe relates in a letter to me that when they shoved off on this Caribbean cruise there was a shortage of coffee, so they were given a large supply of tea to make up for this. This led to an unforeseen burst of indignation from his crew the first time tea was served. It seems that when a young sailor drew the assignment as cook on a U-boat he was given a ten-day course ashore on how to keep hungry sailors well fed and happy. But you can't impart all the secrets of the culinary art to a willing amateur in ten days, and evidently one secret overlooked at the school was how to make tea.

Shortly after arrival in the Caribbean, Loewe's young cook dumped several pounds of tea in a big pot and boiled the hell out of it as if it had been coffee. The indignant howls of protest from the crew when they took their first swig of this poisonous brew brought Loewe scrambling out of his cubbyhole to the mess room to stop a riot.

Loewe says in his letter, "Since my mother was Dutch, I

had learned how to make tea as a child and was able to correct my cook's education. I must have done it well because the crew seemed to like tea—prepared my way." I doubt if many readers have ever imagined that one of the duties of a U-boat skipper fighting the Battle of the Atlantic was to teach young sailors how to make tea!

Loewe relates another little incident of this voyage. One day while cruising on the surface, a messenger came scurrying down to his cabin with a request from the officer of the watch, "Permission to change course and get some turtle steaks." He had sighted a school of huge sea turtles basking in the sun, and thought it would be easy to bag a couple of these proverbially slow leviathans. Loewe promptly granted permission and scrambled up on deck, followed by all hands not on watch, to see the fun.

The officer of the watch stationed a couple of men up in the bow with long handled nets, slowed to creeping speed, and conducted his approach on the school of turtles as carefully as if he were Prien making the firing run on the *Royal Oak*. But this naval engagement, like the Battle of Jutland, turned out to be indecisive. When the battle was over, U-505 retained control of the seas, as did the British after Jutland—but they got no turtles.

Loewe's action report to me says, "Turtles are phlegmatic animals which will let you get close to them but become suspicious when you poke nets at them. We soon found the turtles could submerge just as well as we could!"

To help keep the boys amused Loewe sometimes got up contests among the crew. These were simple affairs in which luck usually played at least as big a part as skill, like guessing the number of dried peas in a five pound bag, or working a series of riddles each of which had a dozen plausible answers but only one of which had been predesignated by the Captain as the official one. They ran checker tournaments for the championship of the boat. Another contest was guessing the last two numbers that would appear on the revolution counter at the precise moment of noon. The prize was that the skipper himself would stand the winner's next watch.

It isn't every skipper that could put up a prize of that kind. To do it you've got to know just about all there is to be known about a submarine, because there's no telling whose watch you will have to stand. It may be the cook's, a lookout's, an engineer's, a radio operator's, or the watch officer's duty. It's a good bet that when Loewe fell heir to a technician's watch the man involved stayed close to the skipper while he was standing it—not because he was afraid that Loewe might make a mess of it, you understand, but because in case of an alarm the monkey business would have to stop and the skipper would be needed elsewhere. Even so, Loewe gained in stature with his crew by showing them he could do the job of any man in the boat.

After twenty-three days of futile prowling following the sinking of the *McKean*, a puzzling entry appears in the war diary of the U-505: "July 22 7.25 a.m. Sighted sailing ship bearing 30°, course West. Three masted schooner *Roamar* from Cartagena with Colombian flag. As he did not stop for my warning shot I sank him with 22 rounds from my 10·5 cm gun. Size 400 BRT. 9.00 a.m., she sank."

"She sank." So far as the war diary is concerned, that's the end of the story. . . . But this ending leaves a number of questions to be answered. In the first place, the shelling of this harmless little sailing ship seems completely out of character for Loewe. When he sank large steamers he always waited, after his first torpedo hit, and gave the ship a chance to lower her boats before firing his second shot. In every case where the ship was unescorted and got off no SOS, he approached the lifeboats after the sinking to see if he could give them medical supplies, provisions or advice on the course to nearest land. Why did he gun this small schooner after one warning shot? Why is there no mention whatever in his log about the fate of the crew?

And why didn't the schooner heave to after the first warning shot? It was impossible for her to outrun the U-boat. It was suicide for her to do anything but luff up and douse her sails. There is no logical explanation for what she did except panic. She had a native crew who knew nothing about the customs of

102

war at sea among civilized nations, and they probably were paralysed with fright, didn't know what to do, and so did nothing.

Even so, it's difficult to see why Loewe attacked her with his second shot. If she had been a submarine trap she wouldn't try to run away from him. The drill for mystery Q-ships called for them to stop, lower boats, and send off the "panic party" leaving the ship ostensibly abandoned. The sinking of this 400-tonner plying between two Caribbean ports could obviously have no effect on the outcome of the great Battle of the Atlantic. Why did Loewe waste twenty-two rounds of ammunition on her and risk disclosing his position, possibly bringing aircraft and destroyers down on his neck?

There is little use speculating and philosophizing about things like this thirteen years after the event. It's just one of the messy little incidents of a global war which are important only to the men concerned in them. Looking back on it now, it is easy to say that this four-hundred-ton schooner could have been spared from the grand total of over twenty million tons sunk, without affecting the final result. But the Germans can also point to some hospitals and churches we blew up in Dresden and say the same thing.

Actually, I can't say that I blame Loewe for sinking her. She *might* have been a submarine trap. About a year later, when I commanded my jeep carrier task group, I met several majestic old full-rigged sailing ships off the Azores. I had a sentimental attachment for these wonderful old ships that link present-day sailors to their adventurous ancestors. But I gave all these seagoing heirlooms a thorough looking-over, had my planes photograph them from all angles, and examined the photos with a magnifying glass looking for suspicious radio antennas, oiling connections, or concealed hatches and side-ports. I will admit, however, that while doing this I felt just a little bit as if I were peeking under my grandmother's skirts, counting the ruffles on her pantaloons and accusing her of robbing poor boxes.

But, looking at it from Loewe's point of view, three-masted schooners that put to sea when a world war is in progress should have a skipper who isn't panicky, and should hire extra hands to be on deck at all times ready to douse sail and heave to the instant a warning shot crosses their bows. If they don't they can expect to get shot at and to have the second shell explode in the middle of the crew's sleeping quarters.

Whether the U-505 was justified in sinking the schooner or not, the U-boat's luck changed from that day forward. Far be it from me to say that this was *because* she had sunk the *Roamar*. But many "superstitious" sailors will shake their heads and say, "It's bad luck to sink a sailing ship."

Her first bit of misfortune was that Loewe got sick and had to request permission to curtail his stay in the operational area. As a matter of fact he had been sick for several days before the *Roamar* sinking and perhaps this explains it. U-boat HQ granted permission to return and ordered a new skipper to relieve Loewe as soon as they arrived in Lorient.

This was indeed a stroke of bad luck for the U-505. Loewe had been a good skipper. He was considerate of his men, he had confidence in them and they trusted him. Until he sank the *Roamar* the U-505 had been quite successful and success is the one thing above all else that creates high morale and a happy ship. Now the U-505 would have to go through the ordeal of breaking in a new skipper, and only time would tell whether he brought good luck or bad luck aboard with him.

On the way back to Lorient, the U-505 had a chance encounter with another U-boat bound for the Caribbean. On August 20 they exchanged recognition signals with U-214, and since they were returning from patrol early and had extra supplies left, they took time out from their return voyage to go alongside U-214 and, as recorded in their war diary, to give their friends two cases of *tea*. (Maybe Loewe's tea wasn't as popular with his crew as he now *claims* it was.)

On August 25 Loewe arrived back in Lorient, having been out for 79 days. This time they had seen six targets and sunk three—counting the *Roamar*. They had seen thirty aircraft but only one had seen them. Their cruising record was 12,842 miles on the surface and 498 submerged.

The U-boats were still able to operate mainly as surface

vessels. But it is worthy of note that whereas on her first cruise the U-505 travelled forty times as far on the surface as she did submerged, on her second the surface travel fell to only twenty-five times as much.

The comment of Doenitz's staff officers on this cruise was as follows: "Mission prematurely ended because of sickness of Captain. Took advantage of few chances of attack during time of almost total traffic stoppage. The sinking of the Colombian schooner had better been left undone."

Two days after arrival in Lorient, Loewe had his appendix removed. He spent the rest of the war on shore duty with Admiral Doenitz's staff.

CHAPTER IX

CSZHECH TAKES COMMAND

KAPITÄN LEUTNANT CSZHECH relieved Loewe early in October 1942. Cszhech came to the U-505 with a good reputation and an impressive record of experience. In fact, he had a great deal more wartime submarine service behind him than Loewe. He had been first lieutenant for a year in the U-124 under Mohr, and the U-124 was a number to conjure with around Lorient in 1942. She was one of the ace U-boats, had already sunk 100,000 tons, and anyone who had served his apprenticeship in her certainly ought to know his business.

But although the transfer of authority from the old skipper to the new becomes final and complete in one instant, transfer of the crew's loyalty is not quite that simple. Usually the crew starts off with a respectfully hopeful attitude towards the new man. For the time being they will take those gold stripes that he wears at their face value. They want to believe in the new skipper and be proud of him, and will give him the benefit of the doubt until he gives them reason to do otherwise.

But this isn't by any means the belligerent loyalty they give a proven skipper. A sailor from a good ship brags about *my* Captain as if he owned a big piece of the skipper. You can start bloody fights along the waterfront by making slighting remarks about a captain who has taken his boys safely through some tough jams and has left his claw marks on the enemy. The new skipper doesn't inherit that kind of loyalty at the change of command ceremony. He has to earn it, just as his predecessor had to.

Cszhech took over command with a somewhat tolerant and condescending air towards his new crew. After all, *he* came from the U-124, which in one two-week period had sunk more tonnage than this crew of newcomers had sunk in two complete war patrols. Of course, Mohr, skipper of U-124, got the credit and the medals for that performance, even though it was *he*, Cszhech, who had trained that crew, and who, in his own opinion, had been the mainspring of the whole boat. Several times Mohr had passed over chances for attacks which he, Cszhech, would have seized. He felt that if Mohr had been a little more daring and had followed his advice, U-124 would have rolled up an even higher score. Now, with his own command, Cszhech would be able to give his initiative full play.

There is no exact parallel for the process that takes place in a ship after a change of command. It's almost as if the heads were amputated from a living body and a new one grafted on without killing the body. If the old and new skippers are of similar temperaments, the change may occur smoothly and the severed nerves and blood vessels will grow together again. The test comes the next time they go into action, and if the operation has been successful the ship performs as she did under the old skipper.

But if the two men are radically different in character, some major upheavals may occur. An ace U-boat can become a dud overnight if she acquires a weak man in command. If an inefficient boat gets a keen skipper aboard, the change in the opposite direction begins immediately. The word gets around, "No more foolishness—this man means business." In the first week a few heads will roll, the slack rigging is set taut, and the former dud is a fighting unit.

A crew's judgment of a wartime skipper is completely objective. If he gives them something to brag about without getting them hurt too badly, he is affectionately called the "Old Man" and you had better not say anything against him no matter what kind of a bastard you think he is. If he doesn't, he's not considered much of a skipper no matter how he may pamper his men trying to get in their good books.

The U-505's reaction to the new skipper was good. All hands knew that in the U-124 Cszhech had seen much more action than they had in the U-505. They expected great things of him.

But Cszhech had seen all his action as first lieutenant, *not* as skipper, and this can make a big difference. A top-notch first officer under an ace skipper can be an utter flop when he is in command himself. Making the life and death decisions yourself is a different thing from just seeing to it that they are carried out after the captain has made them. So, although the U-505 accepted Cszhech on his reputation, time and some successful operations were the only things that could confirm this judgment. Until they had been under fire together everyone in the boat would have some reservations, and would be just a little more formal in speaking to the new skipper than he had been to the old. A few common adventures were necessary to remove the barrier between them.

Cszhech knew that big successes were expected of him, both by the high command and by this new crew, because of his service in the famous U-124. He intended to produce them.

When the U-505 sailed from Lorient on 4 October 1942, bound again for the happy hunting ground in the Caribbean, she had an important new piece of equipment aboard. It was a radar detector, called "Metox," designed to give warning of any active radar set operating in its vicinity. This equipment was designed to pick up any radar pulse that bounced off the hull and show it as a dancing blip on the trace of a scope down in the radio room. It was intended primarily to warn of approaching aircraft, which previously could only be spotted visually by the bridge lookouts. This gadget gave all hands a new sense of security because bridge lookouts didn't always see approaching aircraft in time for a crash dive to get the boat out of danger, particularly on overcast days. Every boat has a few eagle-eyed lookouts who spot everything that comes along, but they can't be on watch all the time. Now the U-505 wouldn't have to worry too much about who was on lookout watch. This new electronic marvel could "see" even through clouds, and would not get sleepy towards the end of a long watch, or indulge in day dreams about a girl back in Lorient.

Cszhech took the boat through the Bay of Biscay, running surfaced all night and submerged during daylight. Twice during the third night out, the Metox gear detected aircraft which the bridge lookouts neither saw nor heard before the "Crash Dive Alarm" was sounded from the control room below.

Five days out of Lorient Cszhech reckoned he was clear of danger. From there to the Caribbean he ran surfaced day and night, except for an hour or so of diving drills each day to check his new crew and keep them on their toes. On the trip across the Atlantic they sighted only a Portuguese schooner and two Spanish ships.

Half way across the Atlantic, a significant incident showed how adjustments must be made to a new skipper. One morning the leading chief requested permission from the officer of the watch to set up the picnic table for lunch on deck. Next time Cszhech came up to the bridge the officer referred this request to him and while the skipper was turning it over in his mind, the officer unwisely added, "Kapitän Loewe used to permit this, sir."

That settled the matter then and there. "No," replied Cszhech. "Captain Loewe is no longer commanding this ship. When you ask me for decisions, I do not wish to be told how you *used* to do things before I came."

At this time Loewe's crest of a lion rampant was still painted on the conning tower. That afternoon Cszhech had it painted out. A few days later the officer of the watch sighted a school of turtles. He ignored them and the turtles continued their siesta undisturbed.

Another incident confirmed to the crew that the new regime was indeed different from the old. Willi Bunger (the "Ostrich") had been studying hard, devoting all his spare time to qualifying himself for promotion to petty officer. En route to the Caribbean he took his test and passed it with flying colours. In due course his petty officer's warrant was presented to Cszhech for signature.

"How many vacancies do we have for this rating in our allowance now?" asked Cszhech.

"None, Herr Kapitän," replied the executive officer.

"None?" said Cszhech. "So if we promote this man we will lose him for a recruit as soon as we get back from this cruise?"

"Yes, Herr Kapitän."

"No," said Cszhech. "I'm not running a kindergarten to train men for other boats. Hold this till later." There was no doubt

109

in anyone's mind now that they had better not use past precedents on the U-505 in drawing conclusions about the future.

The first chance of the new skipper and old crew to size each other up in action came a month after leaving Lorient, just as they arrived in their assigned area east of Trinidad. On November 7th, around 3.00 p.m., Cszhech gave chase to a smoke trail and soon found it led to an unescorted freighter. Four hours later he had worked his way ahead into a firing position.

With his eye glued to the periscope, Cszhech called out his final orders for a double shot from the bow tubes. "Target speed 12, depth setting 4 metres."

The first watch officer set these figures on the attack director and passed them by voice tube to the forward torpedo room. Soon the dials on the attack director indicated that the torpedo room crew had fixed their settings as ordered and confirmation came back over the voice tube, "Speed 12, depth 4."

"Fire," barked Cszhech and punched his stop watch as he felt the jolt of the tubes discharging. After thirty seconds he could see by the wakes of the torpedoes in the periscope that he had overestimated the speed and aimed too far ahead. This was a bad beginning for the new captain fresh from the famous U-124.

"What speed did you tell them?" he demanded of the first watch officer.

"Twelve knots, Kapitän."

"Dammit, I told you ten. Prepare to fire tubes three and four, target speed ten . . . *one-zero*."

"Aye aye, sir. Speed ten—one-zero," said the W.O.

Two minutes later two torpedoes hit the steamer, both forward of the stack. (Even ten knots was a little on the high side.) The war diary reads: "Two mast high black splashes, no fire on deck. Lifeboats set out. Steamer immediately down by the bow. Aft section out of water. Steamer sinks. Did not send SOS. Left her to sink and departed. Estimated size 5500 BRT."*

* Cszhech was a lot more cold-blooded about survivors than Loewe had been. He simply steamed off and left them without even getting the name of the ship.

110

Now the U-505's total tonnage was 46,200, and they could hardly help going over 50,000 on this cruise. Success covers a lot of minor sins in a skipper, and Cszhech had now given them a success. He was not a pleasant man to live with, and nobody would ever get beaten-up along the waterfront for making slighting remarks about him, but that was incidental so long as he kept on sinking ships.

His second chance came the very next morning. At 8.30 he sighted another smoke trail and chased it until 1.30 p.m. He had a difficult time getting into firing position because the ship was escorted by aircraft until about noon. Quoting from the war diary: "Freighter with two tall masts—zigzagging without plan. [The navigator of the U-505 kept a careful plot of all zigs and was convinced that he had analysed the plan and could predict future zigs but Cszhech disagreed with him.] 1323 double shot tubes 5 and 6. Missed. One minute after firing steamer zigged 50 degrees away from me. Probably a chance tack. Because of position astern second shot impossible."

There was furtive discussion of this attack afterwards throughout the boat. Half the crew believed that if Cszhech had followed the navigator's advice on the zigzag he would have known the ship was due to zig fifty degrees to port before the torpedoes could get there. The navigator, of course, kept his mouth grimly shut. The other half of the crew thought Cszhech had pulled a "Totem Pole", stuck his periscope up too far, had approached so fast that it threw up a conspicuous plume of spray, and that the steamer had seen it just in time to turn away. This school of thought pointed out that the steamer held to a course directly away from the U-boat for a solid hour after the attack and therefore must have seen the periscope. Both schools found the Captain to blame for the escape of this ship which would have put them over the 50,000 mark for Iron Crosses.

For the next three days Cszhech patrolled back and forth 150 miles east of Trinidad. There was an RAF base at Trinidad so aircraft alarms were frequent. There were eight alarms, two from actual sightings by lookouts and six from dancing blips on the scope of the Metox gear. In these three days U-505 spent about eighteen hours submerged. Once when the blip caused her to crash dive before any lookout had seen the plane, Cszhech remarked sarcastically to the officer of the watch, "I don't see how you people survived with these lookouts when you didn't have Metox." The officer stared straight ahead, bit his tongue and said nothing.

On the morning of November 10th Cszhech's number came up. The sky was about half covered with white clouds, the bases being at one thousand feet, with bright sunshine and good visibility in between. This was what Loewe used to call perfect air surprise weather, and in such weather he always ran with decks awash so that he could crash dive in a few seconds if necessary. Cszhech was running in normal surface trim. When the first lieutenant pointed to the low clouds and inquired if Cszhech wished him to double the lookouts, the skipper brushed off the suggestion impatiently. A skipper in his first command is apt to be embarrassed when someone else suggests something he should have thought of himself. To justify his hasty decision he added, "With more lookouts it would take us longer to submerge—and we now have Metox."

Half an hour later, with the Metox gear showing a clear scope, a twin-engine Lockheed dived out from the base of a nearby cloud heading right at them. A lookout sighted him only five hundred yards away just as four cylindrical objects dropped off the wings. "Alarm! *Flugzeug!*" he screamed and ducked down behind the bridge spray shield. The officer of the watch and other lookouts whirled round and looked aft just in time to get the blast of an explosion from a direct hit full in the face. There was a blinding flash of flame, a stunning shock, and a few seconds of the unearthly din from steel plates ripping themselves apart while three other bombs exploded in the water close aboard.

Down below, the accustomed quiet hum of the boat was shattered by a tremendous KERBLAM! The steel framework of the submarine and the bones of the crew vibrated in unison for a short period, while the pressure hull rang like a gong hit by a great hammer. "BO-I-I-I-INN-G!" This contact explo-

112

sion on bare metal staggered the boat as if she had smashed into a stone wall.

On deck three lookouts struggled to their feet just in time to hear a WHOOMP in the water off the starboard bow and to glimpse, through the billowing smoke, an aeroplane crashing into the sea a hundred yards away with a great white splash. The plane had come down too low and been destroyed by the blast of its own bombs. The lookouts gripped the coaming and goggled at the carnage aft, blood streaming down their faces. The officer of the watch and one lookout lay in bloody heaps on the deck.

The whole after deck was a shambles. The anti-aircraft guns had disappeared bodily. Pieces of jagged metal were still dropping into the sea all around, raising little plumes of water. Acrid choking fumes from the explosion hung over the bridge and a huge pillar of black smoke rose from the flaming wreck of the aircraft. Two bodies floated face down in the water near the plane.*

Before the fumes had dispersed Cszhech scrambled out of the hatch to the bridge and surveyed his wounded boat. The first glance told him he no longer had a combatant ship. Whether he still had a submarine which could resurface again if she once submerged, remained to be seen. The boat, from the conning tower aft, was a junk heap of bent jagged plates and twisted pipes all tangled up in a rat's nest of metal. Both engines were stopped and the submarine was coasting to a stop about two hundred yards from the column of black smoke marking the spot where the plane crashed. Cszhech's first concern was to keep his smashed boat afloat.

"Report condition of boat," he called down the hatch. ". . . All hands not needed below, on deck."

When the sailors scrambled out of the hatch and saw the

* When I came across this incident in the U-505's war diary, it occurred to me that this might be the only record of what happened to this aircraft and might clear up a minor mystery for the RAF. I sent the information in to London and received a letter of thanks from the Admiralty. The U-505's war diary had supplied final details on a plane and crew which had been listed for twelve years simply as "missing, fate unknown."

carnage aft, their eyes nearly popped out of their sockets.

"Get down there and heave that junk over the side," ordered Cszhech. As the men jumped down off the bridge and began tugging at the wreckage, the reports were coming up from below—"Forward torpedo room undamaged. . . . Acid spilled in Battery Room. . . . All sound and radio gear out of commission. . . . Main Control Room—unable to dive. . . ."

At this point the chief engineer's head appeared in the hatch. "I'm out of commission, Captain," he said. "Port engine is badly damaged and full of water. I need at least ten minutes to check the starboard one before I try to kick her over again."

"Very well, take all the time you need, Chief—but get her going as soon as you can . . . send hacksaws and blowlamps up here," said Cszhech coolly. There was no use getting excited and yelling at people now.

Lying dead in the water on the surface, the boat was in a desperate situation and everyone knew it. Every man had an equal stake in getting her clear for diving again, knew what had to be done, and yelling at them wouldn't help them to do it.

"Clear that rubbish away from the starboard engine's induction and exhaust," Cszhech said quietly, and then called down the hatch, "Send four men up when you can spare them to take wounded below."

For the next hour the men on deck worked desperately with hacksaws, crowbars and cutting torches, clearing away the junk and dumping it overboard, as a surgeon cuts the ragged flesh away from a great open wound. The whole wooden deck aft and all its supporting structure had to be cut free and shoved over the side, exposing the pressure hull and the various nerves and blood vessels that ran along the outside of it. Many of these had to be amputated and plugged off. So far as anyone could see, the pressure hull had not been punctured, but the great pool of oil forming around them on the surface showed that the fuel tanks had been. Probably some of the ballast tanks were too, but the boat was at least ten tons lighter now with guns and upper deck gone, so a few extra tons of water in the after tanks wouldn't sink her.

114

After forty-five minutes the starboard diesel let out a few muffled coughs and started up again. As the submarine got under way and limped off in the direction of France, she was still in a desperate fix. Lorient was almost 4,000 miles away. Unable to submerge, the boat was a sitting duck for any aircraft that came along—and it was quite likely planes would soon be out looking for their crashed comrade. But at any rate, U-505 was now putting distance between herself and the RAF base in Trinidad. It was 11.00 a.m. as they crept away to the northeast leaving a tell-tale oil streak behind. There were ten hours of daylight left.

The most urgent job was to restore the boat's ability to dive. The openings through the pressure hull for the port engine had to be blank flanged. The induction and exhaust for the starboard engine needed numerous patches to make them watertight. Broken air lines had to be replaced, and jammed valves and vents had to be freed. All hands turned to on this task, knowing that whether they got back to Germany or not depended on how well they did it.

At 2.30 p.m., a flying boat appeared on a course that would bring it within five miles of them. There was practically nothing they could do that would have any effect whatever on their fate now.

Everyone knocked off work, scrunched down to make himself inconspicuous, and all eyes remained riveted on that plane. Cszhech changed course gradually to keep the stern of the boat pointed directly at the aircraft, thus presenting the smallest and most easily overlooked silhouette to her. . . . But that damned oil trail was impossible to miss! Nevertheless, the plane missed it!

Many survivors of ordeals in lifeboats told of seeing aeroplanes appear, raising their hopes of early rescue, only to fly on out of sight while the men in the boats sent agonized prayers to heaven. In this case, some prayers went up too, but they pleaded that the plane would keep going—which it did! An hour later the same plane, evidently searching for the one that crashed, appeared on its return leg and again failed to see the crippled U-boat.

By two o'clock the next morning blank flanges had been installed in the intake and exhaust pipes for the port diesel, the holes in the outboard connections of the starboard diesel had temporary patches installed that should hold for a shallow dive just deep enough to get under and out of sight. Although one bomb had hit squarely amidships, a careful check of the pressure hull showed no holes. The blast had expended itself in wrecking the superstructure. At 2.00 a.m., they battened down the hatches and cracked the inlet valves to flood the ballast tanks gradually and take her down in easy stages, double checking every step in the process for any untoward developments. As she went under all hands held their breath and all who could crowd into the control room watched the hand on the depth gauge to see if it stopped at twenty metres . . . or kept on going into eternity.

It stopped at twenty, and Cszhech kept it there until three the next afternoon. By the time he surfaced again many internal pipes and fittings had been repaired and he could make ten knots on the starboard engine. Now his main concern was to stop the oil leak which was leaving that trail behind him. He spent the rest of the day getting that fixed and putting as much distance as he could between his stern and the coast of Trinidad. In another day he would be out in the broad Atlantic where aircraft couldn't reach and would be able to lick his wounds and repair his damage in comparative safety, provided he wasn't unlucky enough to be seen by a fast warship. In that case, he would scuttle the boat, abandon ship, and rely on the British to observe the Geneva Convention and rescue his men.

He was still in a tough spot but he didn't have to go all the way back to Lorient before he got help. Doenitz took good care of his men, and never hesitated to divert nearby boats to the assistance of one that got hurt. Within a few hours of Cszhech's first damage report to Doenitz, orders were cracking out to three nearby U-boats to rendezvous with him and supply him with spare parts and medicines. One of these had a doctor aboard who could tend to his wounded. Meantime, U-boat Headquarters demanded details of the men's injuries and radioed back suggested courses of treatment for two of them who were still semi-conscious and in serious condition.

During the next week they got morphine from the U-105, spare parts from the U-68, fuel and medical advice from the U-462. On advice of the doctor, the injured officer was transferred to the U-462, where he could be given better care. By this time they were well clear of the South American coast, their boat's wounds were reasonably well healed and they squared away on the course for Lorient.

During the twelve days that had elapsed since the bombing, all hands had been so busy repairing the boat to get her out of danger they had had little time to think. Now came a long period of routine cruising with little else to do but think. Cszhech began to feel eyes looking at him when his back was turned, and to notice how they were hastily averted when he turned round. No one spoke to him now except when necessary to answer his questions. If he struck up a conversation it was a stilted one that kept going only as long as he forced it. It was obvious that his men were ill at ease with him and, of course, the reason was that he had brought them bad luck. He spent long hours on the bridge by himself, staring into the sea ahead.

One day in the conning tower thumbing idly through the quartermaster's note book in which rough notes are made about events as they occur, to be transcribed later in the official log, he noticed a page in the back of the book, on which some sort of a tally was being kept. There were bunches of four vertical marks with a horizontal mark through every group of four to keep the count by fives. He noticed that the marks were arranged in three groups. The first group had twenty-four marks in it, the second thirty, and the third eight. The name Freetown was written over the first group, Karibik over the second, and Trinidad over the third. Cszhech, without giving the matter any real thought, realized that this must be a record of the number of times that some recurring event had happened on each of the three operational missions so far. While speculating idly on what this might be, he noticed some doodles drawn on the far side of the page. Opposite Freetown and

117

Karibik, there was a lion rampant clawing an aircraft apart. Opposite Trinidad was a mouse slinking away, looking back over his shoulder with his tail between his legs, pursued by a swarm of planes.

This tally was the number of aircraft sightings on each cruise the U-505 had made so far. There had been fifty-four under Loewe and no harm done. There had been eight under Cszhech. Loewe's name meant "Lion" and the paint was hardly dry over his insignia on the conning tower!

For some moments Cszhech struggled with himself to avoid exploding and making an embarrassing scene. Finally he ripped the page out of the book, clambered up to the bridge, tore the paper into small pieces and flung it over the side. When he went below again his jaw was set and his face pale. The bridge lookouts looked at each other questioningly, shrugged their shoulders, and said nothing.

After two days of internal boiling over this incident, Cszhech sighted a smoke trail and saw a chance to redeem himself. It proved to be an unescorted freighter on a course passing fairly close to him. It was an hour after sunset so he lay in wait on the surface and passed the word, "Target in sight, stand by for double shot from bow tubes."

It was obvious immediately that this was a great boost in the crew's shattered morale. One more normal sized ship would shove the boat's total tonnage over the 50,000 mark and mean Iron Crosses Second Class for some of them after all. The attitude of the crew changed immediately from stolid indifference—almost sullenness—to eager anticipation. At 9.30 Cszhech fired a double shot from tubes one and two and all hands held their breath as the stop watches ticked off the running time. Nothing happened.

Cszhech had paralleled his victim's course to keep his firing position just in case he did miss. "Stand by three and four," he ordered, and twenty minutes later he fired another double shot. Again they both missed. The steamer was still unaware of his presence but was making twelve knots against his speed on one engine of eleven. Cszhech hung on desperately and, his stern tubes being out of commission, reloaded his bow tubes, drop-

118

ping slowly behind all the time. Half an hour later he missed with his fifth shot, and finally an hour afterwards fired a sixth futile shot at extreme range which also missed.

Cszhech notes ruefully in his war diary that some of these shots "may have run erratically or been duds on account of bomb damage." He also logs an occurrence which was misinterpreted by the crew. He states, "The last shot exploded after nineteen minutes run." Some of the crew said sixteen months later, when interrogated by U.S. Naval Intelligence Officers, that this last shot curved back and hit the U-505 but failed to explode. They claimed to have seen the dent in the side when the boat was dry docked in Lorient. Of course, a dent in the side might be explained by one of those near miss bombs, but a recurving torpedo could do it too, if the exploder mechanism had failed.

The upshot of this well-meant attempt by Cszhech to raise the crew's morale, was to sink it even further in the depths. This failure certainly wasn't Cszhech's fault, unless you trace it clear back to the bomb hit which made the torpedoes run erratically, or say that he was foolish to fire torpedoes which he knew might not run straight. But the worst fault any skipper can have in the eyes of a wartime crew is to be unlucky. Napoleon is reputed to have sacked a Marshal of France with an outstanding professional reputation simply because he always had bad luck. Cszhech had now clinched his reputation for being unlucky with the crew of the U-505.

After they had limped into Lorient, on 12 December 1942, Admiral Doenitz's staff put the following comment on the war diary: "Mission broken off because of extremely heavy bomb damage. . . . The air attack came as a surprise without any warning from the Metox. The electronic detection device must never lead to relaxation of the lookouts on the bridge.

"The toughness and stamina of the Commandant who tried to attack despite his heavily damaged boat calls for special mention."

This pat on the back for the six futile torpedo shots did wonders for Cszhech's own morale. But it did nothing to restore his standing with the crew.

On that cruise Cszhech steamed 10,250 miles on the surface and 626 submerged. Loewe went forty times as far on the surface as he did submerged on his first cruise, and twenty-five times as far on the second. On this cruise the ratio was sixteen to one. Although the Allies were still losing the Battle of the Atlantic they were beginning to gain back some of their lost ground.

CHAPTER X

LORIENT

FROM Lorient, where the U-505 spent the next six months, Doenitz directed the far-flung operations of his whole U-boat fleet. Each morning at his headquarters in a villa on the outskirts of town, he held a staff conference at which the night's incoming dispatches were analysed and digested, and the great grid chart of the Atlantic was brought up to date. The staff went over every detail of the previous day's operations and revised plans for the current day's work if necessary.

The huge chart of the Atlantic Ocean, ruled off into numbered six-mile squares, showed the location of all U-boats and the latest reported positions of enemy ships and convoys. Junior officers measured off distances and senior ones framed dispatches to boats in position to intercept worthwhile targets. Intelligence reports on prospective convoy sailings were weighed and scouting lines of U-boats were formed across the expected sailing routes. Sinkings reported the previous day were totalled, added to the grand total of tonnage sent to the bottom so far, and the names of ships sunk were checked off in Lloyd's register. Questionable tonnage claims were discussed, checked against the register, and decided. The exchange rate for the previous ten days was brought up-to-date and boats in unproductive areas might be shifted to better ones.

Ominous little red flags were put up on the grid chart at the last reported position of U-boats which hadn't been heard from recently. When a red flag had been up for a week, headquarters would call the boat periodically for several days. If no answer came back, the duty officer removed the red flag from the master grid chart and corrected the flotilla roster. Next morning Doenitz would be notified, telegrams would go out to relatives of the crew, and the personal effects would be removed from the storage locker in the U-boat barracks, inventoried, and sent home.

At these conferences staff officers reported items of interest culled from the war diaries of recently returned boats, and skippers just back from a war patrol gave Doenitz the highlights of their cruises. The Admiral was no mere figurehead at this headquarters. He personally interviewed every returning skipper and kept the whole Battle of the Atlantic at his finger tips.

All information of any kind, technical, tactical or strategic, which had any bearing on the Battle was funnelled into this headquarters where it was carefully sifted and evaluated. Every significant trend in the statistics of ships sunk versus U-boats lost (exchange rate) had to be explained to Doenitz by the staff experts. As soon as they knew what caused a trend they took action if the trend was favourable to keep it so, if unfavourable to change it back.

If one U-boat skipper was consistently more successful than others working under similar conditions, the staff would study his methods to see how he differed from the rest. It usually turned out that the big factor in outstanding success was the personality of the skipper, and the staff couldn't do much about that. But study of Kretschmer's methods had a lot to do with the adoption of the wolf pack technique, and, even though no skipper came close to Kretschmer's total, the wolf pack tactics took a terrible toll of Allied shipping.

With access to the vast fund of up-to-date data available in headquarters, staff experts could usually put their fingers on necessary changes in tactics even before most of the U-boat skippers, who knew only what happened to their own boats. These staff officers, and Doenitz too, were all former U-boat officers themselves and knew the business from the point of view of the skipper at the periscope. In tactical and strategical matters they were expert and their answers to a U-boat skipper's problems were efficient and practical. If anything, these staff officers were too practical and not scientific enough.

When the research experts in Berlin asserted that aircraft radar was a scientific impossibility, they believed it longer than they should have. It was Doenitz's staff officers who finally learned from their own analyses of war diaries that aircraft radar was an accomplished fact for the Allies. Even then, they had trouble ramming this fact down the throats of the sceptical scientists and forcing them to produce radar detectors for the U-boats.

At Doenitz's villa there was a constant two-way stream of radio traffic, information coming in from all over the Atlantic and orders going out to the boats at sea. I am amazed at some of the things for which U-boats in operational areas broke radio silence and reported to headquarters. Doenitz took a "calculated risk" on the incoming radio traffic and decided it was more important for him to get information than it was for his boats to keep radio silence at sea. Almost daily he arranged ocean rendezvous between U-boats to transfer spare parts for machinery, to transfer a sick man to the nearest boat having a doctor aboard, or for home-bound boats with surplus fuel or torpedoes to transfer the excess to boats remaining in the area. He even held radio musters of his boats at times when he suspected trouble—ordering all boats to "report position and successes." It was by such a muster that he learned he had lost his three great aces, Prien, Schepke, and Kretschmer, early in March of 1941.

When a boat in distress sent an SOS, Doenitz never failed to send nearby boats to her assistance. He was cold-blooded in his orders that they were not to jeopardize their own safety by rescuing Allied survivors, but he took long chances to save his own people.

Most naval men will agree that the outgoing stream of radio traffic from Doenitz was necessary. But some of us think he miscalculated the risk in breaking radio silence and required his boats to do too much transmitting.

Every time a ship at sea touches a radio key, she pin-points her position to an alert enemy with a good direction finder network. Perhaps Doenitz was forced to discard radio silence because he had no air arm. If he had had any help from the Luftwaffe, much of the radio traffic from boats at sea could have been eliminated. But Goering, head of the Luftwaffe, was contemptuous of navies and wouldn't send *his* planes out to sea searching for convoys to help Doenitz roll up a score. If the boats had kept radio silence, Doenitz wouldn't have known what was going on at sea until they returned to Lorient—when it would have been too late.

At any rate, one effect of all this radio traffic was to make U-boat crews feel close to headquarters. They all knew that when and if they got into trouble an SOS to Doenitz would bring immediate help.

Doenitz himself was a sour looking character, but he had a sly sense of humour. They say he had an oil seascape hanging in his headquarters with nothing but the waves visible in it. When visitors asked him what the picture represented, he replied, "The fleet passing in review in 1955." When they said, "But I don't see any ships," his answer was, "There are hundreds of them—submarines cruising in submerged formation." (Note: in 1955 NATO started reorganizing a new German Navy.)

From his headquarters in Lorient, Doenitz kept his fingers constantly on the pulse of the Atlantic Ocean. The Grand Admiral ran the show and knew his business and took care of his people. All hands in the U-boat fleet swore by him and considered him a great leader.

But the citizens of Lorient had every reason to hate him, his U-boats, and everything connected with them. Their presence in Lorient changed a happy, peaceful community into a hotbed of espionage, hate and murder, in which families were disrupted and the only friends you could really trust were those in the graveyard.

Until France collapsed, no enemy soldier had set foot in Lorient since before Napoleon's time. It had been a quiet little community of shipwrights and fishermen, centring around some of the finest shipbuilding ways and best marine repair shops in France. Far removed from the cockpit of Europe where wars are fought, for centuries its inhabitants had been peaceful, industrious, thrifty and God-fearing people.

The first year of World War II affected them little. Even when the phony war exploded into a real one, all the battles were fought far to the east. The surrender of France, instead of bringing peace, plunged the whole Biscay coast of France deep

124

U-boat finishes off burning victim with a final torpedo fired from the surface, and takes this dramatic picture of the explosion

Crew of U-505 working to clear wreckage of submarine's after deck, damaged by R.A.F. plane off Trinidad. The plane destroyed itself with the blast from its own bombs

into the maelstrom of war. During the phony war, and even during the invasion, it had been "business as usual" for the shipbuilders, fishermen and citizens of the Biscay ports. Business was even a little better than usual. But when France collapsed, the grim facts of life in a global war were finally brought home to them and ground into the souls of all inhabitants. For the citizens of the Biscay ports, "Peace" was a will-o'-the-wisp, leering and mocking at them while the rest of France did enjoy peace, of a sort. The German Navy, hemmed in for the first year of the war in bases on the North Sea and Baltic, immediately took over Brest, Bordeaux, Saint Nazaire and Lorient. Lorient's fine shipyards and spacious harbour close to the Atlantic hunting ground, made it an ideal submarine base. But its selection by Doenitz for his HQ brought down a terrible curse on the peaceful inhabitants of the little town for the next three and a half years.

Garrison troops swooped down on their city, billeted themselves on the community, and set up a military government. Their behaviour toward the inhabitants was "correct", but this is a relative term and its meaning depends on whether you are doing the behaving or submitting to the behaviour of conquerors. When a conqueror takes over a town which has spent a thousand years developing its way of life, he simply issues an order telling the people which old customs and institutions they shall abolish and which new ones they shall adopt. The citizens who are able to adjust themselves to this overnight, get along as best they can with the new regime. Those who can't, get shot.

Right behind the garrison troops, heavy anti-aircraft batteries rumbled into place in concentric rings around the town. This gave the citizens a temporary sense of security which was soon dispelled. Other things moving in after the AA batteries provided magnets to attract RAF bombers and make the nights hideous for the next three years, despite the powerful ack-ack batteries.

Thousands of expert U-boat mechanics from Germany swarmed into the shipyards and began converting them into U-boat repair yards. Engineers erected huge concrete structures along the east bank of the river. These bombproof U-boat pens had reinforced concrete roofs fifteen feet thick. The aircraft bombs that soon showered down on them did no more harm than fire crackers. But hundreds of bombs intended for the shipyards or U-boat pens blasted ugly scars all over the town.

By 1942, Lorient was the greatest U-boat base the world has ever seen, and a totally different town from what it had been for several hundred years. Battered by RAF bombs, its swollen population of civilians, soldiers, technicians, collaborating French prostitutes and camp followers, was a simmering brew of arrogance, intrigue, deceit and hate. Lording it over all the rest were the thousand or so of Doenitz's swashbuckling U-boat sailors for whom the whole thing existed.

While their U-boats were in port being serviced for the next patrol, these battle-hardened conquerors had nothing to do but "rest". Resting was a strenuous business, both for them and the local and imported whores. Most of them, knowing how uncertain their future was, lived as hard and fast as possible during each visit to Lorient. For Doenitz's bully boys between cruises it was, "Eat, drink and be merry, for tomorrow . . . you may be in the mud at the bottom of the sea."

Life was hard for the local maids who wished to remain virtuous. They had to be very strong characters indeed to do so. Everything was rationed and plain hunger drove many of the weaker girls to the easy life. A young Frenchman thinking of matrimony had little to offer a nice girl except a chance to share his hardships and privations. The German conquerors controlled everything and could offer many tempting inducements, including food—as much as a hungry girl could eat.

In an occupied town, "correct" behaviour means that physical rape is frowned on. But mental and economic pressures, plus hunger, are normal incidents of war. The military authorities were tolerant of U-boat sailors blowing off steam after a hard patrol, and leading local girls astray. They gave them the benefit of the doubt in cases where there was dispute about what kind of persuasion may have been necessary.

The citizens whose daughters were being despoiled were not

tolerant. Their hate was a terrible, vengeful one. Some opportunists among the local citizens, thinking the Germans would certainly win the war, collaborated wholeheartedly with them, and paid savage penalties to their neighbours when the Nazis lost. Most citizens submitted to the occupation sullenly, but with the necessary minimum of outward respect and obedience.

Beneath the surly submissive surface boiled a venomous hatred which flared out occasionally in the activities of the underground. These activities were many, far-reaching and mostly death-dealing. There were secret Maquis killers who shot German sailors in the back and then disappeared till the war was over, into Southern France. There were spies and saboteurs of many kinds. Every local citizen was a potential enemy of the Germans, and it was almost an impossible job for the military government to separate the "good" from the "bad". About all they could do was to shoot suspects regularly enough to deter the fainter-hearted citizens from getting too far out of line.

Despite the most rigid checks by the Gestapo on the French shipyard workers, underground agents wormed their way into the yard where the U-boats were prepared for their next cruises. These seeming collaborators, ostensibly working for the Germans, slipped little bags of sugar into the lubricating oil tanks of U-boats. The sugar dissolved into the oil and those U-boats came limping back to Lorient with their engines in sad shape. The underground agents made sound-looking welds on pressure fittings that would give way when the boat went deep. Some skippers who didn't take their boats down to maximum depth on trial runs, are on the bottom of the ocean now with their whole crews because these welds gave way under attack. Workmen drilled small holes in the tops of fuel tanks and plugged the holes with stuff that was soluble in salt water. A few days after this boat went to sea, the plug would dissolve and the boat would leave a tell-tale oil streak behind her when she submerged. There was a certain kind of grease you could smear on the gasket of pressure fittings that would cause salt water to eat away the rubber gaskets.

The Frenchmen who did these things took a desperate

chance. The penalty for being caught was death. If a sabotaged boat didn't come back, that was fine. But if she did manage to limp back in, the men who worked on her were in trouble, and the Germans didn't waste too much effort in legal proceedings to pick out the right workmen to shoot. They were apt to execute all suspects in order to be sure that impartial justice was done. Thus the activities of the underground agents imperilled their friends who might be neither saboteurs nor collaborators, but simply citizens trying to stay alive. Sometimes a collaborating French workman would squeal on a saboteur. But when this happened word usually got back to the underground and soon there would be two new graves in the cemetery.

At times it was hard to tell whether the townspeople of Lorient hated the Germans or the British most. The RAF came over frequently at night and scattered bombs around all over the place. If they had done any harm to the U-boat pens, most of the townspeople could have forgiven them for an occasional stray blockbuster in the middle of town. But after it became apparent that the only damage being done was to the town, the townspeople were pretty bitter about it, some directing their bitterness towards the British, some towards the Germans. Many reasoned that their own country had been defeated and surrendered, and they had a right to be left in peace now.

Community life was chaotic and families were often split into factions with lethal designs on each other. Many of the old folks, knowing the best part of their lives was behind them, were content to live what was left to them in whatever way was the easiest. They had no further interest in the war, one way or the other after France collapsed. They knew France was dying and hoped to live out their own lives in peace before she did.

The younger generation took sides violently. Some through hatred of the British or for other reasons, became full-fledged collaborators. A collaborator's brother or sister might be an active member of the underground. This situation eventually produced at least one permanently empty space at the family table.

128

Often members of the same family joined the underground for very different reasons. One might go to avenge the death of a brother killed by the Germans and to prepare himself to assist in the rebuilding of France after the war. Another might join the communists and go underground to prepare for tearing down the old regime after the war. While her brothers in the underground were plotting to kill Germans ashore, a sister might be in bed with one of them wheedling information out of him that would bring about his death at sea.

French public officials and military officers were in a very difficult position. They had been officials of the legal government of France which surrendered to the conquerors and was officially collaborating. They had at least to go through the motions of collaboration or be thrown out of their jobs and put behind barbed wire. If they collaborated too convincingly, they were storing up vengeance at the hands of their countrymen, if and when Germany lost. If their co-operation became too lukewarm, the Germans might suspect them of "treason" and shoot them. There were cases where officials became double agents and worked efficiently for both sides until they could make up their minds which side would win.

In this situation, probably the only people in Lorient who really trusted each other were the U-boat sailors and many of them destroyed each other unintentionally with their wagging tongues.

As the U-boat fleet grew in size, more and more Germans and hangers-on swarmed into Lorient and soon the town was overrun with them. U-boats were either sailing or returning from a mission every day. Either event called for about a week's binge by her crew on the waterfront.

It was impossible to keep secrets in a base such as Lorient. The whole life of the town revolved around the operations of the U-boat fleet and everyone in town rubbed elbows with the U-boats one way or another. The shipyard workers, of course, got right down inside them. Tradesmen delivered food to the boats, and any fool could tell from their grocery orders when a boat was about to sail. A brass band met boats returning from a successful cruise and the boats came up the river proudly displaying pennants with the names of their victims printed on them for anyone to see. Bartenders, waitresses, and girls of the evening took intimate parts in the continual round of arrival and departure binges. Anyone who kept his ears open after the first five or six rounds of drinks, could pick up many items of secret official information.

You can never keep that sort of information from becoming known in the base city itself. Even in one of your own ports, confining this knowledge to the local citizens is a difficult job In a hostile port, it is a very tough job indeed. The Germans didn't succeed very well in their censorship attempts. From an operational point of view, Doenitz gained a great deal by moving his bases six hundred miles to his hunting grounds. From a security point of view, he lost.

In this devil's brew at Lorient the U-505 was plunged for six months following her return from the Caribbean in December 1942. It was during this six months, while the U-505 lay idle, that the tide of battle turned against the U-boats with crushing finality.

The year 1942 had been a year of overwhelming victory for the U-boats. Counting sinkings from all causes 1,570 Allied ships, totalling 7,697,000 tons, had gone to the bottom. Churchill says of this period, "The Battle of the Atlantic was the dominating factor all through the war. Never for one moment could we forget that everything happening on land, sea, and in the air depended ultimately on its outcome and amid all other cares we viewed its changing fortunes day by day with hope or apprehension."

For the Allies, 1942 was a year steeped in apprehension as the awful destruction at sea mounted. But towards the end a ray of hope appeared. Although the shambles on the shipping lanes continued, the exchange rate dropped from forty to one in the first quarter, to ten to one in the last. This was the sign that the flood tide had reached high water and was about to turn.

Turn it did—with dramatic suddenness. When the U-505 limped into Lorient to be repaired, the U-boats were riding the crest of the wave and Doenitz had lost only 86 boats in the whole preceding year. Before the U-505 was ready for sea again, he had lost 150 more. In May, June and July of '43, the Allies rocked him back on his heels by destroying 73 of his submarines at sea. During these months the exchange rate was two to one!

This stunned the U-boat High Command. By the end of June, losses had mounted till the odds were heavy against any boat returning safely from a sortie into the Atlantic. Doenitz was losing U-boats and their trained crews faster than he was getting replacements for them.

There is a limit to the casualties that any military organization can stand and still keep its fighting morale. Most armies when losses approach twenty per cent, pull the units concerned out of the firing line to rest and be reorganized. Doenitz's losses were over fifty per cent. It speaks highly for the discipline and morale of his men that they still obeyed him when an operation order directing a U-boat to sail was practically a death warrant for the whole crew.

At the end of June, Doenitz had to call a halt. He pulled his U-boats off the heavily protected North Atlantic shipping lanes and redeployed them to quiet areas. There would be few targets to shoot at in these areas but at least his trained crews could stay alive and lick their wounds while his staff and the experts in Berlin searched frantically for ways to put them back in action.

This withdrawal from the North Atlantic was Doenitz's retreat from Moscow. His U-boat flotillas never recovered the initiative. The Battle of the Atlantic went on for two more bitter years in which 506 Allied ships of 2,500,000 tons, and 518 German U-boats were sunk. But it was a grim, losing battle for the U-boats from that point on. The exchange rate fell to less than one to one!

The Allies broke the back of Doenitz's fleet in the middle of 1943, and thereafter the once-feared U-boats were hunted down and killed methodically and relentlessly. In 1942 the cry "U-boat in sight" struck terror into the hearts of all merchant sailors. In 1943 it was like the "Tally Ho" of the hunt to Allied airmen and destroyer sailors. The prowling arrogant wolves from the Night of the Long Knives became slinking fugitives creeping beneath the seas submerged even at night. The nature of these prowlers required them to operate as surface ships if they were to do their jobs of destruction. But simple self-preservation made them stay submerged most of the time except when a run-down battery forced them to surface furtively and recharge as quickly as they could.

German accounts of the war still blame the debacle on a new type of Allied aircraft radar for which they were not ready. But that was only part of the story. Had the sudden turn of the tide been due to only one new development, Doenitz's experts *might* have produced a technical device to counter it. But actually there were many Allied developments that all came to a head at once. The new radar was only one. Others were: better weapons for destroying submarines, huge numbers of new long-range aircraft rolling off the U.S. production lines, the new jeep carrier hunter-killer groups, bombing raids on the U-boat building yards and finally, the massive production of U.S. shipyards. All these things coming at the same time simply overwhelmed the U-boats.

If any one factor was more decisive than the others, it was the amazing expansion of the U.S. shipbuilding industry. In the first three months of the phony war our shipyards were practically idle. By the middle of 1943 they were producing 1,000,000 tons per month. Hitler's "experts" had scoffed at a fantastic estimate by Doenitz that by an all-out effort we *might* build a maximum of 8,000,000 tons per year.

The whole economy of the U.S., its industry, and most of its citizens were involved one way or another in this herculean effort. Finished ships put to sea in 1943 which had been almost entirely buried in the ground among the ore deposits of the Mesabi range in Minnesota when the war began. We dug the ore out of the ground, hauled it to Pittsburgh, made it into steel, and rolled the steel into plates, bars, and beams. All over the country we manufactured steam and electric machinery, boilers, pipes and valves, shafts, propellers, anchors and chains, radio and electronic equipment. All this stuff, tailored to fit the places where it had to go, in many cases by workmen who had never seen salt water, was brought together in the shipyards and assembled into sea-worthy ships by workers, many of whom were high school girls.

There were also a number of important technical developments on our side. Until early '43, shore-based aircraft in Iceland, Greenland, Newfoundland, and England, straining to their maximum range had left a mid-ocean gap where the wolf packs were comparatively safe. Now, new types of planes rolling off the production lines in the U.S. in large numbers were closing this gap.

German scientists had fallen down badly on radar. Despite constant warnings and pleas from Doenitz early in the war, the German experts had assured him that aircraft radar was technically impossible, and that his submarine skippers who were attacked by aircraft on dark nights were imagining things. By 1943 the "experts" knew they had been wrong and had hastily equipped the U-boats with a primitive radar detector. But the Allies came out with a new short-wavelength radar that baffled the outmoded detectors and caught the U-boats flat-footed again. We also had developed new and better weapons for killing U-boats after we found them.

Finally, a new deadly enemy to the submarines was just getting into the battle—the jeep carrier Hunter-Killer Group —which put mobile air bases all over the Atlantic and closed the mid-ocean gap.

None of these technical developments alone would have turned the tide of battle. But all of them coming to a head at once early in 1943 cut the head off Nazi Germany's offensive out in the Atlantic Ocean and made a Nazi victory impossible after July '43.

Doenitz, with his finger constantly on the pulse of the battle, sensed the turn of the tide even sooner than his superiors did. He pulled his U-boats out of the North Atlantic and deployed them to what he thought would be comparative safety west of the Azores, where they might intercept some Gibraltar-bound convoys. But while they were basking in the sunlight there and relaxing, the jeep carriers *Bogue, Card* and *Core* tore into them in a daylight version of the Night of the Long Knives and sank two dozen surprised U-boats in a couple of months. After the jeep carriers appeared on the scene, there was no place for the U-boats to hide except deep down in the ocean's depths. There were no more mid-ocean gaps.

Doenitz tried desperately to save the battle which was by now hopelessly lost. Ships were pouring down the building ways in the U.S. twice as fast as he had ever been able to sink them.

He belatedly equipped his boats with the radar detectors which his scientific "experts" had assured him would not be needed. They did more harm than good. By this time the air was full of Allied aircraft and every time one of his U-boats surfaced, he could almost be sure of picking up some sort of a radar indication and being forced to crash dive. As a result, the U-boats spent most of their time submerged.

The World War II U-boat was primarily a surface vessel which could accomplish little of military value if it had to stay under water using up the vital charge in its battery. To overcome this handicap Doenitz started fitting all his U-boats with schnorkel so that they could at least run almost fully submerged on their diesels without using up the battery. He also forced through the development programmes for the type XXI and XXIII U-boats with huge storage batteries and high submerged speeds. He developed the Walther cycle boats, the first true submarines which never had to come up to recharge batteries. But these things came too late to have any effect on World War II.

After the slaughter of U-boats in early '43, Hitler told Doenitz to keep on fighting because the U-boats tied up huge naval forces and reduced the RAF bombing effort on German cities. Doenitz passed this idea along to his U-boat crews and by doing so probably shook their morale instead of helping it. This idea of tying down Allied forces by an offensive *threat* was a far cry from the Night of the Long Knives, and gave the U-boat crews an excuse for being over-cautious. If their mere presence at sea was all that was required, why stick their necks out attacking anything but sitting birds?

CHAPTER XI

THE CAPTAIN DESERTS HIS SHIP

SUCH was the situation towards the end of June 1943, when the U-505 was declared ready for sea again. By then only one-third of her original crew was left on board, the rest having been transferred to other boats while she was being repaired. Of these, about half had been killed in the terrible retribution which the Allies were then exacting out in the Atlantic. Still on board were the four leading chief petty officers and a dozen of those who had put her in commission. All the original officers were gone.

The U-505 was scheduled to sail on July 1, and on the night of June 30 the crew made a final round of the bars and bistros in Lorient to bid adieu to their friends. U-boats always sailed in the late afternoon and everyone could get good and drunk the night before sailing knowing they would have all the next day to sober up.

The U-505's crew threw the usual farewell party on June 30. Theirs was even more frenzied than most because they had spent the last six months in Lorient and knew better than most how heavily the dice were loaded against them. Since January they had said *auf wiedersehen* to several dozen crews that didn't come back. Now it was their turn to go out and act as decoys to keep RAF bombers away from Germany. It was late that night before the last of them got to bed. At noon the next day all hands mustered on board the U-505, bleary-eyed but ready to go to sea for ninety days.

Cszhech, with a bad hangover himself, took his boat down the river that evening and headed out into Biscay. He started this cruise with mingled emotions. A lot of his friends had disappeared for ever into Biscay during the past six months. In a way, he was lucky to be still alive. But others of his contemporaries had come back with good scores, been decorated, promoted, and assigned to shore duty. He had fallen behind them and now he must try to catch up after the tide of battle had definitely turned. But there was no use brooding over his bad luck. This was his fate and he just had to make the best of it. He was bound for the Azores where the opposition would not be too heavy and there were still some targets for a skilful skipper to sink. As the French coast dropped out of sight he probably thought, "If I'm lucky, I'll be assigned to shore duty next time I get ashore."

He was back ashore within twenty-four hours with a long list of minor defects and one major one which couldn't be fixed at sea but wouldn't take long in dock. U-boat headquarters had a crew of experts on the dockside to meet him. They made short work of his defects, freed the jammed valve on one of his ballast tanks and had him ready to sail again by the next evening.

Some of his boys got in another last fling ashore that night, repeating the same ritual as the night before. Like the U-boats at sea, the girls and bartenders of Lorient were on a Yesterday, Today and Tomorrow routine too. One night was the same as another to them. They had already forgotten they had said goodbye to these same men the night before. They said it all over again with equal fervour.

Next evening, July 3rd, the U-505 sailed again, this time in company with four other outbound U-boats, and an escort of seven motor torpedo boats to furnish anti-aircraft protection until they reached water deep enough for them to submerge.

The change in the tide of battle that had occurred in the past six months is graphically shown by the U-505's war diary for the first five days out of Lorient. While trying to get across the Bay to Cape Finisterre, she spent only about twenty per cent of the time on the surface. She averaged twenty hours out of each twenty-four submerged. Her distance run on the surface was only twice that submerged—quite a change from Loewe's first cruise when the surface distance was forty times the submerged run!

After four days of this Cszhech got impatient and decided to make a break for the open sea. It was a clear day with excellent

136

visibility; he should be able to sight any aircraft in time for a crash dive. He surfaced at noon on July 8 and boiled along at eighteen knots until one p.m., when he submerged again feeling that he had stolen a march on the enemy.

It would have taken him at least twelve hours to run eighteen miles submerged. This sprint on the surface in broad daylight put him half a day's run closer to the comparative safety of the broad Atlantic.

Fifteen minutes after submerging six stunning blows slammed into the hull in rapid succession, knocking men off their feet, smashing lights, and jarring great flakes of paint off the bulkheads.

The officer of the watch and Cszhech had been flung against opposite sides of the conning tower. They remained braced there staring at each other silently, waiting for the battering to stop. Some seconds after the sixth explosion had died away, the officer inquired incredulously "Destroyers?"

"No," said Cszhech. "There were no destroyers in sight fifteen minutes ago. It's an aircraft."

"But how could he see us down at forty metres?"

"These new listening buoys they drop into the water . . . they have a microphone and a radio that broadcasts our propeller noises and . . ." There were four more crashing explosions much too close for comfort but not quite as close as the first ones.

Cszhech dropped down into the control room. "All stations report damage," he ordered.

The reports showed no serious structural damage had been done and the engines were all right. But the Metox and listening gear were completely out of commission. Loss of the listening gear was a very serious matter indeed. A submerged U-boat without listening gear knows nothing about what goes on in the ocean around it except, of course, when the explosion of depth charges serves emphatic notice that bad things have been going on.

"You hear nothing whatever?" demanded Cszhech of the sound operator.

"Nothing Kapitän . . . the whole set is dead."

"Silent speed," said Cszhech to the man on the engine-room telegraph, and then to the depth control man, "Hold her at forty metres." For the rest of the afternoon the crew tiptoed through the boat as she crept along about 130 feet below the surface at one knot, gradually putting distance between herself and the scene of the previous attack.

In a situation like this there is little that a skipper can do to influence events. Unable to hear or see, he just has to trust to his luck. When the situation gets tough, a show of nonchalance by the skipper does a lot of good. After a couple of hours of creeping, Cszhech said to the first officer, "I don't think any more planes are coming out. Just hold everything as it is now. I'm going to take a nap. . . . Call me at 6.00 p.m."

For the next few hours Cszhech lay in his bunk wide awake braced for the next series of explosions, but with the curtain drawn so that no one could see. Reassured by the knowledge that the skipper had turned in, many of the crew seized the chance of a nap they would have missed otherwise.

Meanwhile Cszhech kept turning over in his mind the chain of events leading up to the attack, and always came to the same conclusion—he must be leaving an oil trail on the surface. That attack had been too accurate to explain by sonobuoys alone. . . . A sonobuoy only tells the plane there is a submarine within a mile or so of the buoy. But a sonobuoy, plus a tell-tale oil slick would pinpoint the submerged submarine. If he was leaving an oil slick he was in a desperate situation—blind and deaf himself, but plainly advertising his own location, at least in daylight, to aircraft and surface vessels alike. He decided to surface after dark, check for oil leaks and then make up his mind whether to keep going or head back to Lorient.

At 8.00 p.m., before it was dark enough to surface, he got sudden and emphatic confirmation that, despite his forty metre depth and creeping speed, something was indeed revealing his location. A salvo of nine depth charges made the ocean quake like a bowl of jelly. As the thunder subsided and he realized that he still wasn't hurt Cszhech ordered, "Full speed ahead. . . . Fire decoys!"

He now had fifteen minutes when reverberations of the sea

would make it impossible for destroyers to use their sonar gear, and if luck was still with him the enemy might concentrate on the decoys instead of the U-505 when the rumblings died down. Fifteen minutes later six more depth charges exploded, but further away than the others. Apparently the decoys had worked. This gave him another fifteen minutes to run at high speed, and when this reprieve expired there were nine more explosions plainly audible to all in the boat but obviously aimed at the chemical bubble which the decoys had made a couple of miles astern.

Cszhech settled down to creeping speed again for an hour, during which time all was quiet. Evidently the destroyers, or aircraft, or whatever they were that had beaten that chemical bubble to pieces were satisfied that they had destroyed a submarine. With his sound gear inoperative, the only way Cszhech could find out what was going on was to come up to shallow depth and stick his periscope up. An hour and a half after the attack he poked up his periscope cautiously and took a look.

There were three destroyers sniffing around the ocean a mile to the north of him. The sea was glassy calm, and a quick swing of the periscope astern confirmed that the boat was indeed leaving a conspicuous oil trail behind her. But it was nearly dark now, and if those destroyers were convinced they had destroyed him, they might not pay too much attention to a little stray oil on the surface in the area of the "kill." Cszhech went back down to forty metres and crept towards the coast of Spain.

A few hours later he entered Spanish territorial waters, where he surfaced and ran east the rest of the night under the lee of the coast, taking stock of his situation. It would be humiliating to limp into Lorient again and his pride made him want to go on, but common sense told him not to. That oil leak was a conspicuous one and could not be fixed at sea. Without radar or sound gear he could accomplish little even if he went on. And finally, Doenitz had stressed the need for caution and preserving his trained crews until the new types of U-boats were ready. Cszhech decided to go back.

He hugged the Spanish and French coasts close into the

beach, lying on the bottom during daylight and surfacing for a few hours' sprint each night. Oil came up when he sat on the bottom, but a stationary oil puddle in these waters, where there were lots of fishing boats, wasn't as conspicuous as a moving streak out in the middle of Biscay. On July 14 he berthed again in Lorient.

In addition to the troubles Cszhech reported, the dockyard found that all the gaskets in the vent valves had been eaten away by some corrosive substance and that there was a hole the size of a lead pencil drilled into one of the under-water oil tanks. It was two weeks before they got these things put right, repaired the radar and listening gear, and pronounced the boat ready for sea again.

During July thirty-seven U-boats failed to return from the operating areas. Fourteen of these had been sunk in the Bay of Biscay, and every one of the skippers was a personal friend of Cszhech.

On the first of August U-505 sallied forth once more. But they were back again the next day. There were ominous noises when they dived deeper than fifty metres, sounds as if the joints in the hull were coming apart or a ballast tank were being crushed. There were also noises of water coming in somewhere. They could find no leaks, but every time they went down to fifty metres the noises began again, indicating at least that something was being strained close to the breaking point.

For two weeks the shipyard checked the hull rivet by rivet and joint by joint. They could find nothing wrong, but Cszhech and all his men swore they had not imagined these noises. The shipyard sent them out again on August 15, and exactly the same noises were repeated. This time Cszhech took her a little deeper, and when he surfaced he found the main air induction had been crushed in and was full of water. At least this would prove to the dockyard sceptics he hadn't been dreaming about the noises. They were back in the dockyard again on August 16th, for another week to repair the induction.

They went out again on August 22nd, and came back in again as usual the next day. This time they found the vent gaskets eaten away, just as they had been on their first cruise.

140

The gaskets had been in order when they sailed the day before. The dockyard inspectors smelt a rat, and half a dozen French labourers who had renewed these gaskets were arrested on suspicion of sabotage and shot.

On September 18 the U-505 took her fifth departure from Lorient in the two and a half months since her overhaul had been "finished". This time the engineering officer from Doenitz's staff sailed with her to observe her trial dives. Cszhech took this as a not-too-veiled hint that the high command were beginning to think that he got discouraged too easily and magnified his difficulties. With the Staff Engineer breathing down his neck, Cszhech ran through his test dives and as usual found a lot of small things wrong.

But staff officers who are fighting the war in a swivel chair are the same in all navies. This one minimized the difficulties and pointed out that they could all be repaired at sea during the first week of the cruise. So he patted Cszhech on the back, wished him luck, transferred to a motor torpedo boat and headed back for Lorient at a high rate of knots. Cszhech submerged and set off again.

This time he made the transit of Biscay even more cautiously than before. He never came up except to charge batteries and for about ten minutes in the morning to snatch a quick sextant altitude of the sun and verify his run. He averaged less than three hours a day on the surface and in the first four and a half days covered only 200 miles surfaced and 131 submerged. The joint British-U.S. air patrol over Biscay was getting more effective every day.

During these four days, thanks to the ingenuity of the four chief petty officers in the original crew, the men of the U-505 had repaired most of the defects which the staff engineer claimed he could put right over night.

Near midnight on the fifth day out U-505 surfaced to re-charge batteries, but as she was breaking surface she got radar warning of nearby aircraft and had to dive again immediately. There was no reason why this should cause her to blow any fuses. A submarine is always ready to crash dive when she surfaces. But this was the first time U-505 had had to crash dive on this cruise, and in her haste to get down she overloaded her main ballast pump. Some fuses which *should* have blown didn't, and as a result the armature of the main ballast pump went up in acrid smelling smoke.

Cszhech spent the whole night trying to figure out some way of repairing that pump at sea. His war diary records that he considered requesting another outbound boat to bring out a spare armature for his pump, transfer it to him in a safe place at sea, and thus avoid another return to Lorient. Although installing the big armature at sea would be a very difficult job, it was physically possible to do it. But there were no safe places at sea for surfaced U-boats, and it would be suicide for him to go on without this pump. True, he didn't need it for shallow dives, but the way the war at sea was going now, any U-boat had to be ready to go to a hundred metres at any time, and had to be able to get up from there fast to give the crew a chance to scuttle and get overboard if deep diving didn't shake off the pursuers. That main ballast pump was vital. So Cszhech turned back for the sixth time and crept into Lorient on the 30th of September.

In the ninety days since his boat had been pronounced ready by the dockyard and scheduled for operations on 1 July, he had spent twenty days at sea and seventy alongside the dock. During these ninety days, seventy-one submarines commanded by his flotilla mates had been sent to the bottom by the Allies. One hundred and fifteen Allied ships, totalling over half a million tons, had been sunk by the flotilla, but U-505 had done nothing except wear a path in the channel in and out of Lorient. Cszhech was not anxious to see any of his contemporaries when he came in this time, although he had no choice about returning and it wasn't his fault.

But when a boat is lucky the skipper often gets a medal which he didn't really earn. By the same token, if a boat is unlucky, the skipper takes the blame for things over which he had no control. The most damning charge you can bring against a military man is that he is unlucky. As he was bringing the U-505 back to Lorient again, Cszhech in the silence of the conning tower could sense this charge being preferred against

142

him by all the men in his crew, who no longer looked him in the eye when they spoke to him.

As he brought his submarine alongside, the French underground got in a shrewd blow at his morale. Painted in large white letters which could not be seen by anyone standing on the dock, but which couldn't be missed by anyone on the deck of a U-boat coming alongside the dock, was the legend, "U-505's Hunting Ground".

Fixing the motor was a major job that took ten days even in the shipyard. Cszhech spent most of this time brooding over his series of failures. He had been fully justified every time he turned back and no one could have done otherwise. But his contemporaries now were beginning to treat him almost as if he were a cripple, who wasn't to be blamed for his infirmities but who was not the same as other men. When he joined a circle of them at the club there was an embarrassed lull in the conversation. He took to solitary drinking and avoided the company of his friends.

The night before he was to sail on his seventh attempt to get out, he was seated in a booth at a waterfront cafe with a girl, getting drunk. In the next booth, separated from them by only a thin partition, was a noisy group of U-boat sailors hashing over recent events. Cszhech was listening absent-mindedly.

At this stage of the war there were no successes to boast of and most of the talk was about recent losses and boats reported missing.

"U-68 and U-515 sail tomorrow," said a voice on the other side of the screen, "and the way things are going now at least one of them won't come back."

Another voice challenged this statement, "Both have good captains—Henke and Lauzemis—they will be back."

"Many just as good haven't come back . . . the odds are two to one against *anybody* now."

There was a lull in the conversation while that ominous statement sank in. Then a humorist trying to relieve the tension said, "At least we've still got one ace who will always come back."

"Who?" demanded several voices.

"Cszhech."

The blood drained from Cszhech's face. As a roar of derisive laughter from the other side of the screen greeted this quip, Cszhech sat staring at his glass and squeezing his grip tighter until his knuckles were white. The glass shattered in his hand, cut into the flesh, and for several seconds more he squeezed the broken pieces. Then he flung the fragments against the wall, threw some money on the bloody table, and reeled out into the night.

Back at the dockyard a hospital doctor picked pieces of glass out of his hand, bandaged it up and told him it would heal in about a week. The wound to his soul was a mortal one. When he sailed the next day nothing in this world could have induced Cszhech to return from that cruise prematurely.

He crept out of Lorient. To insure against being spotted from the air he stayed submerged twenty-two hours out of every twenty-four. He had to surface for a minimum of two hours each day to recharge his battery and during these two hours he ran at full speed putting about thirty-five miles behind him. But at creeping speed submerged for the other twenty-two hours he covered only about the same distance, so his daily run averaged about seventy miles. He crossed the Bay of Biscay so slowly, keeping radio silence, that U-boat Headquarters sent him a message when he was ten days out, asking if he hadn't forgotten to report reaching the Atlantic. He replied that he had not—and continued at creeping speed.

In the early evening of their fourteenth day out, the U-505 was cruising slowly at forty metres when the sound room reported, "Screw noises at medium distance." Meyer, the first officer, notified the Captain and got ready to come up to periscope depth and have a look.

As Cszhech climbed up the ladder to the conning tower, nursing his injured right hand, he inquired nervously, "What is it, Meyer? What is it?"

"Sound room can't tell yet," replied Meyer. Then nodding at the periscope he asked, "Shall I bring her up to periscope depth, Captain?" This was the natural reaction of any U-boat man in these circumstances. A submarine's sensitive listening gear would nearly always pick up propeller noises much farther away than a surface vessel could hear the echo of a ping from her sonar gear. The submarine, therefore, always had the big advantage of surprise on her first attack, and to a normal skipper any screw noises were a challenge to a battle, with the opening odds heavily in his favour. But Cszhech was not normal now.

"No," he said. "Hold her at forty metres. This must be a destroyer."

Meyer thought it strange that his captain made up his mind so quickly that this was a destroyer rather than a merchant ship and that he had no intention of attacking. But Meyer obediently passed the word below, "Hold her at forty metres."

"What do you hear now?" demanded Cszhech on the voice tube to the sound room.

"Twin screws making 180 r.p.m. . . . diesel engines . . . approaching rapidly," came the answer from below.

"Another submarine?" asked Meyer.

"No," said Cszhech. "There are no other submarines near us. This is a Britisher, just as I thought."

"Maybe he won't find us, Captain," said Meyer. "We can't even hear his sonar pings yet."

"He will find us," said Cszhech, a hunted look coming over his face. "I *know* he will find us."

Soon a report came up from the sound room, "Bearing holds steady—he is heading right at us."

Cszhech cast a furtive look, like a cornered animal, at his first officer.

"Shall I change course ninety degrees, Captain?" suggested Meyer.

For some seconds Cszhech made no reply. Finally he said, "Very well, Meyer. . . . But it won't do any good—we *can't* escape."

"Hard a' port," said Meyer to the helmsman, wondering what had come over the Captain. "Steady on course 180."

Cszhech stared at the dial on the bearing indicator from the sound room as if he were looking at a ghost. "The bearing remains steady," he said in a hollow voice, "He knows where I am."

"Not yet, Captain," said Meyer. "We don't hear any pings yet."

Almost immediately the sound room called up, "Hear pings now on same bearing and screw noises—approaching fast."

Cszhech shot an accusing glance at his first officer as if to say, "I told you so," but took no other action.

"Shall I go deep, Captain?" asked Meyer.

"It's no use, Meyer," said Cszhech despairingly. "We can't get away . . . they have caught us again . . . my luck is bad."

By now everyone in the boat could hear the propeller noises with the naked ear. "Shall I sound the alarm, Captain?" asked Meyer with his hand on the button.

For perhaps half a minute Cszhech made no reply. He stood there in the conning tower as if in a trance, clenching his fists so tightly that he split the scabs on his right hand. "No," he said; "everyone knows now, anyway. . . ."

A minute later all hands heard the tempo of the screw noises change, indicating that the destroyer was slowing down so that she could hear better in the final stage of a carefully calculated attack. There was no doubt whatever now that the destroyer had them pin-pointed. As the destroyer neared the firing point, Cszhech seemed to shrivel within himself as if he knew the battle was hopeless. Screw noises were very loud now and all hands braced themselves knowing that the climax was close at hand.

"Destroyer is firing depth charges," said the sound room.

Cszhech stared at the gauges like a man who was already in another world and said nothing.

"Hard a' starboard," said Meyer on his own initiative.

For fifteen seconds everyone in the U-505 held his breath and prayed silently as the depth charges were sinking. They all knew now from experience that a depth charge attack was a terrifying experience but that unless the charges were set to explode at exactly the right depth, they might come out of this with just another bad shaking up.

146

The charges were set *almost* exactly right, and the rippling salvo of explosions gave the U-505 the worst jarring she had ever received, even worse than that direct hit by the aerial bomb.

Oberleutnant Meyer says the first depth charge smashed the lights. A few seconds later, while the other depth charges were exploding all around him, he heard an explosion which seemed to be from an extra close depth charge and saw a flash of flame in the conning tower. He thought the flame came from an electric switch. He smelt pungent smoke which might have been from burning insulation. In the darkness his Captain slumped against him and fell to the deck.

There was no time to investigate what had happened now. The skipper had apparently been knocked out by being slammed against the periscope. But the boat was in a desperate situation and until Cszhech came to again and could resume command, it was up to Meyer to take over.

"One hundred metres," barked Meyer. "Full speed—fire decoys." Then he yelled down the hatch to the control room, "Come up here and get the Captain. He is knocked out." He concentrated on the gauges again while they lugged the Captain below. "Hard a' port," he said to the helmsman.

As the boat circled to the left, Meyer noted that they were still at forty metres and at creeping speed. He stuck his head down the hatch and yelled, "Full speed! One hundred metres! What the hell's the matter down there?"

The men were all huddled like sheep around the Captain, who was stretched out on the floor plates. One of the chief petty officers looked up at Meyer with despair in his eyes, pointed his forefinger at his temple and moved his thumb like the hammer of a revolver. At this same moment Meyer saw the pool of blood on the deck of the conning tower with the Captain's Luger lying alongside it. Cszhech had shot himself!

Meyer leaped down into the control room, saw at a glance that Cszhech was done for, and then faced what were now *his* crew. This was a change of command ceremony to put the new skipper's soul to the acid test. Cszhech had quit—deserted under fire. The destroyer was circling to make another attack.

147

Discipline, based on regulations, went overboard when the Commanding Officer pulled the trigger of that Luger. Meyer's gold stripes meant nothing now. Why should these men obey a junior with less experience than the man who had just deserted them? What happened now would depend on Meyer the man, not Oberleutnant Meyer. The whole Officer Corps of the Kriegsmarine was discredited in the minds of those terrified men standing on the brink of eternity.

"I am in command now," said Meyer to his dazed men. "Go back to your battle stations."

No one moved. Meyer reached up into the conning tower, picked up the Captain's gun, toyed with it for a moment looking around the circle of faces and then tossed it on to the chart table.

"Anyone who wants to die—help yourself," he said. "The rest of you do as I say and I'll get you out of this. . . . One hundred metres—full speed—fire decoys."

No one was ready to die. The gun lay there untouched.

Some men went slowly back to their stations and began executing his orders. Others hesitated, motionless. Panic was very near.

Willi Bunger (the "Ostrich") broke into uncontrolled sobbing. Meyer slapped him across the face, shoved him toward his battle station, and said, "Get going boy, you're not old enough to die yet." Willi pulled himself together, took his battle station, and all the others did likewise. "The worst is over—we will escape," said Meyer coolly.

"Steady as you go," he called to the helmsman. "Fire two more decoys."

"What shall we do with *him*, Captain?" asked one of the chiefs, nodding at Cszhech's body, as the men resumed their duties.

For the leading chief to call him "Captain" at this moment meant more to Meyer than a direct commission from *der Führer* himself.

"Lash him up in a hammock, put a weight at his feet, and I'll put him overboard when we have time," replied Meyer.

In the face of mortal danger some men come apart if responsibility is suddenly thrust upon them. Others exceed anything they have ever done before. Meyer carried out his promise to his men and got them out of the jam. The destroyer was fooled by the decoys, and for the next few hours the U-505 heard depth charge explosions receding farther and farther astern as the destroyer blasted away at false echoes from chemical bubbles.

At four o'clock in the morning Meyer surfaced. They carried Cszhech's body up on deck and committed it to the deep.

The whole eight-hour period is tersely recorded in the war diary of the U-505 as follows:

1952 Propeller noises in medium distance.
1954 Piston engine noises.
1956 Sonar noises.
1958 Depth charges—very close.
1958 *Kommandant ausgefallen.* (Literally, "Captain fell out of ranks").
2100 Captain dead.
     First Officer Meyer assumes command.
0406 Captain's body overboard.

Above is the whole story so far as the official log of the U-505 goes. Note that although Meyer took over at 1958 and saved the boat, he doesn't officially record assuming command until an hour later when Cszhech dies!

So, after putting Cszhech overboard, the U-505 headed back to Lorient again, Oberleutnant Paul Meyer commanding.

They got back on November 7th. Meyer made his report to Doenitz and was "absolved of all blame".

That is all he ever got out of this operation—absolved of all blame! He had saved a U-boat from certain destruction under almost impossible circumstances, after the captain had deserted under fire and blown his brains out. He had preserved a trained crew for Doenitz and had restored respect for authority in a group of men who had just seen the highest authority there is at sea fail them shamefully. The first officer's reward was to be "absolved from blame".

The only way I can explain this is that Doenitz considered

that the incident had to be hushed up to avoid dishonouring the Officers' Corps and damaging the morale of the surviving U-boat crews. Meyer's outstanding conduct could not be recognized without publicizing Cszhech's cowardice, so Meyer stayed on as first officer of the U-505 and had nothing to show for what he had done—except his own life, and the lasting respect of some fifty men.

CHAPTER XII

THE S.S. *CERAMIC*

WE come now to a minor incident in the Battle of the Atlantic which, although it concerns another U-boat, the U-515, must be told in some detail as it has a bearing on the U-505 story. Among the records of lost ships in the British Admiralty, appears the following item:

Date	Place	Ship	Remarks
Dec. 1942	Near Azores	SS Ceramic	Missing

In the war diary of the U-515, now reposing in the Admiralty archives, appears the following:

Date	Position	Event
7 Dec. 42	40° 50′ N 39° 55′ W	Sank SS Ceramic, 18,800 BRT. Rescued one soldier.

The *Ceramic* was a passenger ship built in 1913 for the Shaw, Savill and Albion Line. She spent a long and useful life on a regular run between England and Australia via the Cape of Good Hope. When war broke out she was too old to justify conversion to a troop ship, and even during a world war *some* civilians must travel back and forth between Australia and the home country. So the *Ceramic* stayed on her regular run.

She was one of the few ships that continued to work at their peace-time trade, and thousands of civilians at both ends of her run had urgent, legitimate reasons for taking passage in her. Getting on her civilian passenger list was a difficult, tedious business involving a long wait and much red tape. She was not a troop ship but she did carry miscellaneous military people and naturally they had priority. Civilians needed affidavits from England and Australia, and had to explain all the facts of their cases to different officials whose duty it was to listen to hundreds of heart-breaking stories and select the most deserving applicants. Every time the *Ceramic* sailed, she left many aching hearts behind to sweat out the long wait for her next trip. One plea always hard for the officials to deny was that of a mother and her children, caught on a visit to England when war began, asking to be reunited with father in Australia. So the *Ceramic* always carried many women and children.

She sailed from England on her final voyage late in November 1942, with convoy ON-149, carrying about four hundred military personnel and civilians on official business, plus one hundred women and children. The convoy was bound for Canada, and the *Ceramic* would break off and proceed independently after clearing the submarine-infested waters around England. Convoys such as this one were given an anti-submarine escort of a dozen destroyers or corvettes, and usually had one or two cruisers to beat off attacks by surface raiders. They sailed northwest out of the Irish Sea and passed within range of the shore-based aircraft in Iceland. As long as possible, the RAF gave them continuous air cover.

No Allied ship was really *safe* at sea during the grim year of 1942. But ON convoys were at least as safe as any.

The North Atlantic in December is cold and blustery, but the run past Iceland was uneventful. By the time the *Ceramic* was southwest of Greenland, skies were bright, the weather mild, seas calm and no submarines had been sighted. England, with its hunger diet, wailing air raid sirens and hideous nights of terror, was a long way astern and out here at sea the world seemed saner.

Off Cape Farewell at the southern tip of Greenland, the *Ceramic* changed course sharply to port heading south and bent on full speed, while the convoy stood on towards Canada. As they parted company, the convoy commodore and the skipper of the ancient liner exchanged identical blinker messages, "Good Luck". Soon the forest of masts in the convoy dropped below the horizon to the northwest and the *Ceramic* was on her own.

She was in reasonably safe waters now. She would run south till she passed the Azores and then head for the Cape, keeping far to the west of the usual shipping lanes. The U-boats' hunting ground was off Freetown, where convoys run close in to the coast. But she would pass Freetown far off-shore and wasn't likely to encounter any submarines out in the South Atlantic.

Loading up a ship with civilians, women, and children and sending her on a 12,000 mile voyage unescorted most of the way, is what military men call a calculated risk—*when they get away with it!* They had got away with this trip by the *Ceramic* several times. She could make seventeen knots, so a submerged U-boat had no chance of getting a shot at her unless she happened to run almost over the U-boat. A submarine on the surface *might* catch her, but if she saw the submarine in time she could make a long race out of it, get off warning signals and probably stay out of range from the U-boat's gun till help arrived. Besides, she had a three-inch gun on her stern. She was well protected in the convoy during the early and most dangerous part of the voyage . . . and, finally, she *had* to sail. You simply can't cut off all passenger traffic to Australia for five and a half years.

At sunset on December 6, the *Ceramic*, four hundred miles west of the Azores, boiled along on a southeasterly course, bucking a choppy sea in a restless empty ocean. The sky was overcast, and a spanking southwest breeze was threatening to blow up into a gale, keeping most of the passengers below decks.

But on the other side of the horizon to the west a baleful eye was focused on *Ceramic's* masts, and a submarine, running at high speed on the surface, obscured from them by the curvature of the earth, had settled down on a course that would intercept the *Ceramic* about midnight.

By ten that night the increasing motion of the ship had sent most of the passengers off to bed. The night was black and the wind was still rising. At this time the submarine to the west was ten degrees forward of the *Ceramic's* starboard beam and had closed to ten thousand yards. The thrashing of the *Ceramic's* screws was plainly audible in the submarine's sensitive listening devices. The U-boat's skipper, coached by his sound operator exactly where to point his powerful night glasses, could see her blacked-out shape well enough for his purpose.

Two hours later eight bells had sounded, the middle watch

153

had just come on and nearly all the passengers were sound asleep, when the *Ceramic* shuddered as if she had hit a submerged rock. All sleepers awoke instantly, not knowing why, and sat up in their bunks while the ship still quivered from the blow—which *might* have been from a big wave. For ten seconds of suspense in the darkened cabins there was no sign of anything wrong, except the decreasing beat of the vibration from the engines. Then the silence was shattered by the clanging of the alarm.

This *couldn't* be another drill—not at midnight! Lights popped on in the cabins behind shielded ports, children looked into their mothers' eyes to find out what it all meant, saw fear written there. Then stewards were passing the word, "Fall in at your lifeboat stations immediately."

Men, women and children scrambled out of their bunks, pulled on shoes without lacing them, threw on overcoats, grabbed life preservers and started hurrying through the passageways to the upper decks. Lights still burned brightly in the passageways and saloons.

When the people got on deck the inky blackness blinded them. For some minutes, until their eyes refocused, they saw nothing. Women with children clinging to them groped their way along the deck. The wind, now nearing half a gale, moaned through the upper works ominously. There was no outward panic . . . just stark, numbing, unbelieving fear. The ship began to wallow in the trough of the sea, but as yet there was no sign on the upper decks that she was badly hurt—no fire, no wreckage, no wounded crying out. It seemed incredible that anything serious could be wrong with the stout ship that had brought them all safely so far.

When the order "Abandon Ship" was swept along the decks by the mournful wind, it was so fantastic that many simply couldn't believe it. It seemed absurd to lower boats on a night like this. It was bad enough just to be at sea on a big ship in this kind of weather; leaving the ship in those tiny open boats would be suicide. The ship was still firm under the passengers' feet, her steel plates brushed the wind aside and her hull rode the seas steadily, supporting the passengers safely forty feet above the waves. Many refused to get into the boats, sobbing and pleading with the ship's officers to wait awhile.

At 0021 another heavy blow as if from a giant sledge hammer struck the *Ceramic* and there was a muffled rumbling inside her. The Captain, knowing that to remain blacked out could serve no further purpose, flashed the deck lights on. To the people on deck, this showed no visible proof that the ship was badly hurt. Many of these people had lived through the blitz in London and that latest jar to the ship was nothing like as terrifying as a near miss exploding half a street away. Maybe some poor men down in the engine room had been killed, but up here on deck everyone was still safe. The seamen all knew when the lights flashed on that this was indeed the end.

"All hands in the boats," came the cry along the deck. "Last call before we lower away." This brought stark reality home to the dazed undecided passengers. Now they had to make up their minds whether to get into those tiny boats where their chance of survival seemed one in a million, or to stay with this still solid but certainly doomed ship. The only choice seemed whether to drown in a large group with the ship or to drown in small groups out there in blackness. Many chose to stay with the ship.

The *Ceramic's* crew of veteran seamen lowered a dozen crowded boats into the water safely before the first casualty occurred. As the next boat started down, the forward fall jammed and the after one slipped off the cleat. The boat hung up vertically by the bow and spilled men, women and children into the stormy water thirty feet below. The first screams heard that night came from these unfortunate people . . . but they were soon drowned out.

At 0040 a third torpedo crashed into the already mortally wounded *Ceramic*. It was just a question of time before she would go down, but an implacable enemy out in the darkness was getting impatient. Now the *Ceramic's* last electric generator coasted to a stop, all lights dimming slowly and finally going out. The *Ceramic* was dead, but her corpse still floated.

There were few children left on board to await the end. Almost all mothers had clung to the last straw of hope, loaded

155

their youngsters into the boats and climbed in with them, knowing in their hearts that they were just prolonging the agony. Though the lifeboats bobbed around crazily, they remained afloat with their cargoes of humanity. But the nearest land was four hundred miles away and the wind whipped sheets of spray off the tops of the waves which were getting bigger.

At one o'clock a quartermaster, on watch on the bridge, struck two bells, as he always had at this time during thirty years of faithful seafaring service. Some of those huddled in the darkness on deck began to think that a miracle was occurring. In the past hour three torpedoes had hit, but the old *Ceramic* still floated. Perhaps that submarine would go away now . . . and perhaps the *Ceramic* would remain afloat.

At 0102 a fourth torpedo hit the *Ceramic* and broke her back. A big ship doesn't suddenly snap into two pieces like a stick of wood when she breaks her back. It takes time—perhaps twenty or thirty seconds. She jack-knifes in the middle, the bow and stern rising out of water and the midship section going under. This happens ponderously with the tempo of a heavy roll from port to starboard. It is accompanied by the unearthly noise of steel plates tearing apart and being crumpled like tissue paper, of internal explosions, escaping steam, and loose gear in the ship smashing down across the slanting decks. For the second time this night screams filled the darkness.

In less than half a minute the bow and stern of the *Ceramic* tilted opposite each other at a forty-five-degree angle with a jumbled mass of humanity clawing at the decks as they slid down into the sea. In a few more seconds the two broken pieces of the ship sank gurgling into the depths leaving behind on the wind-whipped water a welter of wreckage, life rafts, and struggling human beings.

Of the 650 souls on board the *Ceramic*, perhaps only twenty had been killed by the torpedoes. Another twenty had drowned when the lifeboat hung up at the davits. Perhaps a dozen were crushed inside the ship when she broke her back. About a hundred more were dragged down in the suction when the broken fragments of the ship went under. When it was all over, about five hundred must have been still alive, half of them in a score of bobbing lifeboats, and the rest paddling around in the wreckage-strewn sea. There was a deathly silence broken only by the wailing of the wind and of children. The tiny island of Flores in the Azores was four hundred miles to the east.

We flash back seven hours now and shift to the bridge of the submarine U-515, Kapitän Leutnant Werner Henke, Knight's Cross with Oak Leaves, commanding. Henke, an efficient and ambitious U-boat commander, is damning his luck at being out here in the empty ocean when he knows that many convoys are converging on Gibraltar to support the invasion of Africa which started just a month before. As Henke sweeps his eye around the sharp and empty horizon, he thinks bitterly of how some of his rivals and comrades will be piling up big scores now simply because they were assigned to good areas, whereas, he, Henke, through no fault of his own, is out here where there is nothing. In another couple of hours it will be dark and even if there were any steamers out here he might not see them.

Suddenly a flaw in the horizon catches his eye as it sweeps around. When he concentrates on it he can see nothing, but when he puts his ten-power glasses on it, his heart skips a beat. There are two tiny spars sticking up over the horizon, well separated as on a long ship, broad on the port bow.

"Alarm. . . . Topmasts in sight."

He observed the bearing carefully for two minutes and noted that it remained nearly constant. This meant he was already on a good intercept course. "Estimated distance sixteen sea miles," he called down the hatch—"All engines full speed—alter course 30 degrees to starboard." Running at nineteen knots he would be able to hold his present favourable position forward of the steamer's beam, while he slowly converged on her after dark until close enough to fire torpedoes.

Henke soon solved the enemy speed as being seventeen knots —no zigzag. By sunset it became apparent that she was running independently, relying on her speed to escape attack. He estimated her at 20,000 tons, probably carrying troops to Egypt via the Red Sea and Suez.

As it grew darker Henke drove in on the surface at high speed, gaining bearing ahead of the *Ceramic* and working carefully into position by eye and by sound bearings of her screws. In a few hours he would be in perfect position for a close range shot at this juicy target. Henke's trained mind dropped into the groove worn by many previous attacks. His only thoughts now were target, angle, course, speed, depth setting, and the number of torpedoes to fire.

All six of his torpedo tubes were loaded and ready. A fat target like this one, probably loaded to the gunwales with troops, certainly justified a spread of four torpedoes to allow for errors in estimating enemy course and speed. But Werner Henke didn't make such errors. With confidence he ordered, "Stand by for double shot. Tubes one and four. Keep other tubes ready."

Henke never questioned his first judgment that this was a troop ship—and it probably wouldn't have made any difference if he had. By this time the rules of Prize Warfare had gone down the drain and both sides sank enemy ships without warning whether they were war vessels, cargo, troop, or passenger ships. By midnight the U-515 was in position to shoot, 1,200 yards on the *Ceramic's* starboard bow, giving the torpedoes a perfect ninety-degree track angle.

In the forward and after torpedo rooms the expert crews made final settings on the torpedoes as Henke announced them over the loudspeakers. "Depth setting 6 metres, gyro angle zero, $\frac{1}{2}$ degree spread." The chief torpedoman personally checked each setting, reported back to control, "Ready," and stood by with stop watches to check the time of the explosions against the known running time of the torpedoes to the target.

At 0001, Henke, with his eye glued to the attack periscope in the conning tower, gave the order, "Fire one. . . . Fire four."

In the forward torpedo room there were muffled coughs inside tubes one and four and the chief torpedoman punched his stop watches. All hands waited tensely, listening while the sweep second hands of the watches counted out the sands still remaining in the hour glass of Father Time for the *Ceramic*. Henke kept his eye at the periscope.

At 0003 – ½, there was a light tick on the U-515's hull from the shock wave of an underwater explosion, followed a split second later by a rumble heard throughout the boat. Cheers went up in the forward torpedo room and the chief, glancing at his watch, reported, "Number one hit, sir." Henke, peering through the periscope, saw no indication that anything had happened to the *Ceramic*. His torpedoes were set to run deep and the explosion had been swallowed up inside the *Ceramic*.

The sound operator in his cubbyhole just abaft the torpedo room, with the sensitive underwater phones clamped to his ears, sang out, "Number four hit but did not explode."

In a few minutes the Captain's voice came over the loud-speakers, "Target is stopping. . . . Set target speed zero. . . . Target angle ninety degrees. . . . Depth four metres." The readjustments on the next torpedo were quickly made.

For the next ten minutes Henke used his engines skilfully to hold the boat in position for the next shot, if one were necessary. The submarine rode up and down with the seas, the blacked out target clearly visible in the periscope, lying to but apparently unhurt. At 0018, Henke gave the order, "Stand by—fire two." At 0200 – ½, the tick followed by the muffled roar came back and the chief sang out, "Number two hit, sir."

The lights came on along the *Ceramic's* deck and Henke could now see a dozen boats being lowered, but was too far away to make out any details. He waited twenty minutes more until the boats were clear and gave the order, "Fire three." When the torpedo exploded, the *Ceramic's* lights went out, but the dark shape of her hull still riding on an even keel was plainly visible in the periscope. Thinking that perhaps something was wrong with his torpedoes, Henke turned his boat carefully half circle and drew a bead on the *Ceramic* with his after tubes. One hour after his first shot he fired tube five, and two minutes later he let out a yell of triumph. "God, she's breaking in two!"

Turning to his radio operator, Henke asked, "Did she get off an SOS?"

"Yes, Captain," said the radioman. "SS Ceramic, 18,800

tons, but there is heavy static tonight and I doubt if anyone heard it. . . . Shall I send another for her?"

"No," replied Henke. "Bridge watch on deck," he ordered, and led the way up the conning tower hatch himself. A half gale was blowing now, but the U-boat with all ballast tanks blown out rode lightly up and down with the waves like a cork. Occasionally a sea broke across the weather deck, but the bridge was dry, except when a sheet of spray slapped into the men's faces.

"Engines slow ahead," said Henke. Cruising slowly through the darkness he could hear faint cries in the water as he neared the spot where the *Ceramic* had gone down. The people in the water heard his motors and were trying to attract his attention. He still thought he had sunk a troop ship. When the cries were close at hand on both sides he said, "Stop engines. Turn on the searchlight."

The searchlight swung across the water and spotlighted men, women and children huddled on rafts or clinging to wreckage.

A dozen human-beings swam alongside, seized the beading around the edge of the heaving deck, and hung on pleading for rescue, slammed against the side by each wave and alternately submerged and lifted out of the water as the U-boat rode up and down with the sea.

"Half speed ahead," said Henke, and as the submarine gathered headway, some of them lost their holds and disappeared in the darkness astern. Others still hung on to their only hope for life. After he saw that he couldn't shake them off, Henke said to a seaman, "Go down there and get those people clear of the side." The seaman did as his captain had ordered.

Meantime, in the searchlight probing the darkness, a dozen lifeboats and scores of crowded rafts were visible, in addition to hundreds of heads alongside pieces of wreckage. Henke hailed three lifeboats and asked for the Captain, but all denied that he was aboard. Soon the light settled on a raft with three figures on it, obviously men. Henke stopped his submarine about ten feet away from it and hailed, "Who are you?"

"Merchant seaman Jones," came the first answer.

"Doctor Smith," came the second.

"Sapper Munday, Royal Engineers," came the third.

"Heave him a line," said Henke, and Sapper Munday was dragged aboard.

Henke noted that he was wearing a British uniform. "You are a soldier?" he asked.

"Yes sir," said Sapper Munday.

"Take him below," said Henke. "Full speed ahead."

The other occupants of the raft had meantime swum over to U-515 and had dragged themselves aboard the after deck and collapsed, lying face down on the gratings.

"Stand by to dive," ordered Henke.

Three lookouts plummeted down the hatch. The lookout for the after sector paused for a second, and said, "Captain—there are two men on deck. . . ."

"Get below!" said Henke, and followed him down himself, slamming the hatch a few seconds before the U-515 submerged, and departed from the scene.

The rest of that night Henke tossed in his bunk down in his cabin amidships, alone with his conscience. He assured himself that his conscience was clear, and it was—at least so far as his official orders were concerned. U-boat captains had been authorized by Admiral Doenitz since 1940 to torpedo enemy ships of all classes, except hospital ships, without warning. And besides, this one was armed—he had seen the gun on her stern. He was certainly within his rights on that score, although he would not soon forget the pleas of the children that still rang in his ears. So far as rescuing survivors was concerned, there could be no blame put on him—Doenitz had plainly said, "Don't ever endanger the safety of your boat to rescue survivors." A U-boat is jammed to capacity with its own crew of sixty aboard. The only way he could possibly have rescued a couple of hundred survivors would have been to take them on deck—and then he would have given up his ability to submerge and been a sitting target for RAF aircraft. Planes bombed any submarines they saw, not stopping in the heat of battle to count the people on deck or check their identity cards to make sure they weren't friends.

Some of the scenes he had witnessed and the pleas he had

161

heard would be etched into his brain the rest of his life. But war is a ruthless business, you've got to be tough to win, and his conscience was clear. So Werner Henke rolled over in his bunk.

As the U-515 turned away from the scene of the disaster, at least four hundred people were still alive. Had the weather been moderate perhaps fifty or so of those on the rafts might have survived for several days and might have been sighted by passing planes or ships. The lifeboats could have sailed to the Azores in about a week and over half the two hundred and fifty people in the boats would have survived that ordeal.

But that night the wind increased, and next day it blew a whole gale. Huge breaking rollers swept majestically across the surface of the sea. When they broke, they flung lifeboats end over end, spilling the occupants into the boiling waters and smashing the capsized boat down on top of them. By sunset, December 7, there were probably no survivors of the Ceramic, except Sapper Munday.

At noon of December 7, Henke wrote in his log the seaman's terse description of a howling gale: "Wind NW, Force 10, Sea 8 (very rough), rain and hail. . . . Submerging on account of weather."

When Henke returned from that cruise, he made a full report of the Ceramic incident and turned in Sapper Munday to verify his tonnage claim. Admiral Doenitz approved what he had done and credited Henke with twice the Ceramic's tonnage towards another oak leaf because she was a troop ship. Sapper Munday was sent by Doenitz to Berlin and handed from one agency of the Nazi party to another, where they did various things to him which I have no way of knowing about.

Early in 1943 Sapper Munday spoke on a radio broadcast from Berlin and gave the first news that the British had had of the Ceramic's fate. This news made the British very angry and, as will appear later, started an ominous chain of events for Henke.

A year and a half later in April 1944 this chain of events came to a new head when my hunter-killer group sank the

U-515 just a few hundred miles from where she sank the *Ceramic*.

As will be related in due course, the circumstances of the U-515's sinking, in which we rescued Henke and most of his crew, played a key role in starting another chain of events that finally brought the U-505 to Chicago.

CHAPTER XIII

HUNTER-KILLER TASK GROUP

WE now change to the Allied side of the battle and watch the story from the bridge of a jeep carrier operating in the U.S. Atlantic Fleet. In January 1944, at Norfolk, Virginia, I was given command of a hunter-killer task group made up of the small escort carrier U.S.S. *Guadalcanal* and her four escort destroyers. Groups such as this one were used to keep air cover over areas beyond the reach of shore-based aircraft. After these groups made their appearance in the Battle of the Atlantic, there were no more mid-ocean gaps and a U-boat might be attacked by aircraft anywhere at sea.

In addition to being Task Group Commander, I was also the Captain of the *Guadalcanal*, a Kaiser-built prefabricated carrier of 11,000 tons commissioned only three months previously in Astoria, Oregon. On the *Guadalcanal* we had just finished our shakedown period working our way to the Atlantic via Panama and doing everything we could think of to make sailor men out of our crew of young farmhands, shoe clerks and high school boys, eighty per cent of whom had never seen salt water before. It had been a busy time.

When my crew were assembling before commissioning, we gave each new man who reported the following memo:

1. The motto of this ship will be "Can Do", meaning that we will take any tough job that is given to us and run away with it. The tougher the job, the better we'll like it.

2. Before a carrier can do its big job of sinking enemy ships, several hundred small jobs have got to be done and done well. One man falling down on a small job can bitch the works for the whole ship. So learn all you can about your job during this pre-commissioning period. Pretty soon we will be out where it rains bombs and it will be too late to learn.

Note: This ship will be employed on dangerous duty. We will either sink the enemy or get sunk ourselves depending on how well we learn our jobs now and do our jobs later.

ANYONE WHO PREFERS SAFER DUTY SEE ME AND I WILL ARRANGE TO HAVE HIM TRANSFERRED.

D. V. GALLERY,
Captain, U.S.N.

On the day of commissioning, we lined up on the flight deck in our best blue uniforms. Father Weldon said a prayer, I read the orders, and we hoisted the colours. I then made a short speech reminding all hands that we had just become the custodians of a name that was enshrined for ever in American history. We would have to do great things to live up to what the Marines had already done in making this name immortal.

Next day Father Weldon, with my hearty approval, started a custom which I feel had an important influence on our subsequent career. He and I had both read battle reports from the Pacific telling of ships in which the Chaplain said a prayer over the loudspeakers just before going into battle. Father Weldon and I agreed it was poor psychology as well as rather shabby theology to wait till you were looking down the enemy gun barrels before asking for God's help. We decided to ask for it every day as a matter of ship's routine.

From then on each morning at eight bells, right after colours, the boatswain's mate passed the word, "Attention to morning prayer." All hands would knock off whatever they were doing, uncover and face the bridge for a few moments while Father Weldon said a non-sectarian prayer to which Protestants, Catholics, Jews or Moslems could all say "Amen," simply reminding God that we needed His help and would be grateful for it that day. There are no atheists in the combat zones in wartime, so our general prayer was accepted by everybody in the spirit in which it was made: "We will do the best we can, please God help us."

When we shoved off from Norfolk in January 1944 on our maiden cruise, we were a cocky but unproven outfit. Like Doenitz's new U-boats, the big thing we needed was a victory to confirm that we were an effective fighting unit. We on the *Guadalcanal* were all sure that we were a great bulwark to the

165

western world against Hitler's attempt to wrest freedom of the seas from us. But to the rest of the U.S. Atlantic Fleet we were just a big question mark. We had made it from Astoria to Norfolk without getting sunk; now we were going out where they played for keeps and the penalty for making small mistakes could be all hands getting both lungs full of salt water.

We drew our first blood within two weeks. On January 16, several hundred miles west of the Azores, we had a flight of eight "turkeys" out scouring the ocean on all sides of us. They were scheduled to land just before sunset. At this period, as the reader knows, U-boats seldom surfaced during daylight hours, but we had reason to believe that in this particular area, and at this particular time, we might find something.

About twenty minutes before sunset two planes on their return leg to the ship spotted a group of three surfaced U-boats. It was a refuelling operation in which a "milch cow sub" supplied oil to boats of the U-505 type. There was a solid cloud layer that day which made it easy for my boys to approach unseen. They caught the cow with one of her calves sucking eagerly on the six-inch, hundred-foot-long rubber teats from her ample fuel tanks, and the other waiting its turn a few hundred yards away. They barged in on this little domestic scene like a couple of hawks in a chicken yard and plastered depth charges all around the two U-boats that were so encumbered with mooring lines and hoses that they couldn't submerge quickly. When the depth charge plumes subsided there was junk all over the ocean and about thirty Germans swimming around in a huge puddle of oil. All three submarines had disappeared and until we got back from that cruise we thought we had certainly sunk two of them.

The destroyer I sent back to look for those Germans in the oil pool didn't find any. With another submarine nearby he couldn't very well turn on searchlights, and men fighting for their lives in a cold, oil-covered ocean don't live long anyway.

A month later the experts on the Assessment Board told us we had sunk the refueller (U-544) and badly damaged the one alongside her (U-129), which managed to limp home. The other one (U-516) got away.

166

Jubilant cheers went up all over the ship when the loud-speakers announced we had just blasted two submarines to the bottom. But the day's work wasn't over yet. We still had to get those eight planes on deck before it got dark.

As soon as we got word of the kill we recalled all planes. But curiosity is a strong human emotion, this was our first kill, and that oil puddle with the Germans paddling around in it was only 40 miles from the ship. I had detached a destroyer to pick up survivors, but every one of our pilots felt it was essential to the war effort for him to fly over there and take a look at the scene. We put out some peremptory orders on the radio to "get the hell back here and land". But the boys later claimed there was a lot of static.

At this stage of the war we were all still primarily daytime pilots in the jeep carriers. Even on the big carriers in the Pacific, night flying was regarded as a hazardous business to be undertaken only by a few highly trained specialists. Landing on a jeep after dark was perhaps three or four times as difficult as landing on a big carrier, because of the tiny deck, the greater motion of the ship, and her slower speed. By the time my pilots came wandering back from their rubberneck trip the sun had gone down, and under that solid overcast sky darkness was rapidly closing in on us.

The first four lads got aboard safely, but the fifth one landed too far to starboard and wound up with his right wheel down in the gallery walk-way and his left wing and tail sticking out over the deck, fouling the landing area. We still had three planes in the air and the darkness was getting blacker every minute.

Ordinarily, getting that plane back on deck and out of the landing area should have been about a five-minute job. But we were a new ship, the pressure was on us for the first time and we got butterfingered. After we had fumbled around for about ten minutes, the plane suddenly took a sickening lurch, swung its left wheel over the coaming of the flight deck and came to rest nose-down in the walk-way with its tail now sticking out at right angles across the deck into the landing area. The boys messed around with it for five more minutes, getting nowhere, and then I said, "The hell with it—shove it overboard."

This was easier said than done. We heaved and we hauled, we grunted and we cursed, we pried with 4 × 4 beams, we pumped hydraulic jacks, and we even rammed into it with tractors.

Finally, in desperation, I went ahead full speed on the engines, jammed the rudder hard over left, and whipped the ship into a tight turn thus listing her ten degrees to starboard to help jettison the crash. We still couldn't budge her.

By this time it was pitch dark and my boys in the air were running out of fuel. We couldn't fool around any longer. You don't like to turn on the lights when you know for sure there is at least one undamaged U-boat within a few miles of you. But sometimes you have to stick your own neck out for the boys who are sticking theirs out executing your orders, and you've *got* to have light to land on a jeep carrier at night. We lit the ship up like a waterfront saloon on a Saturday night and I sent the following message to the boys in the air by radio phone:

"That tail doesn't stick out very far into the landing area. If you land smack on the centre line your right wing will clear it. So just ignore that plane on the starboard side . . . come on in and land."

Three very dubious "Rogers" came back out of the darkness.

For the next half hour those three lads made the most hair-raising passes I've ever seen made at a carrier's deck, except maybe for dive bombing attacks. Our landing signal officer gave them wave-off after wave-off trying to get them to settle down. It was easy enough for us on deck to make believe that wreck wasn't there but the boys in the air just didn't have enough imagination. They kept edging over too far to port.

Finally, one of them reluctantly drifted over pretty close to the centre line and the LSO gave him a desperate "cut", even though he was way too fast. He hit wheels first, bounced into the air, rolled over on his back and plunged into the sea to port. A plane-guard destroyer fished all three men out of the water unhurt.

168

That was enough of that business. We turned on the searchlights of all ships, pointed them down at the water and ordered the other two planes to ditch alongside destroyers. The destroyers fished everybody out of the water, we blew out the lights, and got the hell out of that area.

What I went through that night was a miniature preview of something that happened to Admiral Mitscher in the Pacific a few months later. On the night of the "Marianas Turkey Shoot", Mitscher got caught with several hundred planes in the air after dark, and half of them wound up in the water. That was the night he gave the famous order, "Turn on the lights". When I heard about this some months later, I knew just exactly what had gone through his mind that night. But I never could see why the feature writers made such a fuss over the decision to turn on the lights and I doubt if Peter Mitscher could either. It was just one of those things that *had* to be done.

On the way back to Norfolk from the hunting ground, I made sure that never again would our flight deck be tied up by a plane in the cat-walk. We had a damaged plane that would ordinarily have to be turned in for overhaul when we got back and I figured that a few more bumps and bruises on this one wouldn't overtax the war effort of the United States. We used the cripple as a guinea pig learning how to get wrecks out of the cat-walks.

We rolled it carefully over to the edge of the deck, eased one wheel down into the cat-walk, and held a stop watch on the deck crew while they wrestled it back up on the flight deck. When they could do this in five minutes we eased both wheels into the cat-walk and cracked a whip over the boys until they could get it out of there in four minutes. After they became real experts and could throw up sheer legs, rig blocks and tackle, knew where to put jacks on 4×4 levers, or to use just plain manpower and could clear any wreck in three minutes, our battered plane wasn't worth overhauling. So I said to the boys, "Start her with a run from the other side of the deck next time and see if you can get rid of it."

By this time the boys were sick and tired of dragging that plane in and out of the cat-walks. All hands gathered around, put their backs into it, and had her going at the rate of knots by the time they got her to the opposite deck edge. But she just dropped both wheels into the cat-walk and stuck there. From the bridge I could almost imagine that poor old plane looking back over its shoulder at me reproachfully. The boys had to drag it out and try again.

That plane became an albatross around the necks of the whole flight deck crew. Try as they would, and believe me they tried real hard, they just couldn't get up enough speed to heave it plumb overboard. The day before we got in to Norfolk I finally let the boys jack it overboard, giving it a proper burial at sea with appropriate ceremony. Meanwhile my lads had become the outstanding experts in the Atlantic Ocean on how to get planes out of the unusual places that pilots sometimes park them in.

When we set sail on our second cruise in March 1944, I had made up my mind to do some experimenting with night flying. All jeep carrier skippers had been toying with the idea of flying around the clock and everybody knew we had to come to it eventually. Some ships had launched planes at midnight with enough fuel to stay up and land after sunrise. Others had installed extra tanks so they could take off at sunset, stay up all night, and land at dawn, even though the planes could carry no weapons with this load. But this was just sticking our toes into the cold water tentatively. Somebody had to take the plunge of simply ignoring the darkness and scheduling operations around the clock.

The skipper who broke the ice would have to risk the necks of his pilots finding out how thick the ice was, and knowing that he would be running no physical risks himself. He also knew that he would be subjected to much criticism in high places if he failed, because the high command had not been willing to go on record and demand night flying. Besides, after you have spent twenty-five years in naval aviation and have attended the funerals of many good friends, you don't like to *order* the younger pilots to do things you haven't done yourself. For these reasons no skipper had yet undertaken full-fledged night operations. As it turned out later, this wartime generation of naval aviators could do lots of things we old-timers had never done.

As we left Norfolk, I got the pilots together and explained what I had in mind to them. I wanted to operate around the clock during the next full moon, feeling our way along as the moon waned to see if we could eventually work into pitch dark operations. They all took it in stride and said they would like to try it. They were a lot more confident about it than I was.

Our hunting area this time was between the Azores and Gibraltar in the well-travelled lane used by U-boats creeping out of Biscay. There were plenty of U-boats coming out of Biscay, but in the first part of the cruise, flying mostly in daylight, we didn't see any. Checking back on war logs now, eleven years later, I can show you one night when a submarine outbound from the Bay of Biscay on her way to Freetown, went almost between my legs when I had all my planes on deck. She was the U-505, but her rendezvous with us in the book of fate was set for about two and a half months later.

The fact that we patrolled over this area for about a month, asking for trouble but not getting any, shows how the U-boats had been beaten down by this time. Just a year before, any U-boat skipper would have rubbed his hands in glee at the prospect of getting a potshot at an aircraft carrier. Now, they avoided us.

Early in April, as the moon got bigger, we started experimenting with our night landing programme. It was scary business, we went at it gingerly, but it worked out well.

At sunset on the evening of April 8th, we launched four "turkeys" to patrol an area extending one hundred miles on each beam and sixty miles ahead. Our planes were all equipped with radar enabling them to spot objects on the surface of the sea below. However, the radar was not accurate enough to conduct an attack blind—you had to see the target visually before you could hope to straddle it with depth charges. And besides, a radar simply tells you there is "something" down there in the blackness—whether it is a Portuguese fishing trawler, an Allied ship running without lights, or a German submarine, is up to you to find out. You can do this either by

171

dropping flares, which warns the submarine to submerge, or if you're lucky and the moon is just right, you can approach so that you see a silhouette in the silver path of the moonglow on the ocean. Tonight we would have a full moon.

After we launched this first flight we had a casualty on the flight deck which put two of our seven arresting-gear cables out of commission. We would have to land the first flight with only five cables working, and I decided that in view of the highly experimental nature of our night landings, I would cancel further flights that night unless we definitely found a U-boat on the first flight. At midnight with a bomber's moon lighting our decks, we landed our first flight and passed the word, "Secure operations till sunrise."

I was down in Combat Information Centre with the Operations Officer and Combat Intelligence Officer waiting to quiz the pilots about any unusual happenings when the flight landed. The last pilot came in with a tense look and his eyes bulging.

"Cap'n," he said, "I almost got him!"

We all looked up from the chart table a bit startled, "Wh . . . Wh . . . what do you mean?"

"That submarine," he replied. "He barely got under in time to get away after I identified him."

We all did a double take, and I said, "What submarine?"

"Didn't you get my radio an hour ago?" the lad demanded.

I glared accusingly at the CIC officer and he shook his head. "Check with communications right away," I said.

After fifteen seconds of tense silence the report came over the voice tube, "Nothing whatever from Four Sail 8, sir."

"Captain, I sent it an hour ago and my radioman says they 'Rogered' for it," protested the pilot.

"We'll go into that later," I said. "Now let's get the dope on what happened." In brief, the lad had picked up a radar blip forty miles on our port quarter, had manœuvred around to get down moon from it and had sighted a small silhouette when only a quarter of a mile away from it. By the time he could be sure it was a submarine, it was too late to drop depth charges so he whipped around in a close turn for another run, but when he completed his circle she was gone.

172

"You're *sure* it was a submarine?" I asked.

"Absolutely certain—I looked right down the conning tower hatch and saw lights inside as I went. . . ."

"How certain are you of the position?" I demanded.

"If you'll give me about two minutes to work it out, I'll give you a real good position on it."

"Okay, get busy," I said, and then turning to the operations officer, "Prepare to launch another flight immediately and have a second group of four ready to back it up."

In fifteen minutes we had four "turkeys" back in the air proceeding to the spot where the U-boat was last seen. I headed the whole Task Group over there so that other planes would have less distance to fly if we regained contact. At 0130, two and a half hours after the first sighting, a "turkey" pilot caught the submarine on the surface again fifteen miles from the first spot. But night bombing on a pinpoint target is a difficult business. My pilot reported, "All depth charges fell short—estimate no damage—Sub has submerged again."

Now we had confirmation of the first sighting, a new fix on it, and the Task Group was rapidly closing on it. The U-boat wouldn't get much of a charge in his battery tonight and would *have* to come up tomorrow. He should be a dead duck within twenty-four hours unless we muffed it.

We had one more sighting by our planes that night as the U-boat kept trying to come up and charge his battery. This time I was only fifteen miles away from him, and peeled off three of my destroyer escorts to be over the spot at dawn and try to root him out by sonar. An hour after sunrise they had him on sonar and the ocean rumbled and shook from depth charge explosions.

But even a surface ship with a solid sonar echo can't be sure of a kill every time. A depth charge must explode almost in contact with the tough pressure hull to get a kill. It takes some seconds for a depth charge to arch through the air and more seconds to sink through the water to its set depth, during which time a skilful U-boat skipper may manœuvre out from under it. If he chooses to go down to say five hundred feet, he has quite a few seconds for his evasive manœuvring. If you miss him once

173

he has that fifteen minutes' reprieve during which he doesn't have to creep silently but can run at high speed while the ocean is reverberating and disturbed water conditions give your sonar false echoes.

This chap that we were after was obviously a tough customer who knew his business. Three times during the morning my destroyers got him on sonar and dropped several full patterns of a dozen depth charges around him. Each time when the ocean quieted down again the destroyers' sonar men could hear tell-tale noises which indicated a U-boat was fleeing for its life somewhere in the nearby depths. Each time the destroyers went into our prearranged expanding search pattern and re-gained sonar contact. After the fourth attack a lot of garbage and oil came up to the surface, but this was an old familiar stunt by this time in the war, and we paid no attention to it. We could still hear the desperate thum . . . thum . . . thum of propellers running very deep.

This submarine we were after gambled on staying deep. About 1300, our destroyers were pinging on him again. One took station about half a mile from him and coached another into firing position. Sonar loses contact on a deep submarine when nearly over it and the firing ship, if relying on its own sonar, would make the last minute of the approach blind. We had already learnt that if you gave this chap half a minute it was too much.

At 1410 the *Pope* dropped a depth charge pattern, and half a minute later the U-boat skipper down at six hundred feet was slammed against the steel walls of his conning tower and knew that the game was up. "Blow all tanks," he ordered. "Prepare to abandon ship and scuttle."

At 1417 the submarine surfaced within a hundred yards of the *Pope, Flaherty, Pillsbury* and *Chatelain*. I could see him from the bridge of the *Guadalcanal* five miles away. There was no way of knowing that he had surfaced *in extremis* to abandon ship and scuttle. A deadly rattlesnake had just reared his head from the depths—ready to strike, as far as we knew! So we let him have it. All destroyers opened up with everything they had, depth charges, torpedoes, four-inch guns, and 20-mm.

174

AA guns. All indications were that the U-boat was structurally sound and was quite capable of firing a salvo of six torpedoes from her bow and stern tubes. In such a situation, you don't count the number of men who pop out of the forward and after escape hatches and dive over the side before issuing the order to cease firing. You watch the snake to see if you have broken its neck.

Four minutes after the U-515 surfaced, she slowly reared herself straight up in the air, her stern going down and her bow pointing into the sky with white water pouring out of all the vent holes in the gingerbread around her pressure hull. I suppose a literary man might say she looked like a cobra rearing its head to strike. But on the bridge of the *Guadalcanal*, my seafaring first officer yelled, "Thar she blows . . . and sparm at that!"

We fished forty-five survivors from this U-boat out of the water and hauled them aboard the *Guadalcanal*. From some of the first we learned that her number was U-515, which meant nothing whatever to me except another U-boat. I directed the boys to bring the skipper up to my cabin when and if they got him.

Soon my chief master-at-arms and his number one escorted a husky, blond, eagle-eyed character, clad in U.S. GI dungaree pants and a dry sweat shirt, into the cabin.

"This is the Captain, sir," the CMAA said.

It was hardly necessary for him to say this. The man had a commanding personality and I knew the instant he came in the cabin that he was the skipper. I discovered later that he was one of Doenitz's aces and that though his crew respected his ability as a U-boat skipper they hated his guts. They said he took unnecessary chances because he wanted an Oak Leaf for his Knight's Cross and they blamed the loss of their boat on his reckless confidence that he would sink the *Guadalcanal* before we got him. They were also bitter because for two years he had frozen promotions on his boat to prevent any of his hand-picked crew from being transferred to other boats when they were promoted.

"Your name?" I asked.

175

"Henke," he said, continuing in English as good as mine, "Werner Henke, Kapitän Leutnant, Kriegsmarine," and gave his serial number.

"The number of your U-boat?" I asked.

Henke stood mute.

"It was U-515," I said, and the look in his eye admitted it.

"How long were you at sea this cruise?" I asked.

Henke made no answer.

"You sailed from Lorient ten days ago," I said. It didn't take a crystal ball to figure that one out. Lorient was the Nazi main U-boat base in Biscay; every time we had sighted him he was on a southwest course away from the Bay of Biscay; and it took eight or nine days to creep out of Biscay now that the RAF and U.S. Navy's Patrol Wing 7 were patrolling over it around the clock.

Henke shrugged his shoulders but said nothing. All this time he had a beaten but defiant look in his eye. Now the look began to harden.

I started to ask another question, "How many ships . . ."

He interrupted, "Captain, I have a protest to make!"

Caught off guard I said, "What is it?"

"You violated International Law and the Geneva Convention," he said.

"How?"

"You killed many of my men while we were trying to surrender."

The answer to that one was easy. I said, "I had no way of knowing whether you were trying to surrender or to torpedo my ships. As soon as we were sure you were harmless we ceased firing and we have rescued forty-five of your men."

"But you killed ten," he said, "in violation of the Geneva Convention."

Henke knew as well as I did that several times wounded U-boats had surfaced to allow the crew to escape and with their dying gasp had torpedoed the ship that had done them in. I've often wondered whether in this situation the survivors from opposite sides should negotiate a truce after their ships go down or should keep on fighting in the water. But there was no

176

point in continuing this argument any further. "Take him below," I said to the MAA.

Some of our skippers in the Battle of the Atlantic treated rescued U-boat captains as guests, and since they themselves lived in the sea cabin near the bridge when in dangerous waters, they turned over their own main cabin to the captured U-boat skipper. I didn't agree with this idea and figured it was better for all concerned to treat U-boat survivors as prisoners of war regardless of rank.

On the *Guadalcanal* we put all officers, including the skipper, in the brig (ship's prison) and separated the enlisted men into groups. We kept all non-rated men in one compartment and all petty officers in another. These three groups could never communicate with each other, so they had no chance to give each other pep talks on security, or to hatch any plots to overthrow the government of the United States, or of the U.S.S. *Guadalcanal*.

So Kapitän Leutnant Werner Henke, Kriegsmarine, just awarded the Knight's Cross of the Iron Cross, was incarcerated in the brig. His cell there was bigger than his "cabin" on the U-515, the air was better, and the food that my chief master-at-arms brought him was at least as good as what he had been eating on his own ship.

Next day the master-at-arms brought word up to me on the bridge that Henke would like to see me. "What for?" I asked.

"Something about the Geneva Convention," said the chief.

"Oh, *that* again," I said. "Okay, bring him up to the cabin after we land the next flight."

When Henke was escorted into the cabin he had lost some of the beaten air of the day before. He registered an official protest against being quartered in the brig and quoted what he claimed was the Geneva Convention to me, saying that under its terms he was entitled to an officer's stateroom and should be allowed to eat in the officers' mess.

This wasn't too hard to answer either. I didn't have my copy of the Geneva Convention handy, but I explained to him that regardless of what the Convention said, we were still in the

177

war zone and had to be practical. I couldn't give him an officer's stateroom without putting one of my own officers out of his bunk, which I didn't propose to do.

"But the Geneva Convention says . . ." he began.

"Besides," I interrupted, "many of my officers and sailors are of Jewish or Polish ancestry. They might not be very polite to you if I gave you the freedom of the ship."

"According to the Geneva Convention, it is your duty to protect your prisoners."

By this time I was getting a little irritated at being lectured on how to run my ship. The next thing I said was just a shot in the dark, on a completely unpremeditated impulse. "Captain, we are going to refuel in Gibraltar about ten days from now. If you don't like the way I'm treating you, I'll be glad to turn you and your crew over to the British. Maybe they will treat you better."

There are several things about this statement of mine which literal-minded people may criticize now. In the first place, we weren't going anywhere near Gibraltar. In the second place, if we had, the whole British Mediterranean Fleet couldn't have taken Henke and those prisoners away from me—I was bringing them home for proof!

My statement had a greater effect on Henke than I had expected. The beaten look came back into his eyes and he said quickly, "Captain, it isn't that bad. I can put up with this treatment for a few more weeks. I withdraw my protest."

So Henke went back to the brig and requested no more audiences with me.

A few days after this interview, my chief master-at-arms, who had been listening just outside the cabin during this discussion with Henke, came up to me on the bridge with a *very* interesting story. (Remember that up to this time none of us on the *Guadalcanal* had ever heard of the *Ceramic*.)

It seems that Henke, knowing that the war was over for him, that he would survive it and could look forward to sitting out the rest of it in comparative comfort in the United States, had done some reminiscing with my MAA. The chief was a sharp operator and had wormed his way into Henke's confidence by assuring Henke that I was a son-of-a-bitch, that all my men would like to shove me overboard, and he personally hated me. This had relaxed Henke so that he did a little talking. The story that the chief brought up to the bridge, given to him by Henke himself was as follows:

Just before the U-515 sailed from Lorient, the BBC had beamed a propaganda broadcast at the U-boat bases, saying they had learned that it was the U-515 that sank the *Ceramic*. (Obviously they learned this from Sapper Munday's broadcast.) They went on to say they had also learned after the sinking the U-515 had surfaced and had machine-gunned survivors in the water. Therefore, the broadcast continued, if anyone from the U-515 ever fell into their hands, they would try them for murder and hang them if convicted.

I don't know what prompted Henke to tell this story to my CMAA, except that the chief had established pretty friendly relations with him. Perhaps something was preying on Henke's mind. He, of course, denied that there was any truth in the part about machine-gunning survivors, and he may have told the story to put the British in a bad light. The British now deny that they ever made such a broadcast, but can offer no explanation as to why Henke, in 1944, should make up such a story. Personally, I do not believe he machine-gunned the lifeboats, but I do believe the British broadcast such a story.

Anyway, this tale gave me food for thought. I had already discovered that Henke was not enthusiastic when you suggested to him that he might go to England. I began to wonder just how far I could push the idea of sending him there.

After weighing a lot of pros and cons, I decided to try a stratagem. I had a message to the *Guadalcanal* written up on an official dispatch blank purporting to come from CinC Atlantic Fleet, saying:

"BRITISH ADMIRALTY REQUESTS YOU TURN OVER CREW OF U-515 TO THEM WHEN YOU REFUEL GIBRALTAR. CONSIDERING CROWDED CONDITION YOUR SHIP AUTHORIZE YOU TO USE YOUR DISCRETION."

I also drew up a statement on legal paper with the ship's seal on it ready for signature by Henke:

"I, Captain Lieutenant Werner Henke, promise on my honour as a German officer that if I and my crew are imprisoned in the United States instead of in England, I will answer all questions truthfully when I am interrogated by Naval Intelligence Officers.

Signed

Kapt. Lt.

Witness:

D. V. Gallery, Capt, USN
J. S. Johnson, Cdr, USN"

Sizing up all the angles on this stunt before going into it, the chance of success didn't seem very good. But it was one of those deals where you have nothing to lose and might win if it worked. The worst that could happen would be for Henke to spit in my face and tell me to go to hell, which wouldn't affect the outcome of the war one way or the other. If it worked, something pretty good might come of it.

I sent for a large-scale anchorage map of Gibraltar, drew some lines on it as if I were studying the best approach to the anchorage, and left it lying on the table with parallel rulers and dividers on it where Henke would be bound to see it. I sent for Commander Johnson to come up to the cabin as a witness and explained the game to him. Then I had the chief master-at-arms bring Henke up from the brig and handed him the phoney dispatch.

His face fell when he read it. A cornered look came back into his eye and he said, "Why do they want me?"

I shrugged and said, "I don't know."

"The Geneva Convention . . ." he began.

"Wait a minute," I said. "The U.S. and England are allies, you can be legally imprisoned in either place."

After a long pause he looked at me rather pathetically and said, "Well, Captain, I suppose there is nothing you can do about it."

"Yes there is," I said. "That dispatch allows me to use my discretion. If you make it worth my while, I'll keep you on board till we arrive in the U.S."

"What do you want me to do?" asked Henke.

"Just sign this," I said, pushing the prepared statement

180

across the table and laying a pen down alongside it.

Henke read the statement carefully twice, thought it over for a while and then said, "Captain, you know I can't sign that."

"It's up to you," I said. "Sign and you go to the United States. If you don't sign, then you and your crew go to England."

Henke was a courageous and tough man, as proved by the decorations he wore. But I had put him in a hell of a spot. Finally he looked at me and I could sense that here was one professional military man baring his soul to another whom he respected even though an enemy. "Well, Captain, what would *you* do if you were in my position?" he asked.

I answered him truthfully and said, "If I were convinced that my country had lost the war and that I could help my crew by signing—I would sign."

Henke and I stood on opposite sides of the table for a few minutes without saying a further word. It was like a scene from a film. I knew nothing of the real story of the *Ceramic* at the time, but I'm sure now that all the harrowing details with which he was so familiar ran through his mind again. He knew that no impartial court would punish him for what he had done, but he believed a British court-martial would hang him. Finally he picked up the pen, signed the paper, looked at me defiantly, and went back to the brig.

I then circulated a photostat of the agreement which the Captain had signed among the petty officers and non-rated men in the two prisoner compartments, and put a similar proposition to them. . . . Sign and you go to the United States— refuse and you go to England. The proposed agreements for the crew went into much more detail as to what they would say than did Henke's. But they all knew the skipper's signature and there could be no doubt that he had agreed to talk. Every man in the U-515's crew signed, promising to tell all he knew.

Upon arrival in the U.S., Henke went back on his agreement as I knew he would, saying quite correctly that it had been obtained under duress and false pretences. But his crew, isolated from him and from each other, never knew this. They

181

figured, "The skipper is talking—why shouldn't we?" When interrogated by our anti-submarine experts they spilt the beans and our intelligence people made quite a haul.

Now that the war is over and we've had time to forget, some may say that I was guilty of using dishonourable tactics on Henke. However, I fed him well, gave him a comfortable bunk to sleep in, used no rubber hoses or drugs on him, and put him ashore in the United States alive, healthy and mentally undamaged. When I think of Buchenwald and Dachau, and of the brainwashed debris of humanity that the Communists have sent back to us from Korea I roll over and go to sleep with a clear conscience in spite of the finale to this episode which I could not foresee.

When Henke went back on his agreement which all his crew carried out as best they could, our intelligence experts decided to hold him to the terms of the agreement. They told Henke, "Either you talk, or you go to England." When he still refused they made preparations to send him to Canada for further transfer to England. The day before he was due to be shipped to Canada, Henke was pacing the exercise compound of the prisoner's camp. It was broad daylight, there was a high barbed wire fence all around the compound, and even if he got over it there were armed sentries outside the fence. Henke's mind must have gone back to the *Ceramic*. The BBC broadcast about it, which the British now claim is a figment of his imagination, apparently was too much for him.

He waited till the sentry was looking right at him and then started climbing the high wire fence. "Halt," cried the sentry, who didn't know Henke from dozens of others in the camp.

Henke kept on climbing despite two more hails.

The sentry let him have it. When you squeeze the trigger of a submachine gun you can't just put one well-aimed bullet in the leg of a fleeing prisoner. You blast a dozen or so slugs in his general direction. Several of the sentry's bullets hit Henke and killed him.

When we hauled the survivors of the U-515 out of the water and aboard the *Guadalcanal* we were smack in the middle of

182

the U-boat lane leading in and out of Biscay and had another moonlight night coming up. Our first night of round the clock operation had hit the jackpot so we repeated the same programme the next night.

Again it paid off. At the crack of dawn on April 10 (Easter Sunday) a group of three of my aircraft got a radar contact and, carefully manœuvring to approach from the west, they made out a surfaced submarine against the anæmic light of dawn in the east.

They caught that U-boat flat-footed. Her lookouts didn't see them boring in from the dark hemisphere of the sky and apparently either her Naxos gear or its operator slipped a cog. At any rate, the first warning her lookouts had of my planes screaming down at them was a hail storm of fifty-calibre bullets bursting on them. Three planes roared over, apart, sowing a field of depth charges all around the submarine and circling back to fire streams of high explosive rockets. The U-boat never had a chance.

When the third plane swooped over for his rocket attack the submarine was gone and my boys could see nothing in the blackness below. They marked the spot with flares, circled, and informed us by radio that they had chalked up another kill.

As the light in the east grew stronger, objects took shape in the dark water below. For a while they thought we had another whole crew in the water. But by the time the sun peered over the rim of the world they found only three human heads in the middle of a huge spreading pool of oil, surrounded by a welter of rubbish, wooden boxes, and torpedo air flasks. My lads dropped rubber boats, we took a careful bearing on the planes by radar, and headed over that way at full speed to rescue seamen in distress.

When we got there three hours later, only two men were left. One of these was dead, but the other, although badly wounded, was hanging on to a rubber boat with one hand and holding up his shipmate with the other. They were from the U-68, a number which together with the U-515 appears often in the U-505's war diary.

Later I tried to pull what I now feel was my only really

unethical trick of the war on this sole survivor of the U-68. I thought I might get something out of this lad by telling him his skipper had slammed the hatch on him and the other lookouts and had submerged and abandoned them, whereas I had gone out of my way to rescue them.

After he recovered enough to walk, I had him brought up to the cabin, sat him down, and tried to question him. I gave him a yarn about his captain deserting him when the going got tough, whereas I had stuck my neck out to save him. He listened respectfully and made no comment. Then I asked him some questions he had no right to answer, but which, in that particular part of the Atlantic Ocean at that particular time, I was very curious about.

I'll never forget how this gaunt kid, who was not yet sure he was going to live, looked me straight in the eye and said, "Captain, I am a German soldier."

He then added to the interpreter that our attack had torn the U-boat in two, so his captain obviously hadn't abandoned him. He went on to say that even if the U-68 had escaped from our attacks it was the captain's duty to submerge and sacrifice the lookouts to save the rest of the crew.

I asked this man no more questions, but had him taken back to sick bay and we restored him to good health. I suppose he is back in Germany now. I'm sure that under similar circumstances a communist brainwasher, confronting a prisoner still shaken by a terrible experience, would not have been as chicken-hearted as I turned out to be. I believe that if I had snarled at this man and threatened him, he might have broken. But I'll never know and I'm glad I won't. I can still look myself in the eye in the morning when I shave—if I had broken him, I don't think I could.

Coming back from the cruise with two pelts in our belt, at a time when U-boats were hard to find, one thing was obvious. Our night flying experiment had paid off and blazed a trail that we had to follow each time we went to sea thereafter. In a twelve-hour period we had sunk two ace U-boats which, as we found out later, between them had sunk 55 ships, totalling 250,000 tons.

But looking back on the U-515, another idea kept cropping up in my mind all the way home—an idea that had originated under the Aurora Borealis up in Iceland almost two years ago. . . . "Why not try to capture the next one?"

Why not? After all, the U-515 was one of the ace boats of the German submarine fleet. Henke was a brilliant skipper and a realistic, tough minded, military man. He fought skilfully as long as he felt he had a chance. But when he knew the game was up, he blew his tanks, came up to the surface and gave his crew a chance to save their lives before scuttling his boat. He didn't shoot at me with either guns or torpedoes after surfacing because he had waited till he knew that he was finished before surfacing.

The more I thought about this the more significant it became. At this stage of the war, if a U-boat surfaced during an attack it probably meant that he thought he was finished and was coming up simply to give his crew a chance. But a skipper who was hounded and battered might surface prematurely before his boat was actually fatally wounded. After all, we had thrown everything but the galley ranges at U-515 before she up-ended and sank. For a while I thought we were going to have to ram her to put her on the bottom. . . . Suppose we hadn't been quite so bloody-minded about sinking her. Suppose we had sent a party of stout-hearted characters over there, to go aboard and make a survey of the situation after the Germans had shoved off. . . .

All the way back to Norfolk a fantastic idea kept thrusting itself forward and would not be swept under the rug.

CHAPTER XIV

CRUISE TO CAPE VERDE ISLANDS

BEFORE shoving off on a cruise, hunter-killer groups always held a departure conference attended by the skippers of the ships in the Task Group, and by numerous "experts" from the staffs of CinCLant, ComAirLant, Anti-SubLant, and Cominch from Washington. At our conference in Norfolk before the next cruise, we ran through the usual routine items, clearing up questions about the communication plan, methods of reorienting our screen when turning into the wind for flight operations, the search plans we would use for both air and surface operations, etc., etc. The staff boys all nodded approvingly as we settled the usual problems according to the book.

Finally, I took the floor and told the boys what I had been thinking about. I said that this time, when and if we brought a U-boat to bay within gun range, we would not shoot it up forthwith as we had the U-515. Instead, we would assume he had surfaced for the sole purpose of saving the hides of his crew and intended to scuttle as soon as the crew got overboard. When he surfaced we would therefore cease fire with ammunition that could do serious structural damage to the boat, such as depth charges, torpedoes or rockets. We would blast away briskly with small calibre antipersonnel stuff in order to expedite the Germans' abandoned-ship drill, keep them away from their guns, and encourage them to get the hell off that U-boat so that we could put an inspecting party on board. If this party, after a diligent survey, closing scuttling valves, disarming booby traps and doing whatever else such a party might have to do, believed we could keep her afloat, we would pass them a tow line and bring the U-boat back to the United States.

When I finished outlining this idea there was a silence in which a flake of falling dandruff would have made an audible thud. Then I went on to review our experience with the U-515 and to point out that even after the Germans went overboard convinced that she was sinking, we expended a lot of armour-piercing ammunition on her before she went down. She probably was finished as a *submarine* when she came to the surface, but maybe if we hadn't co-operated with the Germans by hammering her to pieces she might have survived as a *surface* vessel. I could see several of my destroyer skippers glance at each other and indicate agreement with me on this. I also saw one of the staff officers in the back of the room glance at a cohort and make circular motions with his forefinger pointing at his head, indicating he thought I had barnacles on the brain.

I continued, "I want each ship to organize a boarding party and keep a whale boat ready to lower throughout the next cruise. Also keep your tow line where you can get at it in case we need it. Any questions?"

As we cleared the Virginia Capes the next day, I sent the Task Group a signal reminding them that I expected each ship to have a boarding party organized and ready in case a situation came up where we might use it.

I'm sure that most of us in the Task Group had our tongues in our cheeks when we organized those boarding parties. Even now I'm not sure whether I had mine there or not. Some people may say this was an example of sound imaginative planning, but I feel it's more accurate to call it "wishful thinking". I think most of the boys who were named for the boarding parties figured, "What the hell, this will never come off— I might as well get credit for volunteering." But whatever their reasons, we got plenty of volunteers. We organized the parties and were ready when opportunity hammered on our door the next time.

Our night flying experiment on the previous cruise had paid off so well that this time we made the plunge into full scale round the clock operations. On the way to the hunting grounds we checked out all the pilots in our new squadron for night take-offs and landings. We started with a full moon and

187

flew every night, watching it get blacker and blacker as the moon waned. At the end of two weeks the boys were making good landings in the pitch dark. We smashed up some of our planes learning how to do this, but we didn't hurt any of our men.

You can't just issue an order to your pilots to go out and do this kind of flying. You have to sort of talk them into it and persuade them it isn't as dangerous as they know it *is*. The main reason why we were able to get our pilots into the right frame of mind was that we had made three notable rescues on previous cruises, and the boys felt that if they got in trouble we would go all out to help them.

One was the night we had to turn on the lights. I don't like to think of that one even now, because it was our own incompetence that caused it. But anyway, we washed out four planes that night and didn't lose a pilot or an aircrewman. Pilots and aircrewmen take notice of things like that.

On the previous cruise, while we were disposing of U-515 and U-68, one of our aircraft had a complete radio failure in the middle of the night and missed the Task Group on his return leg from his search sector. It was a black night with a layer of cloud extending from 1,500 to 2,500 feet. Above that layer were the stars—below it was inky darkness.

When our lad failed to check in from his return leg on time and we couldn't raise him by radio, we assumed he had a radio failure. We pointed a big searchlight up in the sky and broadcast instructions to him in the hope he could receive even if he couldn't send. In about fifteen minutes it was apparent that this wasn't going to work. He was either in the water or was very badly lost by now. He still had gas for two more hours so we decided to work on the basis that he was in the air trying to find his way home, and would follow the standard instructions for just this sort of emergency. He did! He climbed through the cloud layer, got up around 10,000 feet where we could see him on our radar over a hundred miles away and circled there. As soon as we spotted the circling blip on our radar, we banged off a couple of other planes to find him and lead him home.

The officers of U-505 when she was captured. Lange is in the centre and on his right Meyer, who saved the submarine at the time of Cszhech's sensational defection

The captured U-505 wallowing at dangerously reduced buoyancy as boarding parties from U.S.S. *Pillsbury* and *Guadalcanal* handle the tow-line

He had wandered so far afield that he was almost out of gas when our "guardian angels" got to him. As the early light of dawn was breaking in the east they closed in on him, and nudged him around to the homeward course, a few minutes before his engine quit. He spiralled down through the clouds and made a good ditching in the rough sea with our other two planes giving us a running account of what was happening. Meantime, we had the whole Task Group headed that way at full speed. After the plane went in, all three men climbed out of it, inflated their rubber boat, got into it and settled down to wait. We were eighty miles away, so one plane stayed under the clouds to keep the tiny raft in sight and the other climbed up through the clouds periodically so we could see him on the radar and talk to him. Every four hours we sent out another pair of aircraft to relieve the watch and make sure we didn't lose track of that little raft in the broad Atlantic. Just before lunch the planes relayed a message to us from the raft, "Please save chow for crew of turkey number six." We saved it for them! They were back on board safe and sound early that afternoon.

In the third rescue episode, we had launched a plane on a black night; he checked out by radio on his initial search leg; and then suddenly disappeared from our radar screen a little sooner than he should have. This, in itself, was no cause for alarm. Maybe he had encountered low clouds, decided to stay under them, and had therefore disappeared behind the curve of the earth before we expected. But my young radar operator had a hunch and stuck to his guns. He put his pencil on a spot on his scope and said, "Cap'n, I think that plane just now went in the water here."

"Call number four and see if he's all right," I said to the watch officer.

"We just completed a radio check with him a minute ago, Cap'n," said the watch officer. "He's okay."

"Captain, I think he's in the water," insisted the radar-man.

"Call him again," I said to the watch officer.

There was no answer to our call.

We headed over to the mark on the radar scope, and half

an hour later we spotted flashlights on the water and hauled three of our boys back aboard.

Their altimeter had been set wrong by a thousand feet. It was a pitch black night and the pilot flew into the water on instruments, thinking he was a thousand feet above it. Many readers will ask how they can make such mistakes, but most aviation accidents are caused by "pilot errors" such as this. Alert, young, highly trained officers occasionally make mistakes just as their elders do.

When our three lads fought their way out of the wreckage of that plane and joined hands with their heads just out of water in the inky blackness, they had little hope of survival. They figured since they had just completed a radio check a minute before the crash we wouldn't miss them for at least an hour and a half, during which time we would be steaming away from them. They figured we wouldn't be looking for them until daylight and then wouldn't have any idea where to start looking. They were the most surprised shipwrecked aviators in the Atlantic Ocean that night when we hauled them out of it half an hour after they crashed. They spread the word among their friends, "This ship takes care of its men."

Rescues such as these inspire confidence in your pilots. On account of them we were able to persuade our pilots on later cruises that our night flying programme was a reasonable one.

By the time we arrived at the hunting grounds about one-third of our planes were out of action because of injuries received during the training period, but the boys were landing aboard on black nights as if they were owls. I figured that flying all night long with two-thirds of our planes we could accomplish a lot more than we would by simply boring holes in the air flying all of them, but only in daylight.

For the next three weeks we scoured the area around the Cape Verde Islands keeping four planes in the air around the clock and having no trouble, except that we couldn't find any submarines. We patrolled across the route from Biscay to the U-boat hunting ground at Freetown where we knew there were U-boats going back and forth, but all we could find were whales, porpoises and Portuguese fishing smacks, plus an assortment of electronic gremlins and false alarms.

We prowled through our assigned area with the carrier three thousand yards behind an aircraft screen of five destroyer escorts, using our planes to scour the ocean for about a hundred miles on each side of our base course and a hundred and sixty miles ahead. With four aircraft you could, during a four hour flight, cover an area of roughly 20,000 square miles. You would expect to find plenty of action in an area that big.

But hunting U-boats is a dull, tedious business ninety-nine per cent of the time. Your planes patrol back and forth, back and forth, combing the same area time and time again. The first time you send a flight out in the hunting area you hang around the radar scope expecting every minute to get a contact. You always feel frustrated and think they sent you to the wrong area when the first flight sees nothing. You become more and more convinced of this as successive flights go out and return with nothing to report. But, of course, the fact that you have combed an area over and over without finding any submarines doesn't mean there are none there. Aircraft can't find a submerged U-boat even with radar, and at this stage of the war the U-boats were submerged most of the time. Our destroyers could find them submerged with their sonar gear, but the maximum range at which it could get an echo off a submarine was about 2,000 yards. Even with five destroyers sweeping a path ahead of us all day long we only searched 3,600 square miles with sonar—about three per cent of the area the planes covered. For the destroyers to find a U-boat, we had to run right over him, and the submarine, with his sensitive listening devices, would hear us coming perhaps an hour before we stumbled over him. During this hour the submarine could do several things, depending on what sort of a man the skipper was. She could go deep and perhaps hide under a layer of cold water which our sonar wouldn't penetrate. She might put on a burst of speed and run out of our path if the skipper didn't mind using up his battery. If he were a real tough skipper he might even run head on at our screen, hoping to break through and get a shot at us before we got him.

191

Our planes could only spot U-boats when they were surfaced. One of the hardest ideas to sell to a young pilot who is just going out on a four hour night patrol is that there really are submarines in an area his pal has just finished patrolling without finding anything. He resents being sent on what he thinks is a wild-goose chase even after you explain that you think the submarines were submerged when his pal searched the area.

There can be three or four U-boats in a 20,000 mile area that you are patrolling constantly and you may *never* see them. If they happen to be lucky and pop up to recharge their battery five minutes after your plane has flown over them, they probably have two hours during which they can remain surfaced safely. The only way you can guarantee that there are no U-boats in an area like that is to keep every square mile of it under continuous surveillance for about thirty-six hours. By that time any submarine in the area would be forced to come up and recharge his battery. But a jeep carrier task group cannot keep the whole area covered all the time. Actually, at any given instant our four night-flying planes would have about six per cent of our total area on their radar scopes. By sweeping this six per cent back and forth at 150 knots for four hours, we stood a good chance of finding any U-boat that surfaced for as long as an hour, but we couldn't be sure of doing it.

Even when our plane's radar picked up a U-boat ten miles away, that didn't mean all was over by any means. The business was just beginning. Usually a submarine would get early warning of our plane's approach and crash dive. By the time the plane got to the spot he would be gone. In such cases the plane circled the spot and reported by radio. Our radar on the ship would pinpoint the circling plane, and we would detach three destroyers to proceed there at full speed and start an expanding sonar search from the point of submergence. We could have destroyers on top of any point in our area within six hours and then if we played our cards properly we should have a kill within twenty-four hours. The U-boat's submerged speed is low and he only has juice in his battery to cover about sixty miles. If he runs full out he will use up his battery before he goes more than about ten miles. If he creeps, he can drag it out to maybe thirty hours and cover sixty miles. At the end of that time he is plumb out of volts and oxygen for his crew, and he *must* stagger to the surface and take a couple of hours to shake the cobwebs out of his head and get juice back in his battery.

Knowing these facts of life about submarines, the proper procedure after you made a *sure* contact was obvious. You concentrated your air search in a circle of an eighty mile radius centred on the point of submergence. Next time he came up to charge batteries and get a whiff of air you should spot him and drive him down again. Your destroyers start another expanding search around the new point of submergence and you reorient your air search. The noose is tightening now. He pops up and down again several times but each time you fence him in a little closer until finally the destroyers or planes, or both, get him at the end of his rope and finish him.

The plane's weapons are 50-calibre machine guns, rockets, depth charges and torpedoes. The destroyer's are guns of various calibres from three inch down to 20 mm., torpedoes, depth charges, and hedgehogs. These last are small weapons, thrown ahead, that look like potato mashers. You shoot a couple of dozen of them a hundred yards or so ahead of you at the spot where you think the U-boat is. If one of them touches the submarine as it sinks past him it blows a hole in his pressure hull. If they just miss nothing at all happens. In this respect they differ from depth charges which are much bigger, are set to go off at a certain depth, and which tear hell out of the ocean whenever you fire them. If you miss with hedgehogs you can make another attack immediately because there were no explosions and your sonar still works in the undisturbed water. If you miss with depth charges the U-boat has about 15 minutes to get away from you before the ocean quiets down enough to use sonar again.

But after a salvo of ash cans explodes all round him, maybe it takes the skipper's nerves that long to settle down too. While they are still agitated he *may* do something foolish. So the standard procedure at this time was to fire a salvo of hedgehogs as you approached and, if you got no explosion as you continued your run, to plant a garden of ash cans around him.

In perhaps half the U-boat killings during the Battle of the Atlantic, the whole action was fought without either side actually seeing the enemy. The battle begins with a radar blip or a sonar contact on the Allied side, and a hydrophone or Naxos warning on the German side. An hour or so later it ends with a blazing surface ship upending and sinking, or a great puddle of oil spreading out across the ocean with pieces of submarine junk in the middle of it.

This is a tremendously exciting game which may go on for twenty-four hours. Sleep is just out of the question till the game is over because the jackpot is a lot of lives, including your own. *If* you had a submarine to begin with and if you play the game the way I have indicated, you will wind up with one submarine credited to your account in the official statistics of the war.

The only hitch to all the above is that right at the beginning the Task Group Commander has to make a difficult command decision on which the whole business hinges. You seldom get a clear-cut sighting and know for sure that you've got a submarine. You get indirect evidence such as a radar blip, a sonar echo, or propeller noises in an aircraft sonobuoy. The Task Group Commander doesn't usually get even these first-hand. He gets a second- or third-hand report of what someone else is seeing or hearing and he has to decide whether the little blip that one of his airborne radarmen claims he saw on his scope was a submarine or something else. If it was a submarine, the Task Group must drop everything and proceed as described above *until* they have killed the submarine. He has no right to leave that area until he has disposed of that "known" submarine. But if the blip was something else and he decides it *was* a U-boat, then his Task Group is out of the war for three or four days, jousting with windmills.

There are perhaps a dozen "something elses" that can give you convincing blips for a few seconds on a radar scope. There are "ghosts", which are simply the electronic version of gremlins. There are bits of small floating rubbish which occasionally present just the right surface to a probing radar beam and send back a strong echo for a minute or so, and then don't happen to synchronize that surface with your beam for days.

194

There are the goddamn balloons that submarines used to turn loose, anchored to a piece of driftwood with strips of tinfoil dangling from the balloon. When you pick up one of these on a radar scope, even those skilled in the art of anti-sub warfare and expert on electronics will swear that you have a submarine periscope on the screen. So you chase the bastard all night and when dawn breaks just as you are closing in for the kill, you see this silly booby-trap bobbing around betwixt wind and water leering at you. The worst part of it is, your men all see it too, and you can almost hear them saying mentally, "Hmmm . . . the Old Man ain't as smart as we thought he was." Of course, if the Old Man is really smart, he notices during the night that this "periscope" is moving exactly down wind, at a few knots less than the speed of the wind. So he calls the "attack" off before dawn breaks, and thus saves himself much face.

There are many natural noises that come out of the sea which sound like submarine noises. When an eager young pilot drops a sonobuoy at the spot where a radar blip has disappeared and hears such noises coming back up out of his sonobuoy, you'll never convince him that he didn't have a submarine. If he has been patrolling long enough with nothing happening, he can sometimes imagine noises where there are none. In fact, I used to say that after about a month of fruitless patrolling a pilot could hear brass bands playing *"Deutschland über Alles"* on a sonobuoy if he tried hard enough.

I know from experience that this business of deciding how to evaluate a radar blip was by far the toughest decision that a hunter-killer Task Group Commander had to make. You stand in the middle of CIC with all your experts around you and the lad who made the contact in front of you. You listen to his story, you get the advice of the experts, and then all eyes bore into you as you make up your mind. The radarman is always sure he had a submarine, otherwise you wouldn't be holding the conference. The experts are never sure of anything, and, if they are real experts, can phrase their advice in such a way that they will be right no matter how the thing turns out.

But "time's awasting", and finally the Old Man has got to make up his mind. I've taken part in many of those midnight conferences, winding up with a dozen pairs of eyes looking at me respectfully while they all thought I was logically analysing the various factors and arriving at a shrewd and penetrating answer. Actually, what I was doing was mentally tossing a nickel.

Many people think that the outcome of the wars of this world are decided by military geniuses. In my lifetime of over thirty years of active duty in the U.S. Navy, I haven't met a single "military" genius. I've met some stuffed shirts who thought they were geniuses, but who couldn't punch their way out of a wet paper bag, unless they had several thousand eager young soldiers helping them. I know and have served under men like Admirals King, Halsey, Nimitz, and Ingersoll, who were the American top naval leaders in World War II. They are all great men, but I would say their outstanding characteristics were that they were fine seamen, knew their weapons systems, and inspired confidence in their subordinates. They surrounded themselves with good men, gave their subordinates authority to act, backed them when they were right, and were cold-blooded about getting rid of incompetents. They had the guts to make weighty decisions and accept heavy responsibility.

Let's get back to the Cape Verde Islands in the spring of 1944. On May 30, after three weeks of fruitless operations, we had to leave the area and head toward Casablanca for fuel. Our route north followed the lane to the Bay of Biscay, and we had a report of a U-boat homeward bound along this route so we centred our operations around him. He was supposed to be about three hundred miles north of us and we planned to run right smack along his track passing directly over him on June 2, *if* our information was accurate.

CHAPTER XV

LANGE

WE now return to the story of the U-505. On November 18, 1943, a new captain had reported aboard, read his orders to the crew, and took command. Oberleutnant Harald Lange was stepping into a tough spot.

His crew's morale, ground thin and brittle by six months of continuous failures, had been completely shattered by the shock of having their captain, Cszhech, desert them in battle. By now the U-505 was known throughout the Second Flotilla as an unlucky boat, the most damning label you can hang on a ship.

This crew should have been broken up and distributed among a dozen other boats. But in wartime you can't always adopt the best solution to problems like this. Shaking down a new crew would put the U-505 out of operations for at least three months. The next best solution was to hand pick the new skipper. Lange was specially selected by U-boat head-quarters as being the kind of man who could handle this tough problem in leadership.

In technical knowledge he was fully qualified, having commanded a similar type boat. But much more important, he was a more mature man than most current U-boat skippers. He was a Reserve Officer who in peace time had been first officer on a merchant ship. He had learned to handle men without benefit of rigid military discipline by winning their confidence and exercising leadership. Not being a professional naval officer, he was perhaps more tolerant of human frailties than a regular might be, although he didn't pamper his men and insisted that important things be done exactly right. But he understood what this crew had been through, was informal in his dealings with them, and made allowances in small things. He was a "big brother" type, which was exactly what this crew needed if it were to be kept together.

197

The boat sailed for her first cruise under Lange on Christmas Day, 1943. The one thing Lange needed more than anything else was some sort of a success to take the curse off their long series of failures. His luck was good, and within three days he had it.

On December 28 there was a battle out in the Bay of Biscay between some British cruisers and a group of German motor torpedo boats and destroyers in which one of the German ships got sunk. The U-505 heard gunfire from this battle about sixty miles away in her sensitive underwater microphones. At sunset she got orders from U-boat headquarters to pick up survivors.

Although the Bay of Biscay was now a dangerous place for surfaced U-boats at night, Lange ran surfaced at full speed for five hours to reach the scene of battle and remained surfaced all night searching the area. At 5.00 a.m. he found seven life rafts lashed together and hauled aboard thirty-three survivors from the destroyer T-25, including her skipper.

As the crew of the U-505 dragged the crew of the T-25 out of the water, their morale got just the kind of shot in the arm it needed. They saw gratitude and admiration shining from the eyes of a group of the men they had rescued. After six months of constant failure, failure so conspicuous that their U-boat comrades were avoiding them along the waterfront, the U-505's crew suddenly found themselves heroes in the eyes of the surface Navy.

But as the boat put into Brest with her survivors on New Year's Day, 1944, her bad luck struck again, and something happened to one of her main propulsion motors. All the war diary says about this is: "0935. Fire in electric motor because of inrush of water and resultant short circuit. 0945 put out fire with extinguishers."

This burned out a main propulsion motor and laid her up in the dockyard again for another two and a half months. But, at any rate, this time they were in Brest, not Lorient. They had no bad reputation to live down here, and their rescue of the T-25's crew gained them some stature.

On March 16 the U-505 sailed from Brest for Freetown on

198

what was to be her last voyage as a German U-boat. This time she finally got out of the Bay. She spent twelve days doing it, running 228 hours submerged and 60 surfaced. Contrast this with her first trip to Freetown under Loewe just over a year before. On her first twelve days of that trip she ran submerged 34 hours and 258 surfaced. This tells an eloquent story of how the tide had turned in the meantime. Submarines were no longer prowling surface raiders that submerged occasionally. They were underwater fugitives that popped up for brief periods when they hoped the coast was clear.

Early in April, the U-505 passed close to the U.S.S. *Guadalcanal*. We were hunting for U-boats coming out of Biscay, but we didn't see U-505 and she didn't see us. A few days later, on April 9 and 10, you will remember, we sank U-515 and U-68, both from the U-505's flotilla, in the area she had just passed through. But her number wasn't up yet.

Proceeding south and starting with Freetown on April 24, she reconnoitred every harbour along the Ivory Coast as far east as Grand Bassam. She looked in at Monrovia, Harpers Village, Port Bouet, and Grand Lahou, but saw nothing. Returning west she took station off Cape Palmas and spent the rest of her time patrolling back and forth across the route from Cape Palmas to the Cape of Good Hope. All she saw there were three neutral steamers, some fishing vessels, and one large British passenger steamer probably home bound from Australia on the *Ceramic's* former run. She gave chase but the liner was too fast and got away. From examination of his war diary, I would say that Lange patrolled diligently, in fact aggressively, but there just wasn't much traffic there any more. The Mediterranean was open to Allied shipping now and Freetown was practically out of business as a shipping centre.

Lange's diary records several serious machinery breakdowns during this period which could have justified a return to base. But he repaired them at sea and remained in his operational area. Perhaps he figured he was better off near Freetown than he would be in France at this stage of the war. And besides,

Doenitz himself had said it was important to keep boats at sea and pin down Allied anti-submarine forces.

While patrolling off Cape Palmas he ran at periscope depth in daytime and on the surface between sunset and sunrise. He only had to crash dive to get away from planes nine times in about a month. Three times his lookouts actually sighted aircraft. Six times his Naxos gear gave warning before any plane could be seen. No aircraft sighted him, and no bombs were dropped near him.

On May 24, the U-505 departed from the Cape Palmas area homeward bound. She was returning empty handed, but so were most of the U-boats these days. At least, after six months of continuous failures, she had now completed a war cruise and her people would get credit for ninety days' front-line service when they got back. She was no longer a barnacle on the pier in Lorient. She was back in good standing as an operational unit of the Second Flotilla.

For the next six days Lange proceeded north, hearing and seeing nothing until the night of May 29, at 10.16 p.m., when he had to crash dive for a Naxos warning. This was the beginning of a series of such warnings which did him more harm than good. It seemed that from here on almost every time he came up to recharge his battery, he would get a Naxos warning from the radio room. Often Naxos "saw" aircraft and cried "wolf, wolf" when the planes were much too far away to be any threat. But the Naxos didn't specify how far away they were and there was nothing that a prudent skipper could do but crash dive. Lange's battery got more and more anæmic because the Naxos wouldn't let him stay surfaced long enough to recharge it.

On May 30, the following entries appear in the U-505's war diary:

30/5/44	*East of the Cape Verde Is.*
0002	Crash dive. Naxos warning.
0045	Surfaced.
0102	Crash dive. Naxos warning. Warnings come in with staccato effect. Immediately after the dive nothing to be seen at periscope depth. Bright moonlight.

0301	Surfaced. Still blowing tanks.
0312	Crash dive. Naxos warning. The radar operator is obstinate; I cannot believe that it is a plane from the Continent since at a distance of 180 m. from the base it could scarcely maintain contact here for 5 hours. Will surface again once more after two hours—after the moon has set.
0534	Surfaced. Dark night with bright stars. Warning at once. A/A guns manned.
	Warnings increasing rapidly from signal strength 3 to 4 and 5. Warning stops for a short time, then suddenly roars loudly in again. After blowing tanks, went off at high speed. Steered deceptive courses in NW part of square.
0540	Two distinct receptions in Naxos gear and Wanze. Both very loud, at times stopping.
0540	Believe there is now a third radar being heard in the receiver.
0549	Crash dive. No bombs. I suspect carrier A/C— Possibly a carrier search group. Nothing in hydrophones. *Determine to set off eastward toward the coast.* On opposite courses to those steered for deception.

[My italics]

So the U-505 took an eighty-four mile jog due east towards the coast of Africa for forty-two hours to get out of the way of an aircraft carrier task group which the skipper thought was breathing down his neck.

This marks the beginning of a strange series of mistakes by Lange and by the only carrier task group that was anywhere near him, which was mine. When Lange was making his detour towards the African coast, I was just starting on his trail and thought I was three hundred miles from him. Actually, we were twice that distance apart, but he thought I was right on top of him. Maybe I smelt something in the air that night. He certainly smelt something from then on, and eventually this proved to be his undoing.

CHAPTER XVI

QUARRY AT BAY

On the *Guadalcanal* we began to get indications that there might be a submarine nearby. We heard strong transmissions on the U-boat's radio frequency. We had disappearing radar blips at night. Some of our pilots thought they heard submarine propeller noises on sonobuoys. We were sure we were close to a U-boat, but it seemed to be a very cautious one who stayed submerged most of the time, and who could detect our radar about as far as we could detect him.

We had several of those midnight conferences trying to decide whether disappearing radar blips were submarines that had seen us coming and submerged, or merely one of the many "other things". On the night of June 2-3, we ran over his reported position. Around 1.00 a.m., we had just had a disappearing blip and a noisy sonobuoy at the spot where the blip disappeared, and our conference of "experts" decided we had him cornered. Our pilots were so sure of the indications that they dropped a lot of high explosive and we took the Task Group over to the spot expecting the sunrise to reveal a big oil pool and a lot of junk. The sunrise revealed nothing. But soon after, my chief engineer, Earl Trosino, came up to the bridge with a long face and said, "Cap'n, we've *got* to quit fooling here and get in to Casablanca; I'm getting down near the safe limit of my fuel."

We resumed course North, leaving the reported position of the U-boat astern of us. By this time I was thoroughly convinced that we had spotted our prey the previous night, driven him down before he had finished charging his battery, and that one more night in the area would cook his goose. He *had* to come up again soon, and I was sure we would find him on the surface in bad shape if we stuck around one more night.

I argued with Trosino all day about fuel and finally, late in the afternoon, I browbeat him into admitting that *maybe*

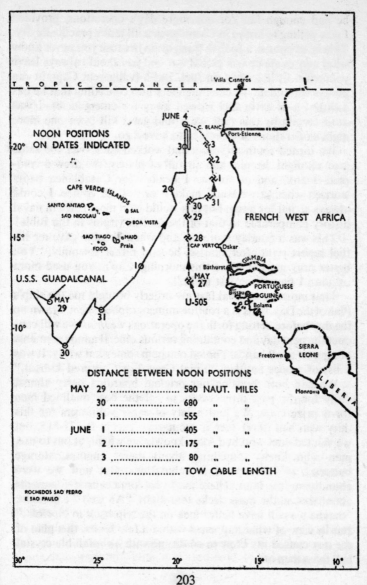

TROPIC OF CANCER   Villa Cisneros

JUNE 4
                                    C. BLANC
NOON POSITIONS   Port-Etienne
ON DATES INDICATED
-20°   30   3
                                        2
                                        1
        CAPE VERDE ISLANDS   2 30   31
SANTO ANTAO   SAL   29
    SAO NICOLAU   BOA VISTA   28   FRENCH WEST AFRICA
-15°   CAP VERT Dakar
        SAO TIAGO   MAIO
            FOGO   Praia   GAMBIA
                                 1   Bathurst
                                        MAY
U.S.S. GUADALCANAL   27   PORTUGUESE
                                        U-505   GUINEA
    MAY   Bissau
    29   Bolama
        31
                                                    SIERRA
    30   LEONE
                                        Freetown
                                                              L
        DISTANCE BETWEEN NOON POSITIONS   I
                                                              B
    MAY 29 .... 580 NAUT. MILES   E
                                                      Monrovia R
        30 680   "   "   I
        31 555   "   "   A
    JUNE 1 405   "   "
        2 175   "   "
        3 80   "   "
        4 .... TOW CABLE LENGTH

ROCHEDOS SAO PEDRO
E SAO PAULO

30°   25°   20°   15°   10°

he had enough fuel for one more day's operations, provided I was willing to arrive in Casablanca with tanks practically dry. This is, of course, a foolish thing to do because you never know what may come up in a global war and you should always leave yourself a little leeway on fuel. But a belligerent Captain can always intimidate his chief engineer into conceding that he has a little bit of extra fuel stowed away for emergencies. I was dead certain by this time we would get a kill from one more night's operations and decided to have a go.

We turned south at sunset and worked back over the same area all night, keeping the air full of planes. We drew a complete blank, and at sunrise I headed for Casablanca badly worried whether we could make it or not. Of course, I could always signal for a tug, but this would gain me a place in naval history comparable to that of the foolish virgins in the Bible!

This was a Sunday morning, and when Trosino gave me his fuel report right after sunrise, he said rather solemnly, "You better pray hard at Mass this morning, Cap'n, you used more oil than I figured on last night."

That morning at breakfast my orderly brought me the ship's Plan of the Day. This is a routine mimeographed sheet, drawn up the day before, setting forth the operations we *think* we will conduct the next day and containing various official announcements of interest to all hands. I noted one item somewhat wryly. It was a list of names entitled, "Final Crew For Captured U-boat."

We had been revising our original boarding party almost daily for the past three weeks to get the best qualified men for a prize crew. We had plenty of eager volunteers for this duty who had never seen a submarine, except the U-515, but we wanted men who had some knowledge we might put to use, men who knew something about diesel engines, storage batteries, or had served in submarines. But now we were abandoning the hunt. There might be some caustic comments about this on the mess decks that night. "Ah well," I thought, "maybe we will have better luck on the trip back to Norfolk." But in view of what happened within a few hours, this plan of the day caused my crew to credit me with an infallible crystal ball from then on.

204

Incidentally, we did find one man on the ship who had served in a U.S. submarine and who immediately became our submarine "expert". He had been a yeoman on an S-boat, and could tell us anything we wanted to know about the paper work or filing system on a submarine!

After attending Mass that morning on the hangar deck, I was up on the bridge, seated in the skipper's chair overlooking the flight deck. It was a beautiful, clear day, with a light breeze and medium sea. We had only two fighter planes aloft maintaining a token patrol, because we figured our only possible target was out of range far astern of us. I was still fuming over the "fact" that we had let him get away from us.

Suddenly, at 1110, the squawk box on the bridge blared forth, "Frenchy to Bluejay—I have a possible sound contact!" (Frenchy was the U.S.S. *Chatelain*, Commander Dudley Knox. I was Bluejay.)

This was nothing to get excited about yet. We had been getting possible sound contacts for the past month on whales, layers of cold water, and other natural phenomena in the sea. But you always treat a "possible" as the real thing until you find out otherwise.

"Left full rudder," I said. "Engines ahead full speed." Then, grabbing the mike of the "Talk Between Ships" radio, I broadcast, "Bluejay to Dagwood—take two destroyers and assist Frenchy. I'll manœuvre to keep clear."

This told the screen commander (Commander F. S. Hall) that it was his party from here on. An aircraft carrier right smack at the scene of a sound contact is like an old lady in the middle of a bar room brawl. She has no business there, can contribute little to the work at hand, and should get the hell out of there leaving elbow room for those who have a job to do. As we gained sea room to the west, I sent up a couple of planes to lend a hand if they were needed, but warned the pilots, "Use no big stuff if the sub surfaces—chase the crew overboard with 50 calibre fire."

As we veered off to the west, *Pillsbury* and *Jenks* raced over to help *Chatelain*, which had picked up her contact at such close range that she ran smack over it before she could make up her mind what it was. She now announced, "Contact evaluated as sub—am starting attack," and, wheeling around under full rudder, she manœuvred into firing position again. She made a complete circle pinging away on her contact, straightened out and fired a salvo of twenty hedgehogs, which arched up in the air and splashed into the water like a huge handful of rocks one hundred yards ahead where the sonar was pinpointing the as yet unseen target. All eyes were glued to the spot and we ticked off each second after the splashes. When the count reached ten, we knew there would be no explosion and began to doubt that *Chatelain's* contact was really a submarine.

Pillsbury and *Jenks* were now prowling warily within hailing distance of the *Chatelain* and probing the contact with their sonar. If this *was* a U-boat and if *Chatelain* missed again, they would pounce on it and plaster it themselves.

Suddenly our two fighter planes, circling over the spot like hawks, opened up with their machine guns, blasted a few bursts of 50 calibre into the water about one hundred yards from where the hedgehogs hit and yelled over the radio, "Sighted sub—destroyers head for spot where we are shooting!"

The *Chatelain* heeled over again under full rudder and headed for the bullet splashes where the pilots saw the dim shape of the completely submerged U-boat trying to go deeper. At 1121, 11 minutes after the first sonar echo, *Chatelain* fired a spread of twelve six-hundred-pound depth charges all set to explode shallow.

From the carrier a few seconds later we saw the ocean boil astern of the *Chatelain* and felt it quake as a dozen geysers spouted into the air from the underwater explosions. As the great white plumes were subsiding, Ensign Cadle in one of the circling aircraft shouted, "You've struck oil, Frenchy, sub is surfacing!"

At 1121½ on June 4, 1944, one hundred and fifty miles west of Cape Blanco, French West Africa, the U-505 heaved itself up from the depths and broke surface seven hundred yards from the *Chatelain*—white water pouring off its rusty black sides. Our quarry was at bay.

CHAPTER XVII

A TERRIFYING SIGHT

WHEN Lange started his eighty-mile jog towards the African coast because he thought I was on top of him, I was 600 miles to the southwest. None of my airplanes had yet been within 500 miles of him, but his Naxos kept seeing planes which he assumed to be carrier-based planes but were not mine at all. All this time he was crossing under the air lane from South America to Africa and there was a constant stream of Air Force transports shuttling back and forth over this route that couldn't hurt him even if they wanted to. Those planes were perfectly harmless as far as U-boats were concerned. Most of their pilots wouldn't know a submarine if they saw one and the unarmed planes couldn't do anything about it if they did.

But all planes look alike on a radar scope at night. Every time Lange came up to charge batteries, a little dancing blip popped up in the Naxos scope and down he went again. I have been grateful ever since to my comrades in arms of the Air Force for this accidental assistance they gave me. It harried Lange and kept him short of volts and air.

By noon of May 31, he was in trouble. Naxos warnings the night before had prevented him from getting any charge in his battery during darkness. It was about to fade out on him —in broad daylight. He surfaced for three-quarters of an hour, ran at full speed and jammed enough juice into it to last him till dark.

Around eight o'clock that evening Lange records, "Heard six aircraft depth bombs in the far distance." (My task group dropped a depth charge pattern on a "possible" sound contact at this time, but we were 550 miles away. If it was our depth charges he heard, "in the far distance" is a classic under-statement!) He surfaced at midnight and stayed up for six hours, getting a full charge in his battery before another Naxos

207

warning drove him down. Just before submerging he changed course north to parallel the coast again.

At noon on June 1, I was 420 miles southwest of U-505, blithely confident that I would nail him either that night or the next. Lange, northbound about sixty miles from the coast, was creeping along submerged waiting to see if that carrier task group which had been "on top of him" had gone away. He surfaced near midnight that night but crash dived an hour later (Naxos again). He came up again at 0330 but was driven down again in sixteen minutes.

The following entry appears in his war diary: "June 2— 0330: Continuous night patrols—here under Cape Blanco!" (Note: The astonished—"!"—is Lange's, not mine. At this time we were still 280 miles southwest and none of my planes had yet been close enough to him to be any threat.)

At 0315 the night of June 3, the war diary records: "Heard one aircraft depth bomb in the far distance." (At this time my planes were bombing around a noisy sonobuoy at least sixty miles away.) Lange tried to surface again at 0710 but another Naxos warning drove him down before he could even start his diesels. He got no juice back in his battery at all that night.

Since 0330 on the night of June 2, he had been driven down every time he stuck his conning tower up. Before he could get the boat aired out and the battery charged, he was down below again using up more air and battery.

By 1338 of June 3, he had spent forty-five and a quarter hours out of the previous forty-eight submerged. His battery was nearly flat again. The air in the boat was rotten and decaying. The crew was getting dopey. Once again he was forced to risk a daylight surfacing. It was a clear day with no clouds, and gambling on the vigilance of his lookouts he surfaced for two hours and two minutes in the middle of the afternoon—and got away with it!

When I first noted from the war diary that he had run on the surface for that long, just sixty miles east of my task group, my only comment was, "Well, I'll be damned!"

I had based all my operations on the assumption that U-boats were submerged all day long. I had been flying only token patrols in daylight and saving my main effort for after dark. In this I was right ninety-nine per cent of the time, and Lange's war diary for the whole cruise proves it. But on June 3, the U-505 and I steamed on converging courses for two hours in broad daylight almost elbowing each other across the horizon and neither one of us detected the other! I'm glad we didn't now, because had my planes caught him on the surface that far away (as they should have) I doubt that we would have captured him. You can't send a boarding party from a carrier based aircraft!

Lange stayed up no longer than he had to that afternoon —just long enough to give the boat a good airing, top off his compressed air tanks, and store up a little juice. He was up again soon after dark to get back on his regular night re-charging routine. He stayed up for over four hours, gave everybody a good whiff of fresh air and didn't submerge until 0213, June 4.

Twice during that night my planes missed him by fan-tastically close margins. At 2200, when he was surfaced, one plane passed within six miles of him, forty-five miles north-east of the task group. Our aircraft radar was supposed to be good for at least ten miles on a surfaced submarine. His Naxos was good for several times that far, and God knows it had apparently been picking up even the seagulls for the past week. My plane's radar didn't see him—he didn't see us. According to her war diary this was the first completely "quiet" night the U-505 had experienced for a couple of weeks!

About 0230, another of my planes flew smack over the spot where he had submerged only a few minutes before. Neither one saw the other. He just happened to submerge because he had got his business finished a few minutes before my plane would have certainly spotted him.

I have plotted this final night's operations out very accurately, using his war diary and my logs. Everyone who looks at this plot notes the two missed contacts by my planes, sees our tracks converge to a point the next day, and just shakes his head and mutters "It doesn't seem possible." We both blundered along practically within hailing distance all night and stumbled over each other at noon the next day!

When he submerged just in the nick of time, Lange had a well charged battery, a good bellyful of fresh air, and had apparently shaken off the aircraft carrier which had been "right on top of him" a few days before. He and his crew settled down on their homebound course for a quiet and relaxed Sunday.

They had just piped down for their noonday dinner on Sunday, June 4, when the sound operator picked up propeller noises. His set wasn't working well and these noises sounded far away. It was 1110 my time, 1210 Berlin time, which the U-boat was keeping.

Lange came up to periscope depth to have a look, expecting perhaps to see masts over the horizon and possibly to get in a shot at a merchant ship. Instead, a terrifying sight confronted him. There were warships all over the ocean, with three destroyers converging on him at high speed, one nearly on top of him, and planes diving at him. He had stuck his head into a hornet's nest.

"Take her down," he ordered sharply and the depth control men wrestled with their big wheels in the compartment below. Lange was in a desperate fix. Obviously he had been spotted and would be depth charged within seconds. He had had a quick glimpse of a carrier and two destroyers in the distance. Six warships and God knows how many planes were on top of him. It would take a miracle to come out of this alive.

If he went deep immediately, the first depth charge attack from those destroyers might smash him so that he couldn't surface. In the undisturbed water their first attack should be pretty accurate. It was better to ride out the first storm of explosions at shallow depth where tons of sea pressure would not be helping the explosions to crush his hull and where he would have some chance of surfacing if they did smash it open. If he survived the first attack then he might go deep under cover of the disturbed water. He held her at shallow depth and manœuvred violently to confuse sonar indications.

In a few seconds all hands, without benefit of ear phones,

210

heard the throbbing of propellers passing right over them. They braced themselves and prayed. Nothing happened. Perhaps half a minute later, all hands heard sounds which they described later as like a cable dragging across their hull. (This was my planes shooting at the water right above them.)

Since no depth charges had been fired and the water was still undisturbed, Lange still couldn't go deep. He squirmed and twisted, fired decoys, and in desperation fired an acoustic torpedo, aimed at nothing. . . . For some minutes the expected attack didn't come. With its defective listening gear the U-505 could only tell that destroyers were still nearby, but not how near.

The sound man reported a muffled series of rippling thuds. That would be a destroyer arching her depth charges into the air. All hands braced themselves again for the explosions. Lange got set to go deep under cover of the disturbed water, *if* he survived the explosions that disturbed the water.

For what seemed like hours but was only two minutes nothing happened. The destroyer had evidently been deceived by a decoy and had fired hedgehogs instead of depth charges at it.

There was another series of muffled thuds. "Hard a' starboard," said Lange, trying to get out from under whatever they were dropping on him now.

Seconds later the whole ocean exploded around them in the most shattering convulsion any of them had ever felt. At least one of the charges in this salvo must have been only inches outside lethal range. All U-boat sailors who felt closer ones are probably on the bottom of the sea.

The lights went out, the rudder jammed hard a' starboard, the boat rolled over on her beam ends and dumped the crew down on what should have been the starboard vertical bulkhead. Mess tables, crockery and junk showered down on top of them in the darkness.

As they were picking themselves "up"—or whichever way it was—someone in the after torpedo room yelled, "Water is coming in!" That meant the end for the U-505. All hands scrambled out of there, slammed the water tight door behind them, and ran forward to the control room shouting that the pressure hull had been split.

Lange had little choice of what to do and only seconds to make his choice. If the after torpedo room was flooding, there was no chance whatever to save the boat. Unless he could blow her to the surface immediately, she would sink taking all hands down with her. Even if the torpedo room were not flooding, his brutally battered boat had a jammed rudder, and with that armada of ships and planes above him further resistance would be foolhardy.

"Blow all tanks," Lange ordered. "Abandon and scuttle the boat."

As the conning tower broke surface and before they could even get the hatch open, a grisly tattoo began beating on the hull—machine-gun bullets!

The captain is always the first man out of the hatch when a submarine surfaces, and just as Lange emerged a 40 mm. shell burst next to him knocking him unconscious, with severe wounds in the face and legs.

As others scrambled out of the hatch, they ducked a torrent of hot steel and plunked into the sea as fast as they could make it overboard. Two men picked up their captain and lugged him overboard to safety with them. Before all hands got up from below, the hail of bullets ceased, and the last few men had time to drag rubber boats out of their stowage places on deck, inflate them, and heave them overboard.

All this time the U-boat was running at six knots on the surface, making a tight circle to the right, and sinking further and further down by the stern. As she circled she drew the line of fire away from the men who had gone overboard, and only one man was killed by all that gunfire. It was Gunner's Mate Fisher, one of the original crew who had put the boat in commission. He was lying face downward alongside the conning tower hatch—the only German left aboard.

In a few minutes the fifty-nine survivors were clinging to the rubber boats, and Lange, lifted into a raft and conscious again by now, led his crew in three cheers for their "sinking" U-boat.

CHAPTER XVIII

THE CAPTURE OF THE U-505

WHEN the cornered U-boat broke surface, we could not be sure whether he had come up to abandon ship and scuttle or to fire a spread of torpedoes and try to take some of our ships to the bottom with him. *Pillsbury, Jenks* and *Chatelain* cut loose with all the guns they had, and for about two minutes 50 calibre slugs and 20 and 40 mm. explosive bullets hammered into the conning tower and tore up the ocean around it. Our fighter planes sent streams of hot metal ricocheting across her decks. Fortunately, all the three-inch stuff we fired missed, as did a torpedo fired by *Chatelain* when she thought the submarine was swinging around to bring her own torpedo tubes to bear.

As the submarine ran in a tight circle to the right, crouching figures popped out of the conning tower and plunged over-board. While these men were leaping for their lives amid our hail of bullets, I broadcast to the Task Group, "I want to capture that bastard, if possible."

After about fifty or so men had gone overboard, Commander Hall ordered, "Cease firing"—and the ancient cry, "Away all boarding parties," boomed out over modern loudspeakers. The *Pillsbury's* party, led by Lieutenant Albert David, had already scrambled into their motor whaleboat and the boat plopped into the water and took off after the U-boat, which was still circling to the right at five or six knots. As that tiny whale-boat took off after the circling black monster, I wouldn't have blamed those men in the boat for hoping that maybe they wouldn't catch her. But cutting inside the circle the gallant band in the boat drew up alongside the runaway U-boat and leapt from the plunging whaleboat to the heaving, slippery deck. As the first one hit the deck with the whaleboat's bow line, it looked for all the world like a cowboy roping a wild horse. I grabbed the microphone and broadcast, "Heigho

213

Silver—rid'em cowboy!"—not a very salty exhortation but readily understood by all hands. On deck was a dead man lying face down with his head alongside the open conning tower hatch, the only man killed on either side in this action.

David and his boys now had a wild bull by the tail and couldn't let go. They were in charge of the upper deck of this submarine, but God only knew who was down below or what nefarious work they were doing. Somebody had to go below and find out.

No one in that boarding party had ever set foot on a submarine of any kind before—to say nothing of a runaway German U-boat. Anyone who ventured down that conning tower hatch might be greeted by a blast of gunfire from below. Even if abandoned, the ship might blow up or sink at any moment. That sewerlike opening in the bridge leading down under the seas looked like a one way street to Davy Jones's locker for everyone in the boarding party.

Lieutenant David, Arthur K. Knispel and Stanley E. Wdowiak jammed all these ideas into unused corners of their minds and plunged down the hatch (David told me later that on the way down he found out exactly how Jonah felt on his way down into the belly of the whale).

They hit the floor plates at the bottom of the ladder ready to fight it out with anyone left aboard. But the enemy had fled and were now all in the water watching the death struggle of their stricken boat. My boys were all alone on board a runaway enemy ship with machinery humming all around them, surrounded by a bewildering array of pipes, valves, levers and instruments with German labels on them. They felt the throbbing of the screws still driving the ship ahead and heard an ominous gurgle of water coming in somewhere nearby.

But the submarine was all theirs. All theirs, that is, if they didn't touch the wrong valve or lever in the semi-darkness of the emergency lights and blow up or sink the boat. David yelled up to the boys on deck to tumble down and lend a hand while he, Knispel and Wdowiak ran forward to the radio room to get the code books. They smashed open a couple of lockers, found the books and immediately passed them up on deck, so we would have something to show for our efforts in case we still lost the boat.

All naval code books have lead covers to make them sink, so why didn't the Germans throw these code books overboard? But why throw a code book overboard from a submarine which you are abandoning in over a thousand fathoms of water, thinking she will be on the bottom in another couple of minutes? *Nothing* had gone overboard except the crew, and we now had in our possession one U-boat, complete with spare parts and all charts, codes and operating instructions from Admiral Doenitz. It would be the greatest intelligence windfall of the war, if David could keep her afloat.

It seemed doubtful that he could, because the submarine was now in practically neutral buoyancy, was riding about ten degrees down by the stern and was settling deeper all the time.

One of the first to plunge down the hatch in response to David's call from below was Zenon B. Lukosius. As soon as Luke hit the floor plates he heard running water. Heading for the sound he ducked around behind the main periscope well and found a stream of water six inches in diameter gushing into the bilges from an open seacock. By the grace of God the cover for this cock had not fallen down into the bilges where he wouldn't have been able to find it, but was lying on the floor plates. Luke grabbed it, slapped it back in place, set up on the butterfly nuts and checked the inrush of water. By this time the boat was threatening to up-end any minute. If she had, she would have taken the whole boarding party with her. Luke got his little chore done just in the nick of time. Another minute might have been too late.

Luke told me later that while he was jamming that cover back in place he was too busy to be scared. But when he tore his Mae West life jacket on a sharp projection in the conning tower, that really shook him—because he didn't know how to swim.

The U-boat was now so low in the water that the swells breaking across her were beginning to wash down the conning tower hatch. David ordered the man left on deck to close the hatch while he and his men continued their work below. The

215

main electric motors were still running and driving the sub-marine in a circle at about six knots.

Meantime, I had reversed course, got back to the scene of action and sent over a whaleboat with Commander Earl Trosino and a group of our "experts" in it. They arrived aboard literally "with a bang". A swell picked up their boat and deposited it bodily on the deck of the submarine, breaking the boat's back and spilling the occupants on deck un-ceremoniously. This blow from above caused some concern even to David and his stout-hearted lads below, who at this time were engaged in ripping electric wires off things which they thought were demolition charges.

When Trosino and his crew scrambled up to the bridge, they couldn't get the conning tower hatch open. It was stuck as if fastened from the inside, a partial vacuum inside the boat holding it down so that they couldn't budge it. The circling U-boat was constantly passing Germans in their rubber boats and Mae Wests, so Trosino's boys grabbed one, hauled him aboard and asked him how to open the hatch. The German showed them a little valve which let air into the pressure hull, equalizing the pressures inside and out and enabled them to get the hatch open.

"Thanks, Bud," said Trosino, and shoved him overboard again.

Trosino then scrambled down the hatch and took over command from David in the same spot where Oberleutnant Meyer had assumed command after Cszhech had shot himself. No other U-boat ever had so many changes of command under fantastically improbable circumstances!

I cannot speak too highly of the job that Trosino did in keeping that U-boat afloat. He too had never been aboard a submarine before. But he had spent most of his life at sea as a chief engineer in Sun Oil tankers. He is the kind of an engineer who can walk into any marine plant, whether it is installed in the *Queen Mary* or a German U-boat, take a quick look around the engine room and know exactly what to do.

He spent the next couple of hours fighting to keep the

submarine's head above water. It was touch and go whether he would succeed or not and they had to keep that conning tower hatch closed. A lot of the time Trosino was down in the bilges under the floor plates tracing out pipelines. Had the boat taken a sudden lurch and up-ended herself, as it was quite probable she would—Earl wouldn't have had any chance whatever to get out. I recommended him for a Navy Cross when we got back to Norfolk. All he got was a Legion of Merit. He did this job in the wrong ocean!

Trosino got the right valves closed and didn't open any of the hundreds of wrong ones. While he was doing this, Gunner Burr went through the boat looking for demolition charges. Our intelligence reports told us we would find fourteen five-pound TNT charges placed against the hull, several in each compartment. We had no information on their exact location or how the firing mechanism worked. Gunner Burr found and disarmed thirteen while Trosino was bilge diving. They found the fourteenth in Bermuda three weeks later! The Germans had been so sure when they abandoned ship that this ship was on the way to the bottom within minutes, that they hadn't set the firing devices! This information is worth only a raised eyebrow now, but when Burr, Trosino, David and their boys were aboard that first day, the knowledge that there was an unlocated demolition charge raised the hackles along all their spines.

Shortly after Trosino got aboard, the *Pillsbury* came alongside to pass salvage pumps over and take the U-boat in tow. Her skipper didn't allow for the fact that submarines have large flippers sticking out from the bow under water on both sides. The port bow flipper cut a long underwater slice in the *Pillsbury's* thin plates as she came alongside, flooding two main compartments and making it necessary for the destroyer to back off and fight to keep herself afloat.

Trosino reported that as long as the submarine had head-way, she rode about ten degrees down by the stern. But when he slowed her down, she lost the lift of her stern diving planes, settled to a steeper angle and submerged the conning tower hatch. The *Pillsbury* reported that a destroyer couldn't do the towing job, so I headed over to take her in tow myself. As we drew near. Trosino pulled the switches and stopped the U-boat.

Working fast, we laid our stern practically alongside the nose of the submarine, threw over a heaving line with a pilot line and an inch-and-a-quarter wire towline bent on. As the lads on the heaving, slippery deck of the submarine were struggling to secure the towline, with four loaded bow torpedo tubes of the submarine practically nuzzling my after end, I said a fervent prayer. "Dear Lord, I've got a bunch of inquisitive lads nosing around below in that submarine—please don't let any of them monkey with the firing switch!"

When the tow line was secured, we eased ahead, took the strain, and got underway again with the U.S. colours proudly flying over the swastika on a boat hook planted in a voice tube on the U-505's bridge. As we gathered speed the stern came up and they could open the hatch again. I cracked off an urgent top secret dispatch to CinCLant and Cominch, "Request immediate assistance to tow captured submarine U-505." That dispatch really shook the staff duty officers back home. At first they didn't believe it and demanded a recheck on the decoding—but lost no time getting necessary action underway in the improbable event that it was true.

It soon became apparent that although we had our bronco roped, she wasn't broken to the halter yet. She sheared way out on our starboard quarter and rode out there listing to starboard and stretching the tow line as taut as a banjo string. Her rudder was jammed hard over. But I couldn't do anything about that now—I had four planes in the air that were getting low on gas.

So, hauling our non-co-operative prize behind us, we swung into the wind and landed our planes. With that submarine dragging its heels back there I could only make about six knots, so the pilots didn't have much wind across the deck for landing. But everyone seems to rise to the occasion at a time like this and they made it look easy—so easy, in fact, that I launched a couple more. Our speed and manœuvrability were seriously restricted by the tow, making us a sitting target for any other submarine that came along, so I figured we *had* to keep our planes aloft.

Meanwhile, the *Pillsbury* had been wallowing astern of us, struggling to stay afloat. She now flashed a message that two main compartments, including one engine room, were flooded to the water line, but that she hoped to get under way again in a couple of hours on one screw. I detached the *Pope* to stand by her, the other three destroyers formed a screen around us and we dragged our prize off at six knots. Next day, knowing that the *Pillsbury's* skipper would be worried about a board of investigation when he got home I sent him the following signal: "This is for your files regarding damage done to your ship this cruise. This damage was done executing my orders and I assume responsibility."

Now I was in real trouble over fuel. One thing was certain, I didn't have enough left to make Casablanca with that U-boat in tow. I was bashful about sending an official dispatch admitting I had made the unpardonable blunder of stretching my fuel supply too far. If I had stopped to think about it, I would have realized that at this point I could have admitted almost anything, and no one would have given it a second thought. Finally, I swallowed my pride and sent a dispatch suggesting I head for the nearest friendly port, Dakar. CinCLant promptly vetoed this and said, "Further orders coming soon."

Sunset was approaching so we now battened the submarine down for the night and brought our boarding parties back to the ship. Trosino informed me he thought she would stay afloat. He also reported that he thought the after torpedo room was flooded but couldn't be sure because the watertight door was dogged shut and he didn't want to open it for fear of flooding the boat. He also said there was what looked to him like a booby trap on the main dog. He had been so busy over there he hadn't noticed that the rudder was jammed but said he could get it amidships for me next morning.

Shortly after sunset the *Flaherty* announced she had a disappearing radar blip and *Chatelain* chimed in with a "Possible sound contact". The only thing I could do was pray and stick on a few extra turns to get the hell out of that area quicker. I must have put on too many because at midnight the tow line snapped and we spent the rest of the night circling the submarine under a full moon and rousing our two-and-one-quarter-inch wire up on deck to put over in the morning.

During the night we got orders from CinCLant to take our prize to Bermuda. (Dakar was full of spies and if we had gone in there news of the capture would have reached Germany before our anchor's splash subsided.) Admiral Ingersoll diverted the fleet tug *Abnaki* from an east bound convoy to take over the towing job and also the oiler *Kennebeck* to refuel the task group.

Next morning we got the big tow wire rigged and when Trosino came back from the submarine he reported he had put the rudder amidships, using the electric controller in the conning tower. But as we gained headway again, it became apparent that the rudder hadn't moved at all. The electric rudder *indicator* in the conning tower had come back amidships, but the rudder was still hard a' starboard. We would have to get into the after torpedo room and hook up the hand steering gear to move it.

I had been itching to get aboard that craft myself and the booby trap on the torpedo room door gave me the excuse I wanted. I was an ordnance post-graduate and knew as much about fuses and circuitry as anyone on board, so I had designated myself as officer-in-charge of booby traps in the capture plans. Trosino and I took along four helpers and went over to investigate.

As we drew alongside the heaving U-boat, riding with its bow out of water, the stern clear under, and seas breaking over the conning tower hatch, I wasn't so sure I had any business being there. After we had scrambled up on the bridge and I could see that we had to close the conning tower hatch behind us after we went down to keep the seas from coming in after us, I could think of a dozen more important things I should have been doing at this time. But the skipper can't back out when he has gone that far. Down the hatch we went, this being the first time *I* had ever been in a submarine. Trosino

220

Rear-Admiral (then Captain) Gallery on the bridge of U-505
as she is being towed to Bermuda

U-505 alongside the Museum of Science and Industry, Chicago

was a veteran by now, so he led the way aft. The battery was practically flat and the lights burned very dimly. The boat was way down by the stern and wallowing heavily. The air stank. That trip through the control room, diesel engine room, and after motor room, seemed endless. As we went further and further aft, I suddenly remembered that one way of correcting trim in a submarine was to have men move to the high end of the boat, and here were four of us trooping aft to the heavy end of a boat that was teetering on a knife edge! But we had passed the point of no return when we went down the hatch. You do your best to look calm, cool, and collected, and to tell yourself, "You can't live for ever anyway".

At the after bulkhead of the motor room, Trosino put his flashlight on an open fuse box and said, "There she is, Cap'n". There were a dozen exposed fuses in the box and many wires leading in and out. The cover of the box opened downward and was lying across the main dog of the watertight door to the torpedo room. To move the dog you had to close the cover of the fuse box. This had the makings of a booby trap and closing the cover *might* complete a circuit that would blow us all up.

But I didn't think so. This was an improbable place for a booby trap—the Germans obviously hadn't expected us to board their ship, so why set booby traps? It looked to me as if that cover had been jarred open accidentally after the door was dogged shut. A close scrutiny of the wiring and circuits revealed nothing suspicious.

You can't hem and haw over a question like this very long when you are twenty-five feet under water in a wallowing submarine, and one nice thing about fiddling with booby traps is that you find out right away, after you have sprung one, whether your calculations were right or not. I eased the cover shut and nothing happened.

Now for the door. Three of us braced our backs against it so we could get it closed again if water started squirting out, and we moved the main dog carefully till we had just cracked the hatch. No water. We swung the door open and scrambled aft to the hand steering gear. In half a minute we had it hooked up and moved the rudder back amidships. As we gave the wheel its final spin, I said, "Let's get the hell out of here". There being no objections—out we went, everybody trying his best to walk up that long slanted passageway nonchalantly. The salt fresh air smelt mighty sweet as we clambered out into the sunlight on the bridge.

While we were below, my lads on deck had been busy with a paint brush. In big red letters across the face of the conning tower they had emblazoned the name "Can Do Junior". My crew always called the *Guadalcanal* the "Can Do". Everyone in the task group has referred to the U-505 ever since as "Junior".

The submarine towed properly now and we proceeded at eight knots for our rendezvous with the *Abnaki*. On June 9, 1944, we turned our tow over to *Abnaki* and refuelled the task group from the *Kennebeck*. Then we formed a screen around the *Abnaki* and "Junior" and headed for Bermuda, 2,500 miles away.

Ever since we opened that booby trap, Earl Trosino had been after me to let him start the U-boat's diesels and bring her in triumphantly under her own power. I wish now I had let him do it. But at the time I was afraid that if we got too ambitious and tried to start the engines somebody might open the wrong valve and sink the boat. I hereby apologize to Trosino and his brave lads for underestimating them. I'm sure that after all the other improbable things they did, they would have brought her in with colours flying.

Trosino did one thing that some of my submariner friends still seem sceptical about when I tell it. At the end of the second day, there wasn't enough juice left in the U-boat's battery to run a bilge pump. By this time Earl had figured out how to pump out the after ballast tanks and bring the boat up to an even keel, *if* he had power to run the pump. But I wouldn't let him start the diesels, so he couldn't charge the battery in the usual way. (Each of the submarine's main shafts had a diesel engine on one end, the propeller on the other, and an electric armature in the middle. When you charge the battery, the diesels turn the propellers and the armature

222

as well, which then acts as a generator and puts juice back in the battery. When cruising submerged you unclutch the diesels and your battery supplies juice to turn the armature and propel the ship.)

Trosino figured out how to set the switches so that the armature would generate juice if something turned it. Then he disconnected the clutches joining the heavy diesel engines to the propeller shafts and asked me to tow at ten to twelve knots that night. I did, and dragging the submarine through the water at this speed with the big diesels disconnected made the propellers windmill in the water. This made the main shafts turn and the armatures had no way of knowing that they weren't being turned in the usual manner. They obediently made juice and recharged the battery. Next morning Earl was able to run a ballast pump and bring the boat up to full surface trim.

By this time we had all prisoners from the U-boat aboard the *Guadalcanal*—fifty-nine out of a crew of sixty. Ober-leutnant Harald Lange was badly wounded and I went down to see him in sick bay. Because of his wounds he hadn't seen our people get aboard his boat and he thought his order to scuttle had been carried out. He wouldn't believe we had her in tow until I sent over to the submarine and got a picture of his family off his cabin desk. This convinced him, and he said over and over again, "I will be punished for this". I tried to cheer him up by pointing out that Germany was losing the war and that a new regime would replace the Nazis. He kept shaking his head and saying, "No matter what happens, I will be punished".

Maybe he was right. I have had some letters from Lange since the war, and reading between the lines I can see that he may be blamed for things which were not his fault. So far as I know, no legal action has been taken against him by the German government, but perhaps other former U-boat skippers exclude him from organizations to which he should be welcome. If so, this is a grave injustice, in my opinion.

Lange was the victim of circumstances. He did exactly what

223

several hundred other U-boat skippers did when they thought the end was at hand and surfaced to give their crew a last chance to survive the war before scuttling their boats. Perhaps a dozen or more of these boats could have been captured if we had been prepared to send off boarding parties. I still think I could have towed the U-515 home if I had exercised proper foresight before she surfaced. Kretschmer, the greatest ace of them all, was captured with most of his crew, and his U-boat lay helpless on the surface with two British destroyers close by for much longer than it took us to get aboard the U-505.

I am told that various false stories have circulated in Germany that the U-505 surrendered. She did not surrender any more than several hundred other U-boats that did the same thing surrendered. If there is any discrimination against her crew in Germany now, it is wrong. In my opinion, the man responsible for her capture was Cszhech. That crew should have been broken up and spread around among a dozen U-boats as soon as she came in from the cruise on which Cszhech ratted on his men by committing suicide. Lange inherited an impossible situation. He and his men, like most other U-boat sailors, were conscientious men who did their duty, were worthy opponents who almost beat us in a fair fight, and should be treated as such now.

On June 19, 1944, we escorted the *Abnaki* and U-505 into Bermuda with the traditional broom hoisted at our main truck. A delegation of experts from Washington swarmed aboard the U-boat and we turned our fifty-nine prisoners over to the Commandant of the Naval Operating Base, Bermuda. They were imprisoned there in a special camp all by themselves till the war was over, when they were returned to Germany.

Some people, in their enthusiasm over this capture, say that the ability to read German naval codes from then on shortened the war by several months. I doubt this. The invasion of Normandy began two days after we got the U-505, and once the Allied Armies got ashore the duration of the war was in their hands. The Navy could still prolong or even lose the war by losing control of the seas, but it couldn't do much to speed up the tempo of operations ashore. The capture did save seamen's lives by providing complete technical data on German submarines and new developments, such as the acoustic torpedo.

It was certainly a big thing capturing the German naval codes. We got the current code books, the cipher machine, and hundreds of dispatches with the code version on one side and German translation on the other. Like all military services, the German Navy changed their code about every two weeks, so that enemy cryptographers wouldn't be constantly working on the same system. But the key to the routine changes was in the code books. We read the operational traffic between U-boat headquarters and the submarines at sea for the rest of the war. Reception committees which we were able to arrange as a result of this eavesdropping may have had something to do with the sinking of nearly three hundred U-boats in the next eleven months.

This brings me to what I think is the most remarkable part of this whole improbable episode. It was very important to prevent knowledge of this capture from reaching Germany. If it had, the Germans would have heaved all the old code books overboard, changed their whole system, and issued brand new ones, which are always kept ready for issue in just such an emergency. While towing the U-boat to Bermuda we carefully explained this to all hands in the task group and directed them to tell *no one*, but no one, what had happened on this cruise.

We had about three thousand young lads in that task group, all of whom had seen the whole thing happen and who came back from that cruise just bursting with the best story of their lives. But they knew they shouldn't tell it. I am very proud indeed of the fact that the Germans never found out we had this U-boat till the war was over. The boys *did* keep their mouths shut.

I think this speaks very highly indeed for the devotion to duty and sense of responsibility of the average young American wearing bell-bottom trousers. When I read the headlines these days about atomic secrets leaking from high level sources and important government officials popping off with top secret stuff just to get in the headlines, I feel even prouder of my lads in Task Group 22.3.

While lecturing the boys on the importance of keeping the capture secret, I also laid down the law on souvenirs. I pointed out that there's no use having a souvenir unless you can show it around and brag about it and that regulations required all captured equipment to be sent to Office of Naval Intelligence in Washington. "So," I said, "if anyone has picked up a souvenir, turn it in to the exec's office tomorrow and no questions will be asked. But we will lower the boom on anyone found with souvenirs after tomorrow."

Next day the Exec's Office was inundated with the damnedest collection of stuff you've ever seen—Lugers, flashlights, cameras, officers' caps, German cigarettes, etc., etc. It was incredible that while struggling to keep a sinking U-boat afloat, the men whose lives were in danger could find time to accumulate all that junk.

I knew that the boys would all rather have turned in their right arms than these souvenirs. So, in accordance with the regulations, we tagged the souvenirs with the names of the "owners" and told the boys that (according to the book) at the end of the war the Office of Naval Intelligence would return them. Most of us, including me, were naive enough to believe this! But nobody ever saw their souvenirs again. After peace broke out the Washington bureaucrats absconded with them.

Checking back on this capture now, it seems as if the U-505 and my task group simply had a rendezvous and there was no avoiding it. The U-505 was never where I thought she was until the moment she popped up almost under foot. I was searching the wrong areas all the time, except that last night when my planes must have missed her by inches once, and by seconds another time.

Plotting my own track that night and the courses flown by my planes against the track given by the U-505's war diary, it is apparent that we should have spotted him about ten o'clock. One of my planes passed within six miles of him when he was surfaced recharging his battery. My radar operator should have picked up a faint blip on his scope but he didn't. By the same token, the submarine's Naxos operator should have picked up our plane's radar, but *he* didn't, although apparently he had picked up every other plane within miles of him for the past two weeks. Two hours later, and only five minutes after the submarine finished recharging and submerged, another one of my planes passed smack over the spot where he had just gone down.

I suppose I can say that at any rate I was right in my decision to turn back and search that area again. But I was right *for the wrong reason*. I had turned back because I was certain we had made contact with him the night before. Actually, he had not been in our search area at any time the night before, and our contacts had been false.

Naturally the advance planning that we did on this thing belongs on the credit side of the ledger. So also does the venture into night flying, although in the final analysis the only real effect it had on this operation was to hold us in the area for one more night. Had we found the U-505 at night, there would have been no possibility of capture—that boarding idea was improbable enough in broad daylight, it was impossible at night.

This whole operation is an example of the fact that a military commander controls events only up to a certain point. He can anticipate certain things, perhaps even set the stage for them to happen, and can be ready to cash in on them if they do happen. But whether they will happen or not depends on many things over which he has no control. One is what goes on in the other commander's mind and another is what goes on in his own.

The only moral I can see to all this is to plan your operations carefully, get the best advice you can from experts, fix it so that if certain things happen you will not be caught flat-footed, and then trust in God. Maybe our daily morning prayer over the loud-hailers had a lot to do with this capture!

CHAPTER XIX

CHICAGO

AFTER Germany surrendered, the U-505, manned by an American crew and cruising under its own power, made a war bond tour of the Atlantic and Gulf coasts. When the Pacific war ended, she tied up at the Navy Yard in Portsmouth, New Hampshire, to await final disposition. She was not decommissioned or mothballed. The American crew simply closed the valves, pulled the switches, hauled down the colours, and walked ashore—taking with them all souvenirs such as name plates, gauges, and small pieces of equipment that weren't double riveted to the hull. For the next nine years the U-boat lay alongside the dock in Portsmouth Navy Yard and rusted.

At the end of the war, all German naval vessels and submarines still afloat were divided among the four so-called great powers, England, Russia, the United States, and France. Each got a dozen or so U-boats under an agreement whereby all these craft would be sunk in deep water or scrapped within two years. As the two year limit approached, we got ready to carry out our agreement and word reached me that the U-505 was to be taken out with the surrendered U-boats and sunk.

I immediately objected on the ground that the U-505 was not included in the Four Power Agreement, which applied only to U-boats surrendered at the end of the war. The U-505 had not surrendered, she was captured in battle on the high seas. She was therefore U.S. property with no strings attached and we could keep her as long as we wanted.

I had no immediate plans in mind for her at this time, but my boys had gone to a lot of trouble to prevent that U-boat from sinking off the coast of Africa, and I took a dim view of scuttling her now. Government bureaucrats always like to have some precedent or a piece of paper to justify what they are doing and there were no precedents for this case. But I raised such a fuss that the Navy Department finally changed its mind rather dubiously and vetoed the scuttling order.

Some years later, after the boat got to Chicago, this question of the Four Power surrender agreement came up again. Molotov visited the Museum of Science and Industry while passing through Chicago on his way to the tenth anniversary celebration of the U.N. at San Francisco. While looking at the U-505, he was heard to ask an aide, "Do you think they really captured her?" The aide simply shrugged.

Molotov obviously didn't believe we had captured her and the implication was that he thought this was one of the U-boats turned over at the end of the war which we should have sunk. Mr. Molotov figured he had stumbled on a little item he could file away for future reference. At an opportune time, he could make one of his sweeping accusations of bad faith and cite this submarine as an example. Major Lohr, President of the Museum, sent the State Department a telegram about this incident and I am told Secretary Dulles straightened Mr. Molotov out on the facts of the case.

After the reprieve on the scuttling order, my brother, Father John Ireland Gallery, had an idea about a possible use for the U-505. He was a naval reserve chaplain and had helped fight the Battle of the Atlantic with the Navy's Patrol Wing 7, which played a big part in the air offensive over the Bay of Biscay. Father John observed that there were monuments all over the country for the land battles in every war that this country has fought, but naval memorials were few and far between. Father John asked himself, "Why not bring the U-505 to Chicago and make it a memorial to the thousands of American seamen who had lost their lives in the two great Battles of the Atlantic? These were two of the crucial battles in our history, and what could be a more appropriate monument to these battles than one of the very submarines around which the battles centred."

One day, while visiting the Museum of Science and Industry near his parish in Chicago, Father John mentioned this idea to Major Lenox Lohr. The Major lit up like a Christmas tree, pushed a button, and told his secretary to bring in the Museum's "submarine file". In this file there were letters going back twenty-four years asking the Navy Department to give them an obsolete submarine for display at the Museum. The Major explained that when Julius Rosenwald endowed and established the Museum back in 1926, he specified that he wanted it patterned after the Deutsche Museum in Munich. This Museum was filled with modern exhibits featuring the technology of the age in which we live and the two principal attractions were a full scale model of a coal mine and an actual submarine hauled out of the water and installed alongside the Museum.

The first exhibit installed in the new Museum of Science and Industry at Chicago, was an accurate replica of a modern coal mine. It had been a feature attraction ever since. The Museum, located five hundred yards from the shore of Lake Michigan, had been trying unsuccessfully for twenty-four years to get a submarine.

The Major, who is one of America's greatest showmen, realized immediately the possibilities of the U-505 for the Museum. This wasn't just any old submarine. It was a historic trophy, the first enemy war ship captured in battle on the high seas since 1815. It could fulfil the founder's dream, but on a bigger scale than Rosenwald had visualized. The Major and Father John agreed that afternoon that they would get a project started to bring the U-505 to Chicago and install it alongside the Museum.

This was easier said than done. It involved acquiring title to the U-boat, making it seaworthy, towing it to Chicago, dragging it out of the water and hauling it across the busiest thoroughfare in the city to the Museum, restoring it to presentable condition, and installing it as a permanent addition to the Museum's main building. Offhand, this looked like an expensive project—and the Museum had no funds for it. Most people with whom the Major and Father John discussed the project agreed that it was a "good idea", but were not anxious to do anything about it. No such project had ever been undertaken before, and there were many difficulties involved. In 1948, most people wanted to forget war rather than erect war memorials. As one critic expressed it, "If you get it here it will just be another cannon on the courthouse lawn."

But, in the course of a couple of years, a few real enthusiasts for the project were found and the idea began to take root. Alderman Clarence F. Wagner got the City Council to pass a resolution asking the Navy Department to give the U-boat to the Museum. Colonel McCormick of the *Chicago Tribune* threw his considerable weight behind it and for the next several years the *Tribune* ran stories periodically about the project and printed editorials favouring it.

Negotiations to secure title from the Navy Department took some time. The Navy was anxious to get this rusty elephant off its hands and would gladly have sunk it in deep water if they could have done it while nobody was looking. But a resolution by both Houses of Congress was necessary before they could give it away. It took two years to get the Congressional resolution because eighty days had to elapse after it was introduced, before Congress could vote on it, in order to allow other interested communities, if any, to put in their bids. No other communities were interested, but the first session of Congress to consider the matter adjourned eight days too soon and another eighty-day waiting period was necessary at the next session. Finally we got Congressional approval and the Navy Department drew up legal papers for the transfer of title.

The first draft of these papers contained a clause typical of the stuff you run into whenever government lawyers get their fingers into the pie. It specified that in case of war, the Museum undertake to return this vessel on demand to the government in the same condition in which it had been turned over to them; I had some fun needling the legal beagles about that one. We finally ridiculed them into reluctantly omitting the clause.

The law says that when an obsolete naval vessel is given away, the recipient must take it over at no expense to the government. The Navy Department interpreted this clause

231

literally and informed the Museum the U-505 would become their property alongside the dock in Portsmouth, and the Museum would have to pay for all repairs necessary to make her seaworthy. I got a sharp rap across the knuckles from the Department for trying to get Senator Dirksen to persuade the bureaucrats that their estimates on these repairs were a little on the high side and that it would be good training for the Navy to tow it to Chicago for us. As a matter of fact, I eventually had more trouble getting that submarine from Portsmouth to Chicago than I did getting her from Cape Blanco to Bermuda.

Early in 1953 Mayor Kennelly of Chicago appointed a committee of leading citizens to take charge of this project, raise the necessary funds, and bring the U-505 to Chicago. Heading this committee as honorary chairman was Mr. Ralph A. Bard, formerly Undersecretary of the Navy. Robert Crown and Carl Stockholm, active members of the Navy League, served as co-chairmen. Estimates of the amount of cash necessary to do the job ranged from $50,000 to two million. It's difficult to estimate a job that has never been done before and which involves taking a strange craft like a submarine out of its element and putting it in a park a thousand miles inland. The committee set a goal of $250,000 to be raised.

Despite the fact that this project had been a *Tribune* baby for years, all Chicago papers got behind it and the co-operation of news media, press, radio and TV for the next year and a half was unprecedented in the history of the city. The U-505 became a household word and the project a civic enterprise in which everyone was interested.

The committee eventually raised $125,000 in cash and obtained a similar amount in free services from civic minded corporations. This was small beer in view of the unprecedented publicity given the project. Had the project been put in the hands of professional fund raisers, I'm sure they could have collected several million. But we didn't need that much and the committee insisted, as a matter of principle, on keeping the fund raising on a strictly amateur basis. There was no cut

232

for any professional fund raisers and every cent collected went into the project.

Two incidents in connection with the free services are typical of the way the whole community got behind this project. One day I got a phone call from a Mr. Leonard Grosse, whom I didn't know from Adam at the time. He announced that his business was making bronze memorial plaques and said, "It seems to me you are going to need some plaques for the sub at the Museum, aren't you?" "Yes," I said rather guardedly. "Well, I can make you some nice ones," said the voice. So far this seemed like a straight inquiry for some business by a man who was alert enough to spot a possible need for his product when he saw it. I replied, "That's fine, we will keep you in mind . . . but those things are expensive, aren't they?" "These won't be," said Grosse, "I want to give them to you." This came out of a clear sky, entirely on Mr. Grosse's own initiative. He presented the Museum with plaques that would have cost close to $5,000.

The other incident concerned getting the use of a floating drydock to lift the U-505 out of the water and put it on the beach. There was only one floating dock in the Great Lakes big enough to do this. It belonged to Great Lakes Dredging and Dock Company. Some of the Great Lakes Company engineers were nervous of this haul-out job, didn't want to have anything to do with it, and informed our chief engineer, Mr. Seth Gooder, that their drydock wasn't big enough. Seth and I got the dimensions of the dock, calculated its displacement and lifting power and *knew* it was big enough.

One day Seth and I called on Mr. William P. Feeley, head of the company, to talk him into participating in our project. He was a poker-faced gentleman who sat back and listened for a long time saying nothing and indicating nothing. I gave him an earnest discourse on the civic aspects of the project, benefit to the school kids, etc., and then Gooder went through all the engineering angles proving mathematically that his drydock could handle this job. When we got through I felt it had all been a waste of time and we had made no impression. Mr. Feeley sat in silence at the head of the table for a few minutes and then fixed a cold eye on us and said, "Just what sort of a proposition did you want to make to us for the use of our drydock?"

I figured we had lost the battle and there was no use wasting time beating around the bush. I said, "Mr. Feeley, we would like to borrow your drydock for six weeks." Mr. Feeley didn't bat an eye. "Okay," he said, "you can have it."

The American Shipbuilding Company of Cleveland and the Fitzsimons and Connel Dredging and Dock Company were equally generous in furnishing special equipment and services.

The committee was very fortunate indeed to secure the services of Mr. Seth Gooder, as project engineer. Mr. Gooder had been one of the leading civil engineers of Chicago for many years and had done some big jobs, including moving large churches, and the whole grandstand of the Cubs' ball park. He had just retired from active practice and found time heavy on his hands. He took over the engineering of this project, at no fee, and gave it his full-time attention for a year and a half. His services were irreplaceable at any price. It might have been possible to hire the best engineers in the city to do this job, but you can't hire the enthusiasm and personal interest that Gooder gave to it. He made complete engineering studies of every possible way of getting the submarine out of Lake Michigan and alongside the Museum. The South Shore Drive, which runs between the Museum and the lake shore, handles 80,000 cars per day, and getting the U-boat across or under this drive with the shortest possible interruption of traffic was the prime consideration. Various schemes for squeezing it under a low bridge into a shallow lagoon near the Museum were discarded because we might damage the bridge. The safest and best method seemed to be the straightforward one of beaching it on the shore of the Lake and hauling it across the drive in the same way that houses are moved. The submarine drew nine feet of water and to beach it the keel had to be lifted about four feet above lake level. She weighed about eight hundred and fifty tons and this weight had to be lifted thirteen feet above its normal position when waterborne. When it looked as though we couldn't get the floating drydock,

Gooder drew up plans for improvising a floating dock, if necessary, by sinking a gravel barge under the U-boat and raising it with the submarine sitting on top. Early in 1954 Gooder had all his plans ready and the Portsmouth Yard pronounced the submarine seaworthy and ready for her last voyage.

On May 14, 1954, the U-505 started her journey to Chicago via the St. Lawrence River, Welland Canal, and the Great Lakes. She was towed by the tug *Pauline L. Moran* to Lake Erie, where the Coast Guard cutter *Arundel* took over.

I rode the tug *Pauline L. Moran* while going from Cornwall to Cardinal on the old St. Lawrence waterway, and had the unforgettable experience of listening for two days to a couple of real old salts trying to snow each other under with yarns about their experiences in forty years of seafaring. The *Moran* skipper and the Canadian pilot had spent their lives at sea, and both were crusted with salt. When you get two characters like that together on the bridge of a tug, each one feels duty bound to outdo the other one with his tales of nautical adventure. When they've got a Rear Admiral, U.S. Navy, standing behind them and listening, in addition to the personal challenge offered by the other's exaggerated tales, each one feels that his professional standing is at stake. In this case, a salt water man was defending his breed of sailors against a character who, although he might be a pretty good seaman, was after all just a river man.

It had never before been my privilege to listen to such a series of colossal tall tales as these two exchanged with perfectly straight faces. No matter what sort of epic one related, the other could top it. While they were doing this, we were clawing our way up the St. Lawrence towing the submarine alongside in a current which often was as high as eight knots. The channel was winding, the stream was full of strong eddies, and every now and then a large ship coming down stream would career around a bend ahead and sweep down at us sidewise.

Time and time again I held my breath in such situations, expecting some frenzied manœuvring on our part to avoid collision. The two old salts seemed to regard these things as minor distractions. Getting the tow safely to its destination was just an incidental job that either one could do with his eyes shut—but not with his mouth shut while the other was within hearing. The really important work of the day was the reminiscing. They went right on relating their sagas until disaster seemed imminent, when the pilot would say apologetically, "Come left a little," the tug skipper would flip his wheel a few spokes, and the tale would be resumed where it had been interrupted, while the down bound steamer swept by a few yards to starboard.

Earl Trosino, who kept the U-505 afloat off Cape Blanco was on this cruise too. He is now chief engineer of a Sun Oil Company tanker, and the company generously loaned him to us for this trip. It was fitting that Trosino, who was mainly responsible for saving the U-505 off Cape Blanco, should be her skipper on her final voyage to Chicago.

In June the U-505 arrived in Chicago and received the biggest civic welcome ever given on the water front. She was met by a fleet of several hundred yachts out in the Lake, escorted to the harbour, saluted by the fireboats, and received at the Michigan Avenue bridge by the Mayor and a huge crowd.

Following the reception, the U-boat spent the next six weeks at Calumet Harbour getting ready for the hauling out job. She had to be drydocked to remove ninety tons of ballast from her keel, and then transferred from the American Shipbuilding Company's 800-foot graving dock to the Great Lakes Company's floating dock. After she was safely ensconced in the floating dock with her keel four feet above water level, a steel cradle was built around her to take her ashore and carry her to the Museum. When this cradle was completed, hydraulic jacks boosted the cradle under the submarine and then lifted the submarine and cradle high enough to insert several hundred two-inch steel rollers between the cradle and the railway rails which had been placed on the floor of the floating dock. When the jacks were let down and removed, she was ready to roll.

Our main concern now was weather, and not entirely local Chicago weather, but weather all over Lake Michigan. We were not worried about a steady blow of any kind. A northeast gale can cause surf on the Chicago side of the lake much too heavy for any beaching operation, but steady gales can be predicted. We only needed about four hours to get the U-boat ashore from the dry dock, and we wouldn't start beaching operations till we were sure that no gales were coming for at least twelve hours.

What we were worried about were small, violent thunderstorms anywhere in the Lake, which produce a phenomenon called a seiche. A seiche is a surge of water caused by sudden changes in barometric pressure such as occur in line squalls. Such a change can start a great surge of water out in the Lake which rolls out, expanding in all directions, toward the shore. The wave produced may be only a few inches in height but over a mile from one crest to the next. When it reaches the beach its action is entirely different from that of the ordinary wave, which lasts for a few seconds and is gone. When a seiche surges in, the level of the Lake rises for a period of five or ten minutes rather than seconds and if it happens to be reinforced by reflected surges, and if the contour of the beach traps the water, the Lake can rise four or five feet in extreme cases as if the tide were coming in. Exactly this happened the day the U-505 arrived in Chicago and seven fishermen were swept off a pier in Lincoln Park and drowned. One or more small seiches occur almost every day in Lake Michigan. The level of the Lake goes up and down at least as frequently as does the sea level in a tidal port, but the variations are almost completely unpredictable. A big seiche at the wrong time, just as we got the U-505 half way ashore, would, of course, produce spectacularly embarrassing results.

While work on the cradle proceeded at Calumet City, a nine-foot channel was being dredged five hundred feet out into the Lake from the beach alongside the Museum. At the inshore end of this channel we built a pier about fifty feet out from the beach capable of carrying a thousand tons, and laid rails on it to receive the cradle and submarine.

On August 13, two tugs brought the floating dock up from Calumet City, eased it up the nine-foot channel and nosed it against the pier. The height of the rails on the pier and in the dock matched to within a sixteenth of an inch, but while we were hooking up the cables to haul the submarine ashore, a small seiche lifted the drydock four inches too high and eased it down where it belonged again in a period of twenty minutes.

But the Lake behaved itself after that one little seiche and the sub came ashore without incident soon after dark on Friday the 13th of August.

Seth Gooder had to do some expert juggling of water ballast to keep the drydock on an even keel during the beaching operation. As the submarine inched forward on to the pier, water had to be admitted to the tanks of the dock just fast enough to compensate for the weight being transferred to the beach. It was like walking a tightrope with a thousand-ton weight.

On the night of September 3, they closed the Outer Drive at 7.00 p.m., we laid railway rails across the pavement and the submarine was dragged across the drive at an average rate of about eight inches per minute. Fifteen thousand people stayed up till 4.00 a.m., watching the U-boat creep across the drive. Every one of these citizens knew a better way of doing the job than the way we were doing it. There were many arguments that night among the sidewalk superintendents, and the only thing they all agreed on was that they wouldn't do it our way. A large sign on the Outer Drive warned motorists, "Drive Carefully—Submarine Crossing". The Drive was open for normal traffic again in time for the morning traffic rush. The U-boat still had three hundred yards to go and a sixty-seven degree turn to make before it reached its final berth, but from here on it was a straight house-moving job.

After the submarine was installed on its concrete foundation at the Museum, holes were cut in her port side and two covered passageways were built connecting her to the Museum. Visitors now enter the U-boat aft, walk forward and return to the Museum through the forward passageway. The U-boat is anchored to the foundation amidships, but the bow and stern rest on rollers. Temperature variations between winter and summer can cause the length of the boat to vary three inches,

238

which would crack a concrete foundation if she were securely anchored.

On September 25, 1954, the U-505 was dedicated as a memorial to the 55,000 Americans who have lost their lives at sea. Admiral Halsey made the principal address, Arthur Godfrey was the master-of-ceremonies, the Bishop Weldon of Springfield, Massachusetts, Chaplain of the *Guadalcanal* when we made the capture, gave the invocation. Mr. William V. Kahler was chairman of the dedication committee. About a hundred members of the task group were on hand for the ceremony, including Captain Trosino and all nine surviving members of the *Pillsbury's* original boarding party. About 40,000 Chicagoans gathered under the trees in Jackson Park to witness the rites.

As I met the various lads in the task group, most of whom I hadn't seen in eleven years, I soon learned exactly what to expect in the way of greeting. After the customary polite preliminaries had been disposed of, each of them would look at me sort of quizzically and say, "Cap'n—where the hell is that Luger you made me turn in and were going to get back for me?"

All I could do was mutter some profane comments on the ONI characters who let us down.

The U-505 has proved a great drawing card at the Museum. During the first year it was on exhibit, attendance at the Museum increased twenty per cent over the previous record-breaking year. A total of 2,400,000 people came to the Museum, of whom 569,349 went through the submarine. Many more would have done so except that only so many can get through it at a time.

But Major Lohr, being the smart showman that he is, refuses to hurry people through the submarine. He says he would rather give people time to look around and digest what they are seeing, even if this means he has to turn some away at the end of the day.

The Museum has done a wonderful job of restoring the boat to its original condition. Major Lohr is a perfectionist who will never be satisfied with it. His hobby is restoring old machines

239

to operating condition and the U-505 gave him something he could really get his teeth into. Every week some fresh piece of equipment is put back in working order. Often it's a piece that looked perfectly all right before, to anyone except the Major, who wants things not only to look right, but to work properly too. He has even fired up the diesel engines and kicked them over under their own power. The U-505 is actually cleaner, more presentable and in better condition today than it was when we took it away from the Germans.

Popular POST

News of THE POPULAR BOOK CLUB for October 1958

BOOK CRITICS...

FILMGOERS...

EVERYONE AGREES...

THIS IS THE LAUGH OF THE YEAR!

★ Compton Mackenzie's riotous comedy ★

★ ROCKETS GALORE ★

★ COMING TO YOU NEXT MONTH ★

CHAPTER XX

EPILOGUE

Now that the war is over and some of the fires of hatred have died down a little, perhaps I can say a word of recognition for the U-boat sailors who fought us almost to a standstill in submarines similar to the U-505. A total of seven hundred and eighty-one German U-boats were destroyed during the war, including twenty-nine still listed simply as "missing, fate unknown". Seventy per cent of all the officers and men who served in the U-boat fleet went to the bottom of the sea with their boats. This is an almost incredible casualty rate. In the Pacific the personnel loss rate for U.S. submarines was only one-third as great. Well trained military outfits have cracked and mutinied in the face of much less. It takes a high calibre of leadership in the officers' corps, good discipline and high morale to keep on fighting despite such brutal losses.

Twenty-eight thousand German sailors rode their U-boats down to Davy Jones's locker. I helped send several hundred on their way there and didn't lose any sleep over it at the time. So far as I was concerned, there was no malice in what I was doing—except when some U-boat skipper made a monkey out of me by outwitting me. I was discharging an official duty just as the U-boat sailors were. Speaking as a professional fighting man myself, I must admit that those men fought well, and observed the code laid down by civilized nations to govern the organized murder that we call war. I have nothing but reluctant respect for the courage and patriotism of the U-boat crews in executing the orders of their Nazi masters even when the odds against them became hopeless. In fact, I look on this U-boat in Chicago as a memorial, of a sort, to our misguided enemies whose devotion to duty deserved a better cause.

It's an ironic proof of war's futility that now, only eleven years after VJ Day, we are wooing the Germans and Japs, and arming them to help protect the western world against our former allies, the communists. Hitler's ghost must cackle sardonically over that one!

Now that we face an evil worse than the Nazis, this submarine in Jackson Park should remind us that men will fight well even for bad causes, and that we can't depend on winning simply because we are right. The U-505 is also a peculiarly appropriate warning that it is folly to stake our security on international agreements, because if solemn treaties had been worth the paper they were written on, it would be impossible for that submarine to be alongside the Museum today. Commerce raiding submarines were abolished by international agreement long before the U-505 was built. The fact that it *is* there in Jackson Park now should be a permanent object lesson to us that international pacts based on good faith and morality have a way of coming apart at the seams when a shooting war starts. Perhaps the best advice ever given to America was Theodore Roosevelt's, "Speak softly but carry a big stick".

After World War I, all great nations agreed that the submarine was an uncivilized weapon which should be outlawed—just as we all now agree the atom bomb should be outlawed. But to outlaw an effective and useful weapon requires more mutual confidence and trust than civilized nations have ever had in each other. The great maritime nations who had little to gain and much to lose from unrestricted submarine warfare against merchant vessels were perfectly willing, between wars, to declare this form of warfare uncivilized and to ban it. But they wouldn't outlaw submarines completely because they might want to use them against each other's warships next time they had to settle their differences in the traditional way employed by the human race ever since Cain settled his with Abel in the Garden of Eden. With this in mind, the great powers, including the United States, foisted off on a gullible world the London Treaty of 1930, saying that if submarines were ever used against merchant ships again they would follow the Rules of Prize Warfare.

These rules, drawn up originally in the days of sailing ships, were as obsolete in 1930 as sailing ships, and everybody who agreed to them knew this. Nevertheless, the United States put its signature on this pious hokum, and (like everybody else) kept right on building submarines.

This hypocritical stuff went down the drain during the first week of World War II. The Germans sank the *Athenia* and the British armed all merchantmen, ordered them to report submarines by radio, and to ram them—things which were impossible in the good old days of sail when Prize Rules originated. Before long, both sides threw the book away and went to unrestricted submarine warfare as in World War I, each side piously claiming it was simply retaliating against the other.

When the U.S. got into the war, our submarines in the Pacific operated in the same way as the Germans, and sank six million tons of ships. We torpedoed without warning and left survivors to their fate. British submarines did exactly the same. That's the only way submarines *can* operate. Admiral Lockwood, who commanded our submarines in the Pacific, tells the story with a few words in the title of his book, *Sink 'Em All*. Naval officers were not at all surprised by any of this. War is a brutal business and no amount of wishful thinking by bubble-headed statesmen between wars will make it otherwise.

When the statesmen louse up *their* job so badly that they have to have the military men pull the chestnuts out of the fire for them, a lot of innocent bystanders are going to get hurt. When nations, by mutual consent, decide to ignore the commandment "Thou shalt not kill", it is very difficult for the military leaders to restrict the killing to just the right people.

You might think that since our submarines fought the same way the Germans did, we would sweep the question of Prize Warfare under the rug after the war and say no more about violation of the laws of war at sea. Our naval officers were perfectly willing to do this, but our statesmen and lawyers were vindictive. When the war was over, they insisted on trying the German Admirals Raeder and Doenitz at Nuremberg as war criminals for permitting their submarines to do exactly what ours did. A justice of our Supreme Court prosecuted them and tried to hang them. To our eternal shame, we convicted the German Admirals of violating the laws of war at sea and sen-

243

tenced them to long terms of imprisonment: Raeder to life; and Doenitz to ten years.

This kangaroo court at Nuremberg was officially known as the "International Military Tribunal". That name is a libel on the military profession. The tribunal was not a military one in any sense. The only military men among the judges were the Russians. Some military titles are listed on the staffs of the secretariat and prosecution counsel, but these belong to a lot of lawyers temporarily masquerading in uniform as military men.

Nuremberg was, in fact, a lawyers' tribunal, although I can readily understand why the legal profession is ashamed to claim it, and deliberately stuck a false label on it.

I'm glad our real military men had nothing to do with the travesty on justice that the lawyers and "statesmen" conducted at Nuremberg. Raeder and Doenitz simply did their duty to *their* country in World War II, trying to straighten out the mess that their politicians got them into as all military men are sworn to do. Our politicians and lawyers set a rather stupid precedent when they tried these officers for carrying out the orders of their own misguided politicians.

Actually, the decision to court-martial the German military leaders was on a par with the "unconditional surrender" blunder, which prolonged rather than shortened the war. From now on, Nuremberg gives enemy military leaders good reason for fighting to the last bullet and dying in the trenches rather than trying to negotiate the surrender of a hopelessly lost cause. There certainly is no use in surrendering if you know you will be hauled up before a kangaroo court and hanged, as most defendants were at Nuremberg.

After all, Doenitz *did* surrender six days after he stepped into Hitler's shoes following Hitler's suicide. He couldn't have surrendered any sooner without leaving millions of Germans in East Prussia to the mercy of the Red Army.

Even today, few people realize that the German Navy, in the days of the war, evacuated several times as many refugees from East Prussia as the British Navy took out from Dunkirk. As soon as Doenitz got his people to safety in West Germany, he

244

surrendered . . . but one of the charges on which our Supreme Court prosecutor tried to hang him was that he prolonged the war!

Had the German people seen fit to try their own military leaders for losing the war, I might go along with that. Or if our statesmen had insisted on hanging the Nazi politicians and had felt that a mock trial was necessary before doing it, I could see some logic in that. But our politicians and lawyers were undermining their own authority when they convicted the German generals and admirals. After all, one thing the much maligned military leaders *must* do, in a democracy as well as a dictatorship, is to swallow their convictions and do as they are told by the politicians.

I have no sympathy for the sadists who operated the death camps at Buchenwald and Dachau. They should have been shoved into their own death chambers and liquidated quietly by the first military commanders to lay hands on them while the rest of us looked the other way. I even approve of their final hanging. But I do *not* approve of the baldfaced hypocritical hocus pocus by which our statesmen try to justify it legally. The mass murderers at the death camps operated on the basis that might was right, and so did we when we hung them.

At Nuremberg, mankind and our present civilization were on trial, with men whose own hands were bloody sitting on the judges' seats. One of the judges came from the country which committed the Katyn Forest massacre and produced an array of witnesses to swear at Nuremberg that the Germans had done it. Maybe crimes of such magnitude as those charged at Nuremberg should be left to the Last Judgment for punishment.

The outstanding example of barefaced hypocrisy at Nuremberg was the trial of Admiral Doenitz. We tried him on three charges: (1) Conspiring to wage aggressive war; (2) Waging aggressive war; and (3) Violation of the laws of war at sea. Even the loaded court at Nuremberg acquitted him on the first charge, but convicted him of the other two. How in the name of common sense a military officer can wage any kind of war except an aggressive one without being a traitor to his country,

I'll never know. I took an oath when I entered the U.S. Navy almost forty years ago, to defend the United States against all enemies—and there wasn't anything said about doing it in a non-aggressive manner. I'm surprised that the Reds in Korea didn't hang all U.S. prisoners, quoting Nuremberg as a precedent, instead of just brainwashing them and sending them back to us for punishment. If the Nuremberg evidence had shown that Doenitz waged a non-aggressive war, the German people themselves would have been entitled to hang him.

Doenitz's conviction on charge three—violation of the laws of war at sea—was an insult to our own submariners. Admiral Doenitz requested early in the trial that our own Admiral Nimitz be summoned as a witness in his defence to testify as to how our submarines operated in the Pacific. Our Supreme Court prosecutor had to back water fast when that hot potato was tossed at him. Admiral Nimitz (God bless him for the honest seafaring man that he is) finally submitted a sworn statement, answering questions put to him by Doenitz's counsel and said that our submarines in the Pacific waged unrestricted warfare just as the Germans did in the Atlantic.

Despite this, we convicted Admiral Doenitz on the charge of violating the laws of war at sea. If the old gentleman ever gets out of jail, I hope I never meet him. I would have trouble looking him in the eye. The only crime he committed was that of almost beating us in a bloody but "legal" fight.

Doenitz's conviction for violating the laws of war in carrying out the orders of his government, raises a serious question. We have just promulgated a Code of Conduct for our fighting men, designed to steel them against brainwashing if captured, and thus to protect them from prosecution in our own courts for improper conduct while prisoners of war. Perhaps, to protect our soldiers from prosecution by tribunals like Nuremberg, we should amend the oath of allegiance they take when they enter the service. After what we did to Doenitz, maybe we should add a proviso to the oath saying, "Before carrying out the orders of my superior officers, I will check to insure that they are compatible with our international commitments, the Charter of the United Nations, etc., etc."

246

The only precedent set at Nuremberg in which I take any stock at all is that they didn't *hang* any admirals!

The Nuremberg trials placed a solemn stamp of approval on a code of war at sea which we not only didn't follow ourselves in World War II, but which may embarrass us in the future. We are, at present, busily engaged in building atomic submarines designed to remain submerged for weeks at a time. It is absurd to think that these submarines will expose themselves on the surface to follow the archaic code of sailing ships, which we confirmed as being the law of war at sea for the atomic age when we threw Doenitz in jail.

Lest there be any mistake about how I feel on this matter, I hasten to say I am not in favour of actually trying to follow Prize Rules with atomic submarines. I'm in favour of denouncing pacts which can't be followed in wartime and of announcing what everybody knows anyway: that in case we are attacked, we will defend ourselves with every weapon in our arsenal.

According to newspaper reports, the Russians now have a trained fleet of four hundred operating submarines. I don't think this fleet is seven times as dangerous as the fleet of fifty-seven with which Hitler started the war, because, in my opinion, the Russians are a little bit stupid on the starboard side. But if the Russians ever get a fleet of four hundred atomic submarines —or even fifty-seven—we will bitterly regret having opened this Pandora's Box of the atomic submarine.

The atomic submarine is a greater threat to America than to Russia, because we are much more dependent on our sea-borne imports, and our coastal cities are more vulnerable. Even if we have complete control of the air we could still be grievously hurt by submarines which our aircraft could never see. We must not allow newer things, such as inter-continental jet bombers and push-button missiles to obscure the fact that sea power is one of the keystones of America's greatness and strength.

The U-505 will be alongside the Museum for many years to come, perhaps over a hundred if it isn't blasted to atoms by a hydrogen bomb in the meantime. It should serve as a constant reminder to us Americans that seventy per cent of

247

the earth's surface is salt water, and that the United States owes a great deal to the sea which carried our ancestors to freedom and a new way of life on a virgin continent, was the bulwark that protected us when the country was young and weak, and gave us access to the markets and resources of the world to make our industry thrive and grow.

In both World Wars, after bloody battles against submarines, the sea was the great military highway over which we deployed our military might to fight the enemy a long way from our home shores. Now that America is the world's greatest industrial nation, the sea's highways bring in the strategic raw materials needed to keep the wheels of our mighty industry turning.

Fifty-five thousand American soldiers, sailors, airmen and merchant seamen have gone down to unmarked graves defending the freedom of the sea. What more fitting memorial could they have, and what more appropriate symbol is there of our victory at sea than an enemy U-boat itself, beaten in mid-ocean battle, towed across the Atlantic, and installed in the mid-West, a thousand miles from salt water?

Even in the atomic age, the submarine is still the greatest threat to our control of the seas. This captured submarine at the Museum of Science and Industry is a tribute to the heroism of our Navy men, a memorial to the dead, and a stern reminder to the living that control of the seas, so vital to our existence, has been purchased at great price.